WE WANT TO BELIEVE

WE WANT TO BELIEVE

Faith and Gospel in *The X-Files*

AMY M. DONALDSON

CASCADE *Books* • Eugene, Oregon

WE WANT TO BELIEVE
Faith and Gospel in *The X-Files*

Copyright © 2011 Amy M. Donaldson. All rights reserved. Except for brief quotations in critical publications or reviews, no part of this book may be reproduced in any manner without prior written permission from the publisher. Write: Permissions, Wipf and Stock Publishers, 199 W. 8th Ave., Suite 3, Eugene, OR 97401.

Cascade Books
An Imprint of Wipf and Stock Publishers
199 W. 8th Ave., Suite 3
Eugene, OR 97401

www.wipfandstock.com

ISBN 13: 978-1-60608-361-1

Cataloging-in-Publication data:

Donaldson, Amy M.

We want to believe : faith and gospel in The X-Files / Amy M. Donaldson.

x + 246 p. ; 23 cm.—includes bibliographical references and index(es).

ISBN 13: 978-1-60608-361-1

1. X-Files (Television program)—Miscellanea. 2. Popular Culture—Religious Aspects—Christianity. 3. Virtues—Religious Aspects—Christianity. 4. Virtues—Biblical Teaching. I. Title.

PN1992.77.X22 .D50 2011

Manufactured in the USA.

Unless otherwise indicated, Scripture quotations are from the New Revised Standard Version Bible, copyright 1989, Division of Christian Education of the National Council of the Churches of Christ in the United States of America. Used by permission. All rights reserved.

Scripture quotations marked (NIV) are taken from the Holy Bible, New International Version®, NIV®. Copyright © 1973, 1978, 1984, 2011 by Biblica, Inc.™ Used by permission of Zondervan. All rights reserved worldwide. www.zondervan.com.

Scripture quotations marked (NIrV) are taken from the Holy Bible, New International Reader's Version®. NIrV®. Copyright © 1995, 1996, 1998 by Biblica, Inc.™ Used by permission of Zondervan. All rights reserved worldwide. www.zondervan.com.

Scripture quotations marked (NCV) are taken from the New Century Version. Copyright © 1987, 1988, 1991 by Thomas Nelson, Inc. Used by permission. All rights reserved.

Contents

Preface | *vii*

Introduction | 1

1 I Want to Believe | 17
2 Faith: The Evidence of Things Not Seen | 35
3 Hope: "I Can't Give Up" | 65
4 Love: "My Constant, My Touchstone" | 97
5 The Truth Is Out There | 143
6 The Way of the Cross: Temptation, Death, and Resurrection | 179

Epilogue | *223*
Appendix: Episodes Cited | *225*
Episode Index | *233*
Scripture Index | *236*
Subject Index | *240*

Preface

Every now and then, you turn on the television and your jaw drops. Networks constantly push the limits of the medium and sometimes broadcast content that makes you think, "I did not just see that on national television." That was my experience one Sunday evening in 2002. My reaction, however, was not to explicit language or gratuitous nudity. It was to a three-word phrase, *Dio Ti Ama*, appearing in place of the regular tagline of *The X-Files'* opening credits. I don't know Italian, but I had a good guess what the phrase said—only, I couldn't believe that was possible. Did I really see "God loves you" flash before my eyes on network television? Yes, in fact, I did.

This moment encapsulates for me one of the reasons why *The X-Files* has held my attention for so many years. It's a show about intelligent characters having intelligent conversations, even if the subject matter is often out of this world. But what is more "out of this world" than the mystical and spiritual truths of the divine? And *The X-Files* has never been afraid to refer to the divine, or the miraculous, as possibilities very much of *this* world. The present book therefore weds two great loves in my life: *The X-Files* and Christian faith. To me, it is a natural union. I find it intriguing, however, that *The X-Files* appeals equally to atheists and agnostics as well as to Christians and people of other faiths. Perhaps this is because the fundamental nature of the show is to present questions rather than answers, and to balance out every argument with alternative points of view. The dynamic of believer versus skeptic is the heart of the show.

The side of the debate that this book takes is primarily that of the believer. In the spirit of *The X-Files*, the purpose of the book is to pose questions and to explore those questions, which may lead to some possible answers. On the other hand, there are several things this book is not: It is not "the real religion behind *The X-Files*" in the same sense as books written on the real science behind the show that correct inconsistencies and explain how the artistically adapted elements of the show would function in the real world. Likewise, the book is not an exegesis of *The X-Files*, or an attempt to argue that the writers and producers intended to develop a particular theology or preach a certain gospel. This book is rather an exploration of the possibilities—the "extreme possibilities" of faith, hope, and love, as exemplified in the Christian tradition—making use of the questions raised by the show and the particular imagery it employs as an occasion for investigating broader truths. It is by no means a comprehensive treatment of every religious metaphor on the series, but an attempt to at least hit on the major themes.

I assume that the reader picking up this book has a general interest in and knowledge of *The X-Files*; I have tried to include enough details about plots, characters, and seasons along the way to aid the reader who may not have an encyclopedic knowledge of the show, without including so many details that it is tedious for the readers who do. For fuller descriptions of individual episodes, there are many useful resources available on the Internet. Here are but a couple: for a synopsis of each episode, see http://xfiles.wearehere.net; for episode transcripts, see http://www.insidethex.co.uk. These and other resources related to *The X-Files* may be found through this book's website, http://www.believex.com. Included there are also episode reviews and discussion questions for several key episodes cited throughout this book. All *X-Files* episodes and movies referenced within this work are available on DVD from Twentieth Century Fox Home Entertainment: *The X-Files: Seasons 1–9* (2000–2004), *The X-Files: Fight the Future* (1998), *The X-Files: I Want to Believe* (2008). The appendix lists the writer(s), director, and original airdate for each episode cited in the text.

There are a number of people I would like to thank for encouraging and assisting me in this endeavor. First of all, thanks to K. C.

Hanson and Cascade Books for giving me the opportunity to write this book, and to Jeremy Funk for his valued editing skills. Thanks also go to my test audience—Marybeth Cieplinski, Angie Cottrell, Mindy Hall, and Jason McBride—who offered much helpful advice to improve the manuscript; to Manisha Dostert, for bringing to my attention the theological value of the episode "The Gift," which I might have otherwise overlooked; and to Kelley VanBuskirk, for her scientific expertise. I owe thanks as well to the many devoted X-Philes over the years who created invaluable resources on the Internet, especially those who spent hours transcribing the episodes and movies. And finally, thank you to Chris Carter for his incredible vision in creating this television series (along with all of the cast and crew, writers, directors, and producers who helped to make that vision a reality), for demanding a high level of quality and integrity in communicating that vision to the audience, and for the many positive ways it has had a lasting impact on my life.

Dio ti ama.

Amy M. Donaldson
February 2010

Introduction

March 1992. Dana Scully, a young FBI agent, approaches the door to a basement office. Trained as a doctor and a scientist, she has been assigned to offer a critical appraisal of the paranormal cases designated "the X-Files." The cross pendant fastened around her neck catches the light from the hallway before she passes into the shadows of the dimly lit office. She scans the walls, which are peppered with clippings of alien encounters and photos of Bigfoot. The centerpiece is a poster of a UFO, proclaiming in bold letters: "I Want to Believe." Right at home in the midst of this clutter sits her new partner, Fox Mulder.

Fast-forward to January 2008. Dana Scully, MD, returns home from a long day of work at Our Lady of Sorrows Hospital. Her cross pendant gleams in the daylight before she steps into the darkened interior of her house and enters the home office of her former FBI partner, Fox Mulder. The walls that cocoon him are papered with news clippings, headlines highlighting the paranormal among us. At the center of the chaos resides a well-worn poster that states: "I Want to Believe."

From the first episode to the latest movie, the cross and the poster's slogan form two major pillars of this 1990s cult classic TV show—a fact made even more explicit by the title of the 2008 movie, *I Want to Believe*, and two main threads of the movie's plot featuring Catholic priests. As creator Chris Carter has often reiterated, "The show is basically a religious show. It's about the search for God. You know, 'The truth is out there.'"[1] What *The X-Files* is primarily known for is not the search for God but the search for aliens. But that search for extraterrestrial life, set against the scientific demand for hard evidence and the traditions of established religion, serves as a metaphor for the human desire to connect with something beyond ourselves. As the standard tagline in the opening credits states, "The Truth Is Out There." The search for the ultimate Truth, fueled by hope and seeking evidence to justify faith, is the prevailing theme of this series. The truth Mulder seeks is first and foremost the truth about what happened to his sister (whether she was abducted by aliens as his recovered memories have led him to believe), but this quest for extraterrestrial life is merely a paradigm for a much larger theme. At its heart, *The X-Files* is not about alien abductions and government conspiracies; it's about the fundamental truth that all people are looking for something, or someone, to believe in.

SCIENCE FICTION AND RELIGIOUS FACT

It is not unusual for science-fiction (sci-fi) narratives to explore religious themes in the guise of encounters with alien races. In fact, a number of books have been written on the subject, such as Gabriel McKee's *The Gospel according to Science Fiction*.[2] McKee sees sci-fi as a vehicle for speculating on how spirituality and faith can adapt to a changing world, through optimism about future possibilities and criticism of past and present failures. But often in this genre, particularly as expressed through movies and television, science fiction represents merely religious fiction: fictional constructions of religion in a fictional universe. Far too rare is the universe—such as the one depicted in *The X-Files*—in which fictional aliens and the real God coexist.

A fictitious world absent the real-world God is acceptable for *Star Wars*, which happened long ago in a galaxy far, far away, where we have no expectation that these people have ever seen a Bible or heard of Jesus Christ, or Buddha or Mohammed for that matter. But (to take two examples of long-running shows nearly contemporary with *The X-Files*) for *Star Trek: The Next Generation*, built on the future of our present reality, or for *Stargate SG-1*, an extension of our present reality, to ignore modern or future human religious experience and faith is a glaring omission, if not an explicit rejection. On the decks of the starship *Enterprise* there is little room for human religion or belief in divinity. (On a ship of that size, where is the chaplain?) Evolved humans have no need of gods; religious themes are therefore left to be explored through more barbaric cultures, such as the Klingons. What is only hinted at in *Star Trek* becomes a major theme in *Stargate SG-1*: what one culture refers to as a "god" is only a more advanced species that seeks to subjugate, use, or at the very least hide the truth from those who would worship them as divine. In neither of these sci-fi universes does the Judeo-Christian God play a prominent role (if indeed he is even acknowledged to exist), nor is there allowance for such a being as a creator God who is more powerful than all alien races and may potentially intervene to protect humanity from hostile aliens.[3]

This is where *The X-Files* distinguishes itself among sci-fi television shows; in fact, Chris Carter has resisted labeling *The X-Files* as sci-fi because he always wanted the show to have a solid foundation in the reality of our present world. As he has often remarked, "the show is only as scary as it is real."[4] Part of that reality is the acknowledgment that real people—real *humans*—have religious convictions and religious struggles. Unexplainable things happen in the real world, and many people attribute these events to the supernatural or divine. But *The X-Files* crosses genres, as not only sci-fi but also drama, mystery, and even police procedural. In presenting the real struggles and ambiguities of faith, *The X-Files* also distinguishes itself from many other shows that explicitly address religion, particularly Christianity, but often do so too simplistically or with a caricatured version of religion.[5] *The X-Files* always counters belief with skepticism, and skepticism with inexplicable experiences, using this dialectic to depict the genuine human struggle with faith and with God.

FAITH IN *THE X-FILES*

As Hebrews 11:1 defines it, "Faith is the assurance of things hoped for, the conviction of things not seen." *The X-Files* is a master of the unseen. The truth lurks in the shadows, obscured to the naked eye, leaving the intellect and imagination to fill in the details. One of the show's trademarks is to leave questions unanswered: Was Scully's cancer cured by a miracle or by alien technology in "Redux

II" (5x03)? Were Father Joe's visions really from God in *I Want to Believe*? While frustrating fans, such ambiguity also leaves open the possibilities for viewers of all persuasions. Questions are posed, issues are raised, but answers are never delivered on a silver platter. As in life, there are clues along the way, open to interpretation depending on your preconceptions and prejudices. In the end, when the credits roll and issues remained unresolved, the question ultimately turns back to the audience itself: what do *you* believe?

In this way, *The X-Files* maintains its appeal to believers and skeptics alike. It always presents both viewpoints, typically through the trusted characters of Mulder and Scully, allowing the audience to draw its own conclusions. When aliens or the paranormal are in view, Mulder plays the believer and Scully the skeptic. But when Christian faith is at issue, the roles are reversed. Mulder has his doubts about organized religion, while it remains a steadfast part of Scully's life, even when she doesn't fully understand it herself. The show thus uses this dialectic between skeptic and believer as the primary way of examining faith and various beliefs. The dialectic or tension is also at times internal, when the believer wrestles with doubt, although this too is often illustrated through external dialogue, usually between the two main characters. In fact, the role of dialectic is so essential to *The X-Files* that it is present even when it feels forced, such as when Scully persistently refuses to believe in aliens even after she's seen them for herself, when Mulder becomes more accepting of Christian ideas to offset Scully's doubts, or when Mulder is missing and Scully must take on the role of the believer to counter a new skeptic.

One of the first episodes to present Mulder's religious skepticism as a backdrop and conversation partner for Scully's struggle with her Catholic faith is "Revelations" (3x11). As Chris Carter describes this episode, "It dealt with faith, not religion with a capital 'R' or Catholicism with a capital 'C.' To me, the idea of faith is really the backbone of the entire series—faith in your own beliefs, ideas about the truth, and so it has religious overtones always."[6] Those religious overtones are expressed in a variety of ways, through legends and superstitions, cults and the occult, fanaticism and complacency, new twists on old religions, and yes, even through Catholicism with a capital C. All manner of beliefs, and lack of beliefs, are depicted by *The X-Files* to explore the underlying truths about the nature of faith.

Religion and the Supernatural

"Religion has masqueraded as the paranormal since the dawn of time."[7] This comment, made by Mulder to Scully, highlights the close connection between the two themes throughout *The X-Files*. For some people (as perhaps for Mulder), religion is purely human and psychological, the opiate of the masses. But *The X-Files* poses the question, What if it's more than that? What if religion truly is an encounter with the supernatural, with a world or consciousness beyond our own? Are "unexplained phenomena" already explained in terms of religious beliefs? If so, can one simply toy with such superhuman forces and expect them to remain in human control?

A wide range of religions and belief systems makes an appearance in X-Files cases. Some of these are closely intertwined with a particular culture, often representing traditional tenets at odds with a more modernist or scientific worldview. In "The Calusari" (2x21), the religion of a Romanian mother is pitted against the abandonment of that faith by her Americanized daughter; the tension between old beliefs and new culminates in the exorcism of the daughter's son by a group of Romanian elders, the Calusari. In "Fresh Bones" (2x15), the clash is directly between the American military (enforcing the government's policy on immigration) and Haitian refugees, who use Voodoo to exact revenge for past and present wrongs. The beliefs and practices of the Navajo recur throughout the series, at one point saving Mulder's life through a healing ritual ("The Blessing Way," 3x01) and at another helping Scully set aside empirical data to look for a more spiritual solution (once again to save Mulder; "The Sixth Extinction II: Amor Fati," 7x04). The negative side of a similar religion is encountered in "Teso Dos Bichos" (3x18) when disturbing the final resting place of a female shaman of the Secona Indians unleashes a curse upon those who would displace her bones from her native soil.

More widespread religions or belief systems also make an appearance, although often in terms of fringe adherents or less-than-mainstream factions and practices. For example, "Kaddish" (4x12) deals with Hasidic Judaism and the hatred and violence that can arise through both anti-Semitism and retaliation against it, but the episode's supernatural element comes from a story unearthed out of medieval Jewish mysticism. Another form of mysticism occurs in

"Badlaa" (8x12): a Siddhi mystic smuggles himself from India to the U.S. in order to use his ascetic training (contrary to its intended practice) to seek revenge. A number of the Christian beliefs encountered in the series are also fringe or fanatical, such as the alternative Church of St. Peter the Sinner set up by Father Gregory in "All Souls" (5x17) or the snake-handling ecstatics in rural Blessing, Tennessee ("Signs & Wonders," 7x09; these episodes will be discussed below).

Various practices associated with Satanism and the occult surface in a number of episodes, at times challenging opinions both for and against these belief systems. In "Sanguinarium" (4x06), for instance, a practicing witch is at first suspected of the murders, but it is discovered she has been attempting to protect the victims from the true murderer, who is using blood sacrifice to enact a more powerful black magic. Potential witchcraft is addressed again, in a slightly less dark but equally disturbing setting, in "Chinga" (5x10), which plays off the historical accusations against witches in New England. Another episode set in the same region, "Die Hand Die Verletzt" (2x14), uses these traditional prejudices in a particularly interesting way. The story opens with the local PTA pausing to pray at the end of their meeting because they've been letting it slide lately. In their later interactions with the FBI agents, these parents and teachers react against suspected Satanism in their area as though they are conservative Christians. The truth is that these upstanding citizens are themselves the Satanists, praying to the Lords of Darkness. They have become the complacent hypocrites that they believed Christians to be and are now suffering the consequences, as the dark powers they have invoked surface and take blood sacrifices to make up for all the sacrifices they've neglected. As Mulder asks one of the PTA members, "Did you really think you could call up the devil and ask him to behave?"

Every religion has its hypocrites and heretics, as well as its faithful adherents and fanatics. People want to believe in something, even when they're not ready to commit themselves wholly to that belief and what it requires of them. One of the questions that *The X-Files* raises is whether religion is just mythology (story) or has real power (supernatural and paranormal manifestations). Episodes like "Revelations" and "Miracle Man" (1x17) present a mixture of charlatans and true practitioners, justifying the opinions of both skeptics (that religion is just a sham to deceive the simpleminded) and believers (that the divine or supernatural is real and is relevant to and involved in our lives today). This theme is well encapsulated in an episode that is not directly about religion but still addresses the major themes of belief and hope. In "Quagmire" (3x22), Mulder believes the disappearances he and Scully are investigating have been caused by the lake monster Big Blue. Locals like Ted Bertram swear that Big Blue is real, even though the creature has never been caught on film. Late one night, we see monstrous feet slopping through the mud—but it is only Ted, creating fake tracks to help sell more Big Blue T-shirts. Yet Ted isn't alone out there. Something large attacks him in the dark, and Ted becomes the next victim. He is the charlatan, someone who concocts manifestations in order to dupe others into believing for the sake of his own prosperity; but when he is confronted by the reality, he is no match for the Truth.

Cults and Charismatics

While complacency and charlatanism populate one end of the spectrum, it is the other extreme that appears perhaps the most often in *The X-Files*, particularly in the form of cults, whether the object of devotion is God or aliens. Sometimes the cult's beliefs are recognizable derivatives of mainstream (typically Christian) religion, and other times they are a bit more "out there." In "The Field Where I Died" (4x05), the cults led by David Koresh and Jim Jones are referenced, foreshadowing the fate of a group called the Temple of the Seven Stars (cf. Revelation 2–3), established by a man who calls himself Ephesian (after the church of Ephesus in Revelation). Another doomsday cult, built more on Eastern religion than on Christian Scripture, is encountered in "Via Negativa" (8x07): psychotropic drugs that are used to open the third eye instead lead to mass slaughter by a hallucinated axe murderer. New Age beliefs undergird the Church of the Red Museum ("Red Museum," 2x10), a group of vegetarians who wear white robes and red turbans and have planted themselves on a ranch in the middle of beef country to preach the gospel of walk-ins, enlightened spirits from the past who return to inhabit new bodies. Yet they might be considered downright normal compared to the inhabitants of a small town in remote Utah, who worship a parasitic slug as the second coming of Christ ("Roadrunners," 8x05). There is also the interesting case of the Kindred, who are in a class of their own ("Genderbender," 1x13). The members of this reclusive community live like the Amish and are known for their "pure Christian ways," but they apparently can also change genders at will and live unnaturally long lives. The entire community disappears, leaving behind only a large crop circle—suggesting that they were actually aliens living among us.

The isolated communities that congregate around their common, and often extreme, beliefs in aliens are socially similar to the religious cults such as the Red Museum or the Seven Stars. The group encountered in "This Is Not Happening" (8x14) follows a man with the biblical name Absalom, who quotes from Scripture and says that the Bible is prophecy misread; for him, the true interpretation relates to the alien invasion. Even more directly, Josepho, the leader of the alien cult in "Provenance" (9x10)/"Providence" (9x11), interprets Ezekiel 1:4–5 as a reference to alien Super Soldiers, and he speaks of prophecies about the role aliens will play in the future. This cult lead by Josepho especially intersects with a theme that previously arose in the "Biogenesis" (6x22)/"Sixth Extinction" (7x03–04) trilogy, when a spaceship was unearthed and found to be inscribed with excerpts from the Bible, the Koran, other religious texts, and even the tenets of science—all written in Navajo. With the implication here that the aliens were somehow connected to the genesis of humans and human culture, the series for the first time drew a direct connection between the themes that had previously been a metaphorical parallel: the search for aliens and the search for God. The UFO cults particularly highlight this parallel, using the same prophetic biblical texts as the doomsday cults to preach about the alien apocalypse.

While cults take mainstream beliefs to an extreme by isolating themselves in separate communities, other fringe groups, often seen as extreme by those who hold a more moderate or majority position, do not go so far as to break off into separate societies. As noted above, the portrayals of organized religions in *The X-Files* frequently deal with these more fringe or fanatical adherents. One example already mentioned is the Church of Signs and Wonders, a congregation that gathers in a remote, rustic building and practices snake handling as a test of faith ("Signs & Wonders"). This ecstatic group is juxtaposed against a more moderate and progressive congregation in town. The comparison comes to a head one evening when both churches are meeting, and both cite Revelation 3:15–16 (about the dangers of being lukewarm), but each uses this biblical passage very differently from the other. There is an implicit message here, as with "Die Hand Die Verletzt" and the backslidden Satanists, about complacency and dabbling in religion while ignoring its true power. Once again, Mulder voices the underlying truth (referring to their suspect in "Signs & Wonders," the pastor of the progressive church): "People think the devil has horns and a tail. They're not used to looking for some kindly man who tells you what you want to hear" (see chapter 5, below). While it is a natural reaction for most of us, like Mulder, to identify with the moderate point of view and reject the fanatics, their extreme level of commitment and alternate view of reality raise interesting questions about perception. Do those of us who consider ourselves progressive and therefore open minded not see the supernatural because it isn't really there, or have our own prejudices blinded our eyes to the truth? If we looked at the world through the eyes of the extremists, what would we see?

Mainline Christianity

The one form of organized religion or mainstream Christian tradition occurring most frequently in *The X-Files* is Catholicism, due largely to Scully's Catholic upbringing and return to her childhood faith. Yet even this established religion is often encountered through its extreme, or even excommunicated, element. In "All Souls," Scully's involvement with the case begins in her own congregation, but the focus soon shifts to the separatist church started by Father Gregory. In the end, it is Father Gregory who appears to see the truth that Scully's priest, Father McCue, dismisses as an apocryphal story and as therefore untrue. In some ways, these two priests parallel the dynamic between the congregations in "Signs & Wonders." The second *X-Files* movie, *I Want to Believe*, also juxtaposes two priests: a disgraced but penitent priest, Father Joe, and a stern hospital administrator, Father Ybarra. (Scully stands somewhere in the middle—or on the outside—and rails against both.) Both "All Souls" and "Revelations" deal with apocrypha and hagiography rather than central Christian stories, but both episodes also represent crucial moments in Scully's rediscovery of her Catholic faith.

The Catholic Church is also featured in the somewhat satirical episode "Hollywood A.D." (7x18). Cardinal O'Fallon is confronted with an ancient religious text (later revealed to be a forgery), which he sets out to destroy because he is afraid of what its contents might reveal about who Jesus really was. The unstated irony here is that in spite of this man's apparent devotion, his faith actually quite weak—he immediately accepts the words of the text as true and damaging rather than trusting in established Church doctrine and what he already knows of Jesus personally. On the other hand, the forger, Micah Hoffman, so immerses himself in the "role" of Jesus (as though a Method actor) in order to compose the forgery that he is transformed by his encounter with the true Christ, like "Saul to Paul on the road to Damascus." In a more surreal twist that is never fully explained, Hoffman also seems to be dead (and autopsied) and then resurrected, which shows how completely he has identified with Jesus. While Hoffman comes off as somewhat bizarre, O'Fallon is to be pitied, referring to himself as having been made a fool of by believing in the truth of the forgery. As shepherd of his flock, he was attempting to protect his people from the "truth," only to find out that they needed no such protection. The real truth, about the nature of Jesus, is what converted Hoffman when he immersed himself in the Gospels while in pursuit of a lie.

In this example, as in many of the others, the key to the story is not one overriding moral that is handed to the audience as the absolute answer, but the juxtaposition of opposing poles that points to a truth somewhere in the middle and allows the audience to arrive at their own conclusions. In this dialectic, this continual tension between believer and skeptic, the Catholic Church often stands in as the representative of organized religion, traditional teachings, and Scully's simplistic childhood faith. If at times there is an implicit criticism of the position that the Church represents, such as Cardinal O'Fallon's lack of true faith, it is presented as a judgment against that position, not a judgment against the entire faith (i.e., not as a condemnation of Scully and all Catholics alongside her). This too represents a reality not always depicted by science fiction or on television: an institution such as Catholicism, although an easy target when one is criticizing authority, is not a unified whole but comprises a complex interaction of beliefs, teachings, leaders, and adherents.[8] Scully may be Catholic, but she is not Catholic in the same way as "St. Owen" ("Revelations"), who believes God has directly charged him to be the guardian of a young stigmatic, or as Father Joe, who believes (or at least hopes) that God can forgive even the most heinous sinner. The reality is the tension inherent in all belief systems as the believers struggle against old teachings and new manifestations, against each other, against the divine or supernatural, and ultimately against themselves in deciding what is truth and what to believe.

Biblical Imagery

While Chris Carter has stated that the religious themes of the show—religion with a small *r*, that is—are not about Catholicism or Christianity, those themes are frequently couched in Christian imagery. (We will return to many of these examples throughout the book.) Several episode titles illustrate this tendency: "Eve," "Lazarus," "Born Again," "Ascension," "Excelsis Dei," "Apocrypha," "Talitha Cumi," "Gethsemane," "Orison," "Signs & Wonders," "Providence," and so on. In addition to presenting messianic parallels in "Miracle Man" (healings, resurrection), "Talitha Cumi" (healings), and "Hollywood A.D." (resurrection), the show often portrays Mulder as a Christ figure, most explicitly with images like the "Last Supper" in "Requiem" (7x22) and his display on the "cross" in "Amor Fati." He undergoes multiple resurrections, even outdoing Jesus by staying in the grave for three months instead of simply three days ("DeadAlive," 8x15). Even Mulder's son is messianic: the use of Nativity motifs is hard to miss in "Existence" (8x21; baby William is born in an isolated, run-down building, to which Mulder is led by a bright light in the sky, and the baby and his mother are visited by three wise guys bearing gifts).

Apocalypticism is another favorite theme in the series, especially using texts and imagery from the book of Revelation, as well as from other biblical prophecy. The most obvious example is the Millennium Group—prominent in the television series *Millennium* (another brainchild of Chris Carter) and intersecting with *The X-Files* in an episode with the same name as the series (7x05)—reflecting the social angst about the approaching end of the millennium. Both the Millennium Group and the Temple of the Seven Stars ("The Field Where I Died") believe in hastening the end of this world in order to achieve the new world promised in Revelation, and so the adherents commit themselves to extremist ideas and practices to help bring about the fulfillment of prophecy. Representing the other side of the final battle between good and evil, the antagonist in "Revelations" is dubbed "Millennium Man" because he apparently believes he is called by Satan to kill the twelve stigmatics in order to usher in the new age and the new world order.[9]

Biblical quotations also appear in a variety of contexts throughout the show, some expected and some less so. For instance, it is not surprising to see a verse etched into Scully's (premature) headstone in "One Breath" (2x08): "The Spirit Is the Truth" (1 John 5:6). A verse on a church sign at the end of "Fearful Symmetry" (2x18) delivers the final statement: "Man has no pre-eminence above a beast: for all is vanity" (Ecclesiastes 3:19). Mulder uses biblical phraseology, such as "seek and ye shall find" ("Quagmire"), as a way of connecting to Scully's own faith and therefore bringing the conversation into terms with which she will agree. Less conventional is the use of Scripture by the "unholy trinity" of vampires (or vampire wannabes) in "3" (2x07), who write Scripture (John 6:54) on the wall in blood and fancy themselves the father, son, and unholy spirit. Appearing on the mirror of a practitioner of black magic in "Sanguinarium" is the refrain from Ecclesiastes, *vanitas vanitatum*—"vanity of vanities"; as Mulder quotes later in the episode, "All is vanity" (1:2; 12:8).

In addition, certain points of Christian theology are referenced. Mulder brings up the Eucharist, or communion, in "Our Town" (2x24) as an example of the connection between consuming flesh and prolonging life (a connection also made by the unholy trinity in "3"). Agent Monica Reyes later makes a more explicit appeal to this sacrament in "Underneath" (9x09), using transubstantiation as an example for how one man could literally become another, just as the bread and wine become body and blood. The theme of divine judgment is raised by a character nicknamed Preacher ("Sleepless," 2x04), who helps his fellow sinners find rest by allowing them to face the retribution of those they have wronged. On the other end of the spectrum is Father Joe (*I Want to Believe*), who lives every day in self-judgment for his sins but may be a living example of divine mercy, if God has truly chosen to bless him with visions that in the end save the life of a young woman and even Mulder. Many overarching questions about fate and free will and God's involvement in the universe culminate in "Improbable" (9x14)—while God may not play dice with the universe, he does indeed play checkers.

Although the biblical and Christian themes throughout the series are pervasive and unmistakable, it would be a leap to deem *The X-Files* a Christian show. Rather than preaching a particular gospel, the show instead uses this imagery to bring up questions about faith, the supernatural, and the divine not simply as sci-fi allegories but in a real-world way. There is an honesty in its depiction of the characters. Like Mulder, there are many people who consider themselves open to all perspectives and possibilities but are closed off to the Christian faith. Like Scully, there are many Christians who believe in God simply because they were taught to do so, but who don't fully understand the nature of their faith or their relationship with God and continue to struggle with the deeper questions in life. Like Father Joe, many people cannot see past their own history or wrongdoings to understand how God could truly love them or accept them into heaven. Like Micah Hoffmann and Cardinal O'Fallon, many grapple with the true identity of Jesus Christ, his humanity and divinity, and how we should respond to the witness of ancient writings (such as the Bible itself). Like all of these, we simply want to believe, in something or someone—in some truth greater than ourselves.

THE STRUCTURE OF THIS BOOK

The two major symbols that drive *The X-Files* series—Mulder's "I Want to Believe" poster and Scully's cross necklace—are also the driving force for this book. The chapters follow a path between the two, starting with the question of wanting to believe and ending up at the cross. The intervening chapters are shaped around two other themes from the series: the standard tagline, "The Truth Is Out There," and the message of the last scene in the series finale ("The Truth," 9x20). In this scene, Mulder and Scully discuss what they should believe in and whether there is hope for the future, cementing their resolve in the foundation of their devotion to each other. The scene is an enactment of the three theological virtues, encapsulated in 1 Corinthians 13:13: "And now faith, hope, and love abide, these three; and the greatest of these is love." These three virtues, along with truth, are revisited throughout the series and so provide the major themes to be addressed in this book.

Chapter 1 examines the desire to believe and the various objects of belief. Imagery and dialogue from "Talitha Cumi" (3x24) that intentionally parallel Dostoyevsky's story "The Grand Inquisitor" are discussed, along with the theme of faith and the role it plays in science versus in religion. Chapter 2 shifts from the desire to believe to the fact of belief. Mulder's and Scully's own faith journeys, their beliefs in both the paranormal and God, serve as paradigms for exploring the larger question of what constitutes faith. Chapter 3 moves on to the second theological virtue: hope. Associated with hope are issues of certainty about the present and future, including fate versus free will and apocalypticism. Chapter 4 addresses the last of the three theological virtues, the greatest of these: love. The relationship between Mulder and Scully, in its various facets, is examined to illustrate different types of human love, which are also metaphors for God's love for us and our reciprocal love for God and others. Chapter 5 turns to the theme of truth, and with it issues of absolutes in a postmodern context, notions of justice, and good versus evil. Chapter 6 concludes the journey by arriving at the cross, investigating the gamut of Gospel themes throughout the series and particularly the nature of messiahship and the meaning of the crucifixion and resurrection.

The intention of this book is to remain true to the nature of *The X-Files* by posing and exploring questions, but also to move forward and propose some answers. Some of the questions are more metaphorical or metaphysical: What is the Truth? Whose truth? What do we believe in? Based on what evidence, and whose interpretation of it? In what or whom do we find hope? Is the future already written, or do we have free will to change it? But some of the questions relate to the practical, and challenging, realities of our lives: Why do bad things happen to good people? Why would God bring a child into the world only to let it suffer? Is God really speaking, or does he only read the box scores? While there are many different ways to respond to these questions, this volume investigates the answers within the Christian tradition, a tradition often appealed to by the show itself. What *The X-Files* presents us with are perplexities and possibilities, constantly interweaving the themes of belief, trust, perception, truth, and ultimately faith, hope, and love. This book endeavors to explore these extreme, and not-so-extreme, possibilities in a way that is faithful to the show. The truth is out there, and hopefully, through the course of this book, we will catch a glimpse of it.

NOTES

1. Russ Spencer, "A Close Encounter with Chris Carter," Salon.com (April 28, 2000) (http://archive.salon.com/people/feature/2000/04/28/chriscarter/index.html).

2. Gabriel McKee, *The Gospel according to Science Fiction: From the Twilight Zone to the Final Frontier* (Louisville: Westminster John Knox, 2007). I find it disappointing, however, that this otherwise impressive and thorough book appears to make no mention of *The X-Files*. While McKee covers a broad range of sci-fi narratives, including literature and movies, another recent book focuses more on television (and does include *The X-Files*): Thomas Bertonneau and Kim Paffenroth, *The Truth Is Out There: Christian Faith and the Classics of TV Science Fiction* (Grand Rapids: Brazos, 2006).

3. *Star Trek: The Next Generation* (1987–1994) was ending its run just as *The X-Files* was beginning (in 1993), and *Stargate SG-1* (1997–2007, based on the 1994 movie *Stargate*) started up after *The X-Files* was well on its way to becoming a cultural phenomenon. Subsequent installments of both the *Star Trek* and *Stargate* franchises have continued to address religious themes in various ways (see the references to both throughout McKee, *The Gospel according to Science Fiction*), usually in terms of alien races rather than human faith. In an interesting departure from the dearth of references to Christianity in *Stargate*, the second episode of the latest incarnation, *Stargate Universe* ("Air," original airdate October 9, 2009), features a main character having visions of Christ on the cross, which leads him toward the lime deposit that will become the salvation of his shipmates. In this experience, he has more in common with Scully than with any previous *Stargate* characters.

4. For example, see Ian Caddell, "Vision Quest," *Reel West* (October/November 1994) (reprinted online at http://www.mjq.net/xfiles/mediwest.htm). On the genre of the show and Carter's reluctance to refer to it as "sci-fi," see Jan Delasara, *PopLit, PopCult, and "The X-Files": A Critical Exploration* (Jefferson, NC: McFarland, 2000), 62–63.

5. Paul C. Peterson declares that *The X-Files* "has provided one of the deepest and most sophisticated treatments of religious phenomena ever found on network television" ("Religion in *The X-Files*," *Journal of Media and Religion* 1 [2002]: 181–96 [quote on p. 181]).

6. Brian Lowry, *Trust No One: The Official Third Season Guide to "The X-Files"* (New York: HarperPrism, 1996), 139.

7. "All Souls" (5x17). This statement is admittedly ripped out of context, but that context (Mulder's preceding sentence is, "Why do bad things happen to good people?") is an important one to which we will return in the following chapters.

8. McKee, *The Gospel according to Science Fiction*, has a chapter (chapter 8) specifically on the treatment of the church in sci-fi. As he summarizes it, "Where churches appear in SF [sci-fi], they are frequently the center of authoritarian corruption. By contrast the heroes of SF tend to be daring individuals who stand against such conformist institutions, praising reason and personal freedom over inherited dogma. SF as a genre has its roots in secular humanism, and thus it is unsurprising that so many works of SF take up the theme of the individual versus the institution in the context of organized religion" (207). This description of the hero could well apply to Mulder.

9. For the designation "Millennium Man," see Lowry, *Trust No One*, 135–39.

1

I Want to Believe

> MULDER: I guess I just wanted Big Blue to be real. I guess I see hope in such a possibility.
>
> SCULLY: Well, there's still hope. That's why these myths and stories have endured. People want to believe. ("Quagmire," 3x22)

"From the first episode of *The X-Files*, you see this poster with a spaceship on it, and it says, 'I want to believe.' And that really is Mulder's mantra. He doesn't believe—he *wants* to believe, he wants to find reason to believe."[1] As Chris Carter describes here, the slogan on Mulder's poster is a major theme throughout the series. I *want* to believe. This implies both passion and doubt, volition and uncertainty. Behind it lies the fervent desire to find something worth believing in, accompanied by the nagging possibility that the search for proof will eventually prove one wrong. Mulder wants to believe that there is other intelligent life in the universe, but the very heart of his quest is to find evidence to justify such a belief.

The search for the truth by Mulder, and Scully alongside him, symbolizes the most basic of human needs. We all long to believe in something, in some truth, that provides meaning for our everyday lives. For some people, it may be the truth about extraterrestrial life. For others, it is the truth about our existence on this planet, how we came to be here, why, and to what end. For yet others, it is the truth about experiences that defy explanation—whether there really is a divine hand behind them, and whether that divine being is personally engaged in our lives. Although many of us pursue these truths on an individual basis, we must also rely on one another in our search, on each other's experiences and interpretations of reality. Whether or not we will proclaim it explicitly with the poster on Mulder's wall, we all have an innate desire to believe.

THE SEARCH FOR ALIENS AND THE SEARCH FOR GOD

For Mulder, the slogan "I want to believe" refers to the truth about alien life, but the phrase can apply more broadly to the variety of places in which people search for truth or meaning. The slogan also represents the parallel that may be seen between the search for aliens and the search for God. The correlation is significant particularly in two ways: the desire for something to believe, and the nature of faith itself. The second point will be the focus of chapter 2, but it is also wrapped up in the first point, wanting to believe.

The first episode of Season 2 ("Little Green Men") opens with a voiceover by Mulder, which begins: "We wanted to believe." He recounts past efforts by humans to send a welcome message out into space, and SETI projects that search for possible extraterrestrial radio signals. When Mulder, at an abandoned radio-telescope observation post, experiences what might be alien contact, he still expresses doubt: "Is this just some elaborate joke played on those who want to believe?" What Mulder continues to seek is the truth about what happened to his sister, who he believes was abducted by aliens, and so he also seeks the truth about alien life. He is looking for answers to the event that forever changed his life. Therefore, his is more than simply an intellectual curiosity. He has a personal stake in whatever his search will uncover. Later in that season ("Colony," 2x16), Mulder believes he has found some of the answers that he seeks. As he expresses it there in another voiceover, he has found justification for his belief "that there is intelligent life in the universe other than our own." This statement sums up what many other people are looking for as well: evidence that humans are not alone in the universe, that there is other intelligence out there, usually perceived as superior or more powerful intelligence—whether that be aliens or God.

The X-Files mirrors the search for aliens and the search for God in a number of ways. In "Gethsemane" (4x24), Mulder makes this parallel explicit by comparing his quest for the truth about aliens to Scully's belief in God. As they debate the significance of what is possibly an alien corpse, he tells her, "Definitive proof of sentient beings sharing time and existence with us, that would change everything . . . There is no greater revelation imaginable, no greater scientific discovery." But when Scully counters, "You already believe, Mulder . . . What will proof change for you?" he replies, "If someone could prove to you the existence of God, would it change you?" This dialogue exemplifies the theme found throughout the series: the quest for the truth about alien life is a metaphor for the human search to understand whether God exists and what our relationship to God might be. This metaphor provides a vehicle for exploring what people believe about a higher power or greater intelligence, and how that is related to the evidence we find to argue for or against the existence of such a being.

At times in *The X-Files*, the metaphor becomes the reality, making the parallel more overt. For the alien cults, such as those led by Absalom and Josepho during Seasons 8 and 9, and for other characters who describe alien encounters in terms of religious experiences, the aliens have themselves become a type of god. For example, Cassandra Spender reports that the aliens, who abducted her repeatedly over the years, have told her "that I am an apostle, here to spread the word of a dawning of a new age of supernatural enlightenment"; Mulder thus sarcastically refers to her as "the prophet" ("Patient X," 5x13). In a scholarly panel discussing Cassandra's testimony, one of the panelists, Dr. Fazio, proposes that our relationship to the aliens is that of "subjects, much like we think of our relationship with God." This is clearly Cassandra's understanding, although others would interpret her experiences differently.

While Cassandra Spender is a fictional character, she represents a truth that extends beyond mere science fiction. In fact, in real life as in *The X-Files*, the line between alien and religious phenomena sometimes becomes blurred. One example is the phenomena experienced at Fatima in Portugal, beginning in 1917. The lights and otherworldly encounter are largely understood as religious, a vision of Mary. However, Jacques Vallee has described the same phenomena in terms of an alien encounter.[2] He refers to the clouds parting to reveal a silver disk, an image that in other contexts is often interpreted as a UFO. What may be perceived by one person as a vision of the Holy Mother is in the eyes of another an alien visitation. Vallee assesses: "As a society, we are developing a great thirst for contact with superior minds that will provide guidance for our poor, harassed, hectic planet."[3] People are longing for something to believe in, something greater than ourselves. And in this desire, we often look to the heavens to find the ultimate truth. The fact, then, that so many people are searching the skies for "superior minds that will provide guidance" illustrates the basic human need to find a sense of meaning and purpose that transcends ourselves.

WE ARE NOT ALONE

After the opening credits, "Jose Chung's *From Outer Space*" (3x20) begins Act 1 with a close-up on Mulder's poster—"I want to believe" dominates the screen. The entire episode revolves around various perceptions of reality and truth, and therefore the various beliefs that people hold about what really happened. The primary story line is about an alien abduction, which seems to be in part a government hoax. But no one can quite explain the appearance of another alien, Lord Kinbote. The encounter that one character, Roky Crikenson, has with this alien (who looks more like King Kong than like one of the little green men) is a perfect example of the blurred lines between alien encounter and religious experience. The scene, as Roky remembers it, resembles an angelic visitation. Lord Kinbote even uses religious language, of the type that usually occurs in an encounter with a divine or heavenly figure—in other words, the alien speaks in King James English: "Roky, be thou not afraid. No harm will come unto thee" (cf. Luke 1:13, 30; Revelation 1:17). What other characters describe merely as a perplexing and unexpected encounter has become for Roky quite literally a religious experience. He uses his memories of the visionary tour of the earth's core by Lord Kinbote as the basis for a new religion.

The episode closes with an update on several of the characters. As for Roky Crikenson, his encounter with Lord Kinbote has turned him into a preacher sharing the gospel of the enlightenment in the inner core of our souls and the inner core of the earth (where we must watch out for the lava men). But the fate of other characters is, relatively speaking, more mundane. Blaine Faulkner, the stereotypical UFO nut, continues to search for meaning in extraterrestrials and for new worlds where he can be taken away from the cares of this one (i.e., where he isn't expected to get a job). Chrissy Giorgio has taken her experiences as a calling to better her own planet, so she has devoted herself to humanitarian causes. But for Harold Lamb, his search for meaning is much more simple and basic: he loves Chrissy and wants her love in return. As Jose Chung's closing voiceover tells us, there are some, like Harold, who seek meaning not in extraterrestrials but in other human beings: "For although we may not be alone in the universe, in our own separate ways on this planet, we are all alone." Each of these people is searching for meaning, for something beyond themselves to which they can devote their energy and in which they can find fulfillment. Whether it's through aliens, religion, social causes, or human relationships, everyone is searching for some meaning in life.

This common search for meaning is described by the philosopher Blaise Pascal as an attempt to fill an "infinite abyss" within us, but that void "can be filled only with an infinite and immutable object; in other words by God himself."[4] This abyss is often referred to as a "God-shaped hole" within the human soul. The exact phrase may have derived from Jean-Paul Sartre, but the sentiment goes back to St. Augustine in the fourth century. As he says in his *Confessions*, "Man is one of your creatures, Lord, and his instinct is to praise you . . . The thought of you stirs him so deeply that he cannot be content unless he praises you, because you made us for yourself and our hearts find no peace until they rest in you."[5] The first half of the *Confessions* is a narrative of Augustine coming to this realization, doing the very thing that Pascal describes: searching in vain through philosophies, relationships, and any experience he can find to fill the longing in his heart. Finally Augustine comes to understand that the longing, the God-shaped hole, was made for and by God and therefore can only be filled by God himself. Augustine's heart only finds peace once it rests in God.

More recently, Huston Smith, a student of world religions, has reiterated this same point: "Having been created in the *imago Dei*, the image of God, all human beings have a God-shaped vacuum built into their hearts. Since nature abhors a vacuum, people keep trying to fill the one inside them."[6] *The X-Files* illustrates this notion of the *imago Dei*, the image of God imprinted on each of us by our Creator, through alien DNA. Initial tests show that the wunderkind and chess prodigy Gibson Praise has extraordinary activity in part of his brain called "the God module" ("The End," 5x20). When Scully performs further DNA tests, she finds something more incredible: there is DNA in Gibson that matches DNA from an alien claw and an alien virus, DNA that is actually common to all humanity (a genetic remnant that is usually inactive but has been turned on in Gibson). Mulder concludes that this means Gibson is part alien, but Scully voices the real implications: "It would mean that all of us are" ("The Beginning," 6x01). Using aliens as a parallel, this is a modern, scientific way of explaining an old idea. The *imago Dei* is like God's DNA within each of us. It is a part of us that is latent and waiting to meet its potential but only does so when returning to its Creator, when reuniting with God. Until that time, it leaves a longing within us to find something "out there" that will put into perspective who we are and why we are here.

With the longing for the divine, there is also hardwired into us, into our spiritual DNA, a longing for each other. "Then God said, 'Let us make humankind in our image, according to our likeness . . .' So God created humankind in his image, in the image of God he created them; male and female he created them" (Genesis 1:26–27). God himself is a being who lives in community, and he has created us, in his image, to be communal beings. "Let us make humankind in *our* image." In ancient Near Eastern terms, God here consults the divine council; in Christian terms, he addresses the other two members of the Trinity (the Son and the Spirit). The implications for this become clearer in the next verse: "male and female he created them." It is together that the two genders represent the image of God. Whether through male-female relationships, through friendships, through family, we most exhibit the image of God within us through our relationships with each other. God is a being who loves and who lives in relationship. Our longing to find meaning in other people, to love and be loved, is part of God's own character and personality built into our very nature (see also chapter 4, below). It is no wonder that Harold Lamb, as narrated by Jose Chung, is searching for his meaning not in the heavens but in his love for Chrissy Giorgio. As humans, we desire to no longer feel alone, either on this planet or in the universe.

At the end of the pilot episode, an FBI superior asks Scully what her new partner thinks about the alien-abduction case they have just completed; Scully answers simply, "Agent Mulder believes we are not alone." This sets up a major theme for the series: Are we alone in the universe? On the surface, the question applies to extraterrestrial life, but on deeper levels, it also applies to the supernatural and even to human relationships. Underlying the question are two basic points, both of which reflect essential human needs: (1) people don't want to be alone, so we seek to connect with something or someone beyond ourselves; and (2) we feel the question is worth answering, and so we constantly push further into the universe, or into the mystical, in order to discover the truth. Mulder, then, symbolizes the fundamental human quest to answer the question and its corollaries: *Are* we alone? If not, who's out there? And what is their relationship to us?

"THE GRAND INQUISITOR"

One other way *The X-Files* explores the parallel between the extraterrestrial and the divine is by portraying the aliens themselves with godlike qualities. This imagery especially emerges in the final episode of Season 3, "Talitha Cumi." The story opens with the all-too-familiar scene of a gunman gone crazy in a public place. The disgruntled, and recently fired, man manages to shoot several people before he is stopped by the police, who drop him with a single bullet. But an onlooker who has tried to reason calmly with the gunman tells him that no one is going to die—and then proceeds to make good on that promise by laying hands on each of the shooting victims and healing them. Before long, we learn that this healer, Jeremiah Smith, has an additional secret: he is one of many, a clone, who is pursued by the Alien Bounty Hunter for veering from the greater plan. Smith is arrested and imprisoned, then visited by the nefarious Cigarette-Smoking Man for a series of philosophical conversations. The dialogue that ensues is directly shaped from the story "The Grand Inquisitor" told in Fyodor Dostoyevsky's *Brothers Karamazov*. Other elements of the episode intentionally echo this narrative, such as the healings, the name of the restaurant where they take place (The Brothers K), and the very title of the episode ("Talitha Cumi").

In book 5 of *The Brothers Karamazov*, two brothers, Ivan and Alyosha, are conversing about the heavy matters of God and immortality. Alyosha is a believer, headed for the priesthood, while Ivan remains a cynical skeptic. Ivan shares with his younger brother the reasons for his skepticism, including how difficult it is to love one's neighbor and why humans, especially children, must suffer. As an illustration of his point of view, Ivan narrates the story of the Grand Inquisitor. In the tale, Jesus Christ has returned to sixteenth-century Seville and begins to perform miracles like those in the Gospels (including commanding an apparently deceased young girl to arise, or in Aramaic, "Talitha cumi"). However, Jesus is arrested by the leaders of the Inquisition, and the bulk of the story is the dialogue between Jesus and the Grand Inquisitor.[7] Much of the Inquisitor's diatribe focuses on Jesus's temptation in the wilderness by Satan at the beginning of his ministry (Matthew 4:1–11). The Inquisitor states: "There are three powers . . . that are capable of eternally vanquishing and ensnaring the consciences . . . —those powers are: miracle, mystery and authority. You rejected the first, the second and the third, and yourself gave the lead in doing so."[8] He sees the three temptations that Jesus overcame, then, as a rejection of miracle, mystery, and authority.

Regarding the first temptation (command these stones to become bread), the Inquisitor ridicules Jesus for turning down this opportunity to do a *miracle*, all because Jesus wanted humanity to love him freely, not merely in response to signs and wonders. The Inquisitor interprets the underlying issue as the fundamental human question, Whom shall we worship? Because, while free, humans seek something or someone to worship (i.e., someone to whom they may relinquish their freedom). But Jesus rejected the one thing that would have been his ticket to making everyone worship him—providing them bread through a miracle—in favor of allowing them free will. In place of the clear-cut Jewish law and its consequences, Jesus burdened them with the freedom to choose for themselves between good and evil. While humans are enticed by such freedom, it is also their greatest cause for sorrow. The Inquisitor then gladly will offer the people bread in exchange for their freedom, and in so doing will appease their consciences.

The Inquisitor interprets Jesus's response to the second temptation (jump from the pinnacle of the temple to test whether God will save you) as not looking for a miracle, and thus not unveiling the *mystery* of faith. He condemns Jesus for setting an example that humans cannot possibly imitate, because in their weakness they will always opt for the miracle, to test God and see if he will act; and if they reject the miracle, rather than choosing in favor of true faith, as did Jesus, they would reject God as well. Regarding the third temptation (worship me [Satan] and I will give you all the kingdoms of the world), the Inquisitor says that what Jesus rejected, he himself (and the church) has accepted: Rome and the sword of Caesar. In laying claim to that *authority*, Jesus could have answered the three basic needs of humans: someone to worship, someone to appease their consciences, and unity. By accepting the offer of the third and final temptation, the Inquisitor has sold his soul to the devil, and in doing so he feels he has made himself a martyr (taken on the role of the messiah) so that people can live happily in their lack of responsibility for their own choices and sins.

Some parallels with the episode "Talitha Cumi" are immediately obvious: Jeremiah Smith plays the role of Jesus, performing miraculous healings, but for his efforts he is arrested by the powers that be. During his incarceration, two conversations between him and the Cigarette-Smoking Man (CSM) mimic the interchange between Jesus and the Grand Inquisitor, even directly borrowing some of the lines. Echoing the Inquisitor (as shown here in italics), CSM states, "*Men can never be free, because they are weak, corrupt, worthless, and restless. The people believe in authority.* They've grown tired of waiting for *miracle and mystery*. Science is their religion. No greater explanation exists for them." Jeremiah Smith later returns to this theme: "*You think when man ceases to believe in miracles, he rejects God?*" When CSM replies, "Of course," Smith then accuses him of hypocrisy and faulty logic: even though CSM says people no longer believe in God, he still *rules over them in God's name*. He preys on their inherent fear of divine judgment to *appease their consciences*, and he thereby *takes away their freedom* and enjoys the absolute authority that they give him. Smith declares, "And if you can't appease their conscience, you kill them. But you can't kill them all. You can't kill their love, which is what makes them who they are, makes them better than us—better than you."

Interweaving dialogue from Dostoyevsky with references to *The X-Files'* mythology (about aliens and conspiracy), the conversation between Jeremiah Smith and CSM brings up a number of interesting themes: faith, hope, love, free will, fate. (We will return to some of these themes in later chapters.) One of the main points that "Talitha Cumi" borrows from "The Grand Inquisitor" is whether people have ceased to believe in God, and where instead they have placed their faith. The Inquisitor repeats the sentiment of Augustine, although more negatively: "So long as man remains free he strives for nothing so incessantly and so painfully as to find someone to worship."[9] CSM, like the Inquisitor, and like Pascal and Sartre, recognizes that if people do cease to believe in God it leaves a void in their lives, which they will fill with things like science (a new source of "wonders") or another type of authority (here, CSM and his co-conspirators). In a voiceover in "Patient X," Mulder expresses something similar: "Before the exploration of space, of the moon and the planets, man held that the heavens were the home and province of powerful gods . . . But in time man replaced these gods with new gods and new religions . . . And while we've chosen now our monolithic and benevolent gods and found our certainties in science, believers all, we wait for a sign, a revelation. Our eyes turn skyward, ready to accept the truly incredible, to find our destiny written in the stars." In the absence of God, people still look to the heavens in a search for meaning, even if only through the lens of science.

SCIENCE IS THEIR RELIGION

The dialogues from "Talitha Cumi" leave us with the questions: Has humanity ceased to believe in God? Has science become our new religion? Behind these questions are some basic assumptions: first, that science and religion are in some way mutually exclusive, or that science replaces belief in God; and second, that science and God are similar in one main respect—they both require faith. The answer to the first question, for humanity in general, is clearly no. There are people who still believe in God. But for those who can personally answer yes, that they no longer believe in deity, the second question remains: Instead of putting their faith in God, do they put their faith in science? If faith is described as something that requires a leap, a blind step forward into the unknown, then many people would deny that science involves faith. After all, isn't science built on evidence, a reliance on what can be proved and verified? Science is also built on hypothesis, on evidence that is open to interpretation—methods for deriving evidence and interpretation of evidence both change over time—and on explanations that are fully understood only by a select few.

In fact, "Herrenvolk" (4x01)—the sequel to "Talitha Cumi"—has an excellent example of this last point. Scully has found evidence of a nonrandom protein through a biopsy of her smallpox vaccination scar. When she puts the colorful image up on a screen to show her superiors, one of them says it looks like something from the Hubble telescope. They understand neither her science nor her scientific explanation of the evidence. Therefore what she sees as irrefutable proof, hard evidence, the others view only as an outlandish theory ("something we might have expected from Agent Mulder") because they do not understand it well enough to accept it as true—they don't believe her. Later in the episode, Mulder puts this into words, telling Scully, "You put such faith in your science." The same point also comes across in "The Beginning": Scully has analyzed DNA that Mulder insists is extraterrestrial, but Scully is willing to conclude only what the scientific evidence tells her. Mulder isn't interested in her "evidence," only in the proof of his own personal experience, what he knows to be true. Scully believes in the answers that science will provide, while Mulder does not believe that scientific analysis can override all other forms of arriving at truth. In the end, it is his evidence, what he has seen and experienced, weighed against her evidence, what the test results say. The deciding factor for each of them is which evidence they choose to believe.

While Mulder presents a good example of science requiring a degree of faith for the individual to accept its conclusions as true, Scully is a paradigm for the relationship between science and religion. Although Scully does have faith in science, that does not negate her faith in God. But as a scientist and a Catholic, she must at times reconcile the two. The episodes where Scully particularly grapples with this issue are "Revelations" (3x11) and "All Souls" (5x17). In the latter, she tells a priest in the confessional, "As much as I have my faith, Father, I am a scientist trained to weigh evidence. But science only teaches us how, not why." Are religion and science competitors, so that they are mutually exclusive? Or are they compatible, answering different questions, science the how and religion the why?

Various scientists and philosophers weigh in differently on these issues. While the scientist Carl Sagan admits that science does have its limitations in the questions it can answer, he asserts that science is still superior to all other means of knowing. Therefore, any answer science can provide would always override an answer given by religion.[10] Stephen Hawking, on the other hand, would agree with Scully's statement that science can only explain how, not why. What he represents is a different worldview from that of Sagan: Hawking leaves open the possibility of a creator God as the origin of all scientific knowledge. Thus, to discover the one unified theory that would explain everything in the universe would not be to replace defunct religion with science, but to wed all science and philosophy, "for then we would know the mind of God."[11] Addressing the issue from the other perspective, that of religion, Huston Smith describes science and religion as two alternate forms of understanding. It is not that religion merely picks up where science leaves off, allowing science to answer the how, and then coming in behind it to answer the lingering whys. Rather, each has its own worldview and set of presuppositions so that science itself is a form of faith.[12]

At several points throughout *The X-Files*, science and faith may seem at odds, or simply pose two different answers to the same question. One example is the cure to Scully's cancer. Through Seasons 3 and 4, it becomes apparent that the removal of the microchip once found at the base of Scully's neck has resulted in her cancer. When Mulder recovers a new microchip and suggests once again implanting it to cure her, Scully's brother refers to the idea as "science fiction," and it clearly is outside her doctor's "conventional treatment" ("Redux II," 5x03). Still, the chip is assumed to be alien—or at least advanced—technology, so there is a science to it, even if that science is not fully understood. At the same time, however, Scully returns to her Catholic faith, willing to pray with the same priest whose assistance she rejected earlier in the story arc. So, when Scully's cancer goes into remission by the end of the episode, is it the chip that has healed her? Or is it a miracle, in response to her prayer? As Mulder replies to Assistant Director Skinner's question on this very point, "I don't know. I don't think we'll ever know." But a deeper question is whether it must be either-or. If the chip is the cure, does this mean there has been no divine intervention? Or could the very fact that Mulder has found the chip be an answer to prayer?

Another instance of science and faith standing in tension occurs in the second *X-Files* movie, *I Want to Believe*. Scully is working as a doctor, and her primary case is a boy with a rare and apparently fatal disease. But she's not ready to give up on him, no matter how experimental or uncertain the treatment. The advice Scully gets from the administration through Father Ybarra is to let the boy go into hospice to manage his final days in a more comfortable setting. Is Scully "playing God" by attempting to prolong the boy's life when others believe she is only prolonging his suffering? Is she putting her faith in science rather than in God? When the boy's parents choose to stop treatment, they say they want to put their faith in God now, implying that trusting God is contrary to Scully's experimental procedures. On the other side, the disgraced Father Joe is telling Scully, "Don't give up," which she takes to be a direct word (a divine word?) to persist in her treatment of the boy. Scully struggles throughout the movie with issues of faith—whether she should believe Father Joe, whether she should have faith in her science, or whether she should turn the boy over to God's hands and accept his current fate. In classic *X-Files* fashion, the end is left open. In the final scene,

Scully continues the procedures, despite her doubts, and despite the hostile looks from her superiors and colleagues. Does the treatment work? Was she right to listen to Father Joe and not give up? We don't know. Once again, the audience must decide: What do you believe will happen? This example, like the mystery of the cure for Scully's cancer, also raises the issue of whether science and faith are truly at odds here, even though the two seem to be at war in Scully. If Father Joe did receive a message from God to tell Scully not to give up on her medical treatment, then the results of the treatment may be in part from divine intervention. As the creator of the universe and its workings, God is also the creator of the stem cells that Scully uses to treat her patient. And if God is the author of science, then science can be an answer to prayer.

To understand the universe and how it works, then, is to understand the Creator; or, as Hawking has said, to "know the mind of God." This is the underlying premise behind the episode "Improbable" (9x14), which depicts the world in terms of intricate mathematical and numerical patterns, all put in place by God to direct humans along the way. In the midst of apparent chaos there is a fundamental order, and there are larger patterns to be found even if we cannot see them. In this sense, it is not merely humans but all creation that bears the image of God—illustrated in the final scene as the camera pans out to show that from a great distance (a God's-eye view) the orderly image that emerges on the earth below is the face of God. By this understanding, science would not replace religion as now defunct, nor would the two necessarily answer different questions (science the how and religion the why). Rather, science would be itself a form of revelation, witnessing to God's character and creativity. But science alone is not enough to reveal the mind of God. This is the other half of the premise behind "Improbable." God didn't simply create an ordered universe and step back to watch the box scores (as Mulder describes in "Orison" [7x07]); God created the order out of love for his creatures, and he remains actively involved in their lives, so far as they will allow him, without violating their free will. Here again resurface the major themes of "The Grand Inquisitor" and "Talitha Cumi": the cost of human freedom and the ultimate triumph of love. If science has *become* our religion, then we're lacking a key variable in the master equation. Science instead can be a *part* of our religion, pointing us toward the care and attention of a loving God.

WE ALL HAVE OUR FAITH

If in the modernist era "God is dead," as Nietzsche declared and as the Grand Inquisitor would concur, then postmodernism has since resurrected him. Although, as sometimes happens with resurrection, God's nature has been fundamentally transformed in the process. Hence the tenets and belief systems that have emerged in postmodernism are more universal and pluralistic, also causing the reactionary rise of more fundamentalist movements (those who would return to the "fundamentals" of the faith, before God was declared dead). The significance, though, is the return of religion and faith, and the recognition that all truth claims are based on specific worldviews. We all have a set of beliefs about the world and how it works. Everyone believes (or wants to believe) something about the origin of our existence, our meaning and purpose, the foundation for our behaviors, our ultimate fate. Even atheism is a type of belief. If we don't answer the big questions with religion, then we answer them with philosophy or science or maybe science fiction. But they are questions that we all share, and that we all seek answers to. The Grand Inquisitor himself recognizes this: "For the secret of human existence does not consist in living, merely, but in what one lives for."[13]

As Mulder declares to his partner, "We all have our faith, and mine is in the truth" ("Redux II"). We all *want* to believe, but in what, and how? What is the nature of faith, and how does it relate to evidence and experience? That is the subject of the next chapter.

NOTES

1. Chris Carter, "Threads of the Mythology," *"The X-Files" Mythology: Super Soldiers*, DVD (Twentieth Century Fox Home Entertainment, 2005).
2. Jacques Vallee, "The Spiritual Component: A Morphology of Miracles," in *Dimensions: A Casebook of Alien Contact* (New York: Ballantine, 1989), 173–95.
3. Vallee, *Dimensions*, 242–43.
4. Blaise Pascal, *Pensées*, trans. A. J. Krailsheimer, rev. ed. (London: Penguin, 1995), 45 (10.148).

5. Augustine, *Confessions*, trans. R. S. Pine-Coffin (London: Penguin, 1961), 21 (1.1). On Sartre and the phrase "God-shaped hole" (which he used in the opposite sense from Pascal and Augustine, referring to an absence that is better filled by something else), see, for example, Karen Armstrong, *A History of God: The 4,000-Year Quest of Judaism, Christianity, and Islam* (New York: Ballantine, 1993), 380.

6. Huston Smith, *Why Religion Matters: The Fate of the Human Spirit in an Age of Disbelief* (San Francisco: HarperSanFrancisco, 2000), 148.

7. "The Grand Inquisitor" is actually more of a monologue than a dialogue, dominated by the Inquisitor's speech while Jesus remains silent (as he does at his trial in the Gospels); the discussion between the brothers is similar in that Ivan does most of the talking and Alyosha hardly gets a word in edgewise. Jesus's only reply, at the end of the diatribe, is to kiss the Inquisitor full on the wrinkled old lips that have just condemned and denounced him. This is both a final statement about loving one's enemies as the better way and a reverse Judas kiss, here not to betray the Inquisitor but to acknowledge the Inquisitor's betrayal.

8. Fyodor Dostoyevsky, *The Brothers Karamazov*, trans. David McDuff, rev. ed. (London: Penguin, 2003), 333. The verbal parallels in "Talitha Cumi" are most obvious in the translation by Constance Garnett (1912), but its English is more archaic, although at times more fluid (the Garnett translation may be found online at http://en.wikisource.org/wiki/The_Brothers_Karamazov).

9. Garnett translation. McDuff (*Brothers Karamazov*, 331) reads: "There is for man no preoccupation more constant or more nagging than, while in a condition of freedom, quickly to find someone to bow down before."

10. Carl Sagan, *The Demon-Haunted World: Science as a Candle in the Dark* (New York: Random House, 1995), 28, 30. Sagan does not see science as "replacing one faith by another," nor does he see science and spirituality as mutually exclusive endeavors; however, his definition of spirituality is based on spirit as matter, not Spirit as divine (29–30). Sagan also derides *The X-Files* for always letting the paranormal win out over the scientific explanation (374–75), which Chris Carter addresses in his foreword to Anne Simon, *The Real Science behind "The X-Files": Microbes, Meteorites, and Mutants* (New York: Simon & Schuster, 1999), 13.

11. Stephen W. Hawking with Leonard Mlodinow, *A Briefer History of Time* (New York: Bantam, 2005), 140–42 (quotation p. 142); cf. Hawking, *A Brief History of Time: From the Big Bang to Black Holes* (New York: Bantam, 1988), 171–75. More recently, however, Hawking has apparently discovered a viable candidate for the "one unified theory," which he believes now makes God unnecessary to the equation (Stephen W. Hawking and Leonard Mlodinow, *The Grand Design* [New York: Bantam Books, 2010]). (That theory is the "M-theory"; since the exact meaning of "M" remains unknown, Hawking posits as possible referents "master," "miracle," or "mystery" [p. 117]—ironically, these are very similar to the "miracle, mystery, and authority" referred to by the Grand Inquisitor, who also deems God unnecessary.) Hawking stands as an example of how science shifts depending on personal interpretations of data and how scientific theories require acceptance, or belief, in order to be perceived as truth.

12. Smith, *Why Religion Matters*, 71, 137. Smith also makes the important distinction between *science*, which may have much to contribute to religion and vice versa (193–200), and *scientism*, which claims "that the scientific method is, if not the *only* reliable method of getting at truth, then at least the *most* reliable method; and . . . that the things science deals with—material entities—are the most fundamental things that exist." These claims "are at best philosophical assumptions and

at worst merely opinions" (59–60). Thus, scientism is a worldview that competes with, rather than complements, religion. While Smith does not name Sagan here, the two points he makes reiterate the exact claims made by Sagan.

    13. Dostoyevsky, *The Brothers Karamazov* (trans. McDuff), 332. On the postmodern return of religion, see, for example, the introductory essay by Jeffrey W. Robbins in John D. Caputo and Gianni Vattimo, *After the Death of God*, ed. Jeffrey W. Robbins (New York: Columbia University Press, 2007), 1–24, who bookends his discussion with references to "The Grand Inquisitor," a story that he says "anticipates . . . the postmodern return of a religion based in the love of Christ" (24).

2

Faith

The Evidence of Things Not Seen

> WAYNE FEDERMAN: You want my advice? You're both crazy.
>
> MULDER: Well, why do you say that?
>
> WAYNE FEDERMAN: (to Mulder) Well, you're crazy for believing what you believe, (to Scully) and you're crazy for not believing what he believes. I'll leave you with that. ("Hollywood A.D.," 7x18)

Faith is a prevalent theme in *The X-Files*, and it is expressed in a number of different ways. It goes beyond merely belief in aliens or belief in God. Faith can be placed in a concept, a person, or an object; it includes trust and confidence, assumptions and perceptions. Scully struggles to regain faith in herself when she's emotionally shaken by a case in "Irresistible." Both Mulder and Scully confide in each other, "You're the only one I trust" ("E.B.E.," "Wetwired"), while their informant Deep Throat warns with his last breath, "Trust no one" ("The Erlenmeyer Flask"). Beliefs can be shaped by, or shape, reality (seeing is believing). Faith, belief, trust—these are key themes that reverberate throughout the series, but they are explored most compellingly through the dynamic between Mulder and Scully.

In the series finale, titled "The Truth" (9x19–20), the "truth" that Mulder and Scully learn is about the coming alien invasion. The episode closes with a scene between the two characters, as they discuss faith and hope and exhibit love. Scully asks, "You've always said that you want to believe. But believe in what, Mulder? If this is the truth that you've been looking for, then what is left to believe in?" As he has many times throughout the series, Mulder stands at a crossroads, confronted with new evidence about his belief in extraterrestrial life, and faced with a choice about how that will impact his beliefs. Mulder's reply encompasses not only his beliefs about aliens but his beliefs in general: "I want to believe that the dead are not lost to us. That they speak to us, as part of something greater than us—greater than any alien force. And if you and I are powerless now, I want to believe that if we listen to what's speaking, it can give us the power to save ourselves."

The question that Scully asks could be addressed to many of us as well: You want to believe, but believe in what? And based on what? How does evidence for or against that belief system impact your faith? This is exactly the type of conversation that Mulder and Scully had five seasons earlier, in "Gethsemane" (4x24). Mulder seeks evidence to prove that aliens exist, but Scully asks how evidence would affect the faith that he already has. Mulder challenges her by comparing this situation to her belief in God. Executive producer Frank Spotnitz reflects on this scene: "What became increasingly clear to Chris [Carter] and me in years of working on these mythology episodes was that Mulder's quest for extraterrestrial life was akin to trying to prove God existed. And there's this wonderful scene in that episode with him and Scully on the stairs, where he says, 'C'mon, if you could prove God exists, wouldn't you?' And she says, 'No, I take it on faith,' which is so profound and correct. That *is* what religion is about. You *must* take it on faith. God is not going to prove it to you."[1]

In the language of Hebrews 11:1, faith *is* the evidence: "Faith is the substance of things hoped for, and the evidence of things not seen" (KJV). When the object of belief—such as the existence of God, the resurrection of Christ, the existence of aliens, or the big bang theory—cannot be proved or disproved to our satisfaction with empirical evidence, then we are left to choose whether or not to believe the assertion. We are left to rely on faith, and that faith itself reinforces the evidence to support the claim. The potential tension between faith and evidence is explored throughout *The X-Files*, often by juxtaposing the views of Mulder and Scully. When it comes to the paranormal or aliens, Mulder stands for faith while Scully represents evidence. But in matters of religion, especially Christianity, the roles are typically reversed. Despite the differences between the characters, they have one thing in common: what drives them both is the power of their beliefs. Mulder believes in the paranormal, in the supernatural, in aliens, in extreme possibilities; Scully believes in science and in God. The conflicting beliefs of the two constantly lead them to differing conclusions, but they both passionately continue to search for the elusive yet attainable Truth. For each of them, faith provides the lens through which they interpret experience. As their beliefs differ, so may their interpretations of reality.

The two scenes from "Gethsemane" and "The Truth" provide snapshots of the progression of this dialectic both between Mulder and Scully and within each of their individual journeys. By the end of the series, in that final scene from "The Truth," it appears that the pair have reached some middle ground—in response to Mulder's answer, Scully says, "Then we believe the same thing." Yet tensions still remain (more within Scully than between the two) in the subsequent movie, *I Want to Believe*. With this ongoing tension, there is an honest depiction of the struggle that faith often can be. For Chris Carter, this struggle is foundational to Mulder's entire quest to find evidence for his faith, to find a reason to believe: "That's kind of, for me, the basis of faith . . . Faith is a struggle, it's an effort. And Mulder's faith was a struggle and an effort, his faith to find the truth about his sister."[2] Or, as Mulder puts it, "You think that believing is easy?" ("Nisei," 3x09). As Mulder and Scully show us, believing is often anything but easy, yet the assumption is that the struggle is worthwhile.

MULDER'S FAITH JOURNEY

In the very first season of *The X-Files*, the fourth episode ("Conduit," 1x03) closes with a scene of Mulder sitting in a church. He is weeping over a picture of his lost sister. Over the scene plays the audio from Mulder's regression-hypnosis session as he recalls the memories of his sister's abduction. He remembers being unable to move, yet not being scared because a voice, speaking inside his head, was telling him not to be afraid. "It's telling me that no harm will come to her, and that one day she'll return." The doctor asks him, "Do you believe the voice?" Mulder replies, "I want to believe." While the description of his sister's abduction changes further into the series, this early scene depicts well the significance that event and his memories of it hold for Mulder's beliefs. There are two threads to Mulder's faith journey: his belief in aliens and his belief in God. His life-shaping event, the abduction of his sister, stands at the center of both.

Faith to Keep Looking

The moment that his sister, Samantha, was abducted certainly had repercussions for Mulder's life, but his recovery of the memories of that night had the greatest impact on his career and his quest. The regression-hypnosis session when he resurrected those memories functions like a conversion experience. The bright light, the presence in the room (as he describes in the pilot episode), the voice telling him not to be afraid—all of these sound much like an encounter with a divine being (cf. Roky Crikenson's close encounter in "Jose Chung's *From Outer Space*," 3x20). This "conversion" is the moment that changes his career and shifts his focus toward finding the truth about what happened to his sister, a truth that he pursues with a religious fervor. Mulder wants to believe the voice in his head, real or imagined, that Samantha will be returned to him safely. He wants to believe that aliens do exist, in order to confirm his memories of that night and to give him a place to look for his sister. But what he does believe in is the Truth—about aliens, about Samantha's abduction, about all other phenomena that defy conventional wisdom—and that the truth can be made known. This is his faith as he defines it to his partner: "We all have our faith, and mine is in the truth" ("Redux II," 5x03).

Mulder persistently claims, like the UFO poster on his wall, "I want to believe." What will allow him to move from "I want to believe" to "I believe"? Not faith, but evidence. Whether this is something he has learned from his partner or is only reinforced by her presence in his life, he is constantly searching for undeniable proof of alien life—such as a recording of first contact ("Little Green Men," 2x01) or an alien corpse ("Gethsemane")—something that will convince not only him but everyone else. His faith is tenuous enough that it waxes and wanes depending on what story someone tells him or what supposed evidence he has encountered. Mulder himself describes it as "a fragile faith built on the ether of vague memories from an experience that I could neither prove nor explain" ("Colony," 2x16). Although Mulder does not directly answer Scully's question, "What will proof change for you?" ("Gethsemane"), it seems, especially from the faith crisis he suffers in the ensuing months, that proof would change everything for him. The truth he believes is that the existence of aliens can be proved or disproved, and he is awaiting the definitive evidence to make a final decision.

The vulnerability of Mulder's faith becomes apparent even in the first two seasons. In "E.B.E." (1x16), he and Scully come at supposed UFO evidence, and the shadowy source providing it, from differing viewpoints. Mulder says to her, "Why don't you just admit it, Scully? You're determined not to believe him." But Scully fires back, "Well, maybe you're too determined to believe him." Mulder declares his true motive: "I am determined to follow a lead that may result in the proof of the existence of extraterrestrial biological entities." As always, he *wants* to believe what he is being told, but he needs verifiable proof. But does that desire to believe make him too gullible in his acceptance and evaluation of the "evidence"? Scully warns him of this: "I have never met anyone so passionate and dedicated to a belief as you. It's so intense that sometimes it's blinding. But there are others who are watching you, who . . . will use it against you. Mulder, the truth is out there, but so are lies." Later in the episode, Mulder admits to her, "Maybe they're using me against myself, like you said before. That I want so badly to believe, that I'd just accept the obvious conclusions and walk away."

The desire for evidence, then, can work both for and against Mulder. At the beginning of Season 2, he is starting to doubt not only the existence of aliens but even his own memories of his sister's abduction. His hope is renewed, however, by possible alien contact ("Little Green Men"). Later in the same season, he faces a faith crisis again. A woman comes forward who claims to be Samantha, but Mulder then learns that she's only a clone who has been using his longing to find his sister in order to manipulate him and get his help. Still determined to find the truth, he goes to extremes, following a lead to northern Alaska. In a violent confrontation with the Alien Bounty Hunter, Mulder begs not for his own life to be spared but only for information about Samantha. Mulder comes up empty, and barely alive, but he does find one thing: "Faith to keep looking" ("End Game," 2x17). He may not have evidence or the truth, but he has hope that the truth can still be found and is worth pursuing.

These two themes—Mulder's willingness to believe being used against him and a crisis of faith—emerge again in Seasons 4 and 5. Scully's cancer provides the impetus for Mulder's doubts: in "Gethsemane," Mulder is told that the alien corpse he's investigating is a hoax, and that Scully's cancer was orchestrated to make him believe in aliens. Mulder comes to believe this story, that the "truth" he has been fed about aliens is only a smokescreen by people in the government to cover their own reprehensible deeds and to divert the blame. Mulder becomes a skeptic. His faith crisis culminates midway through Season 5, when Scully again provides the counterpoint. She has faced experiences of her own that make her question whether Mulder was originally right about extraterrestrials; his memories, which he now doubts, are pitted against her own lack of memories about an event that might involve alien activity.

> SCULLY: Mulder, when I met you five years ago, you told me that your sister had been abducted, by aliens. That that event had marked you so deeply, that nothing else mattered. I didn't believe you, but I followed you, on nothing more than your faith that the truth was out there, based not on facts, not on science, but on your memories that your sister had been taken from you. Your memories were all that you had.

MULDER: I don't trust those memories now.

SCULLY: Well, whether you trust them or not, they've led you here. And me. But I have no memories to either trust nor distrust, and if you ask me now to follow you again, to stand behind you in what you now believe, without knowing what happened to me out there, without those memories, I can't. I won't.

MULDER: If I could give you those memories, if I could prove that I was right and that what I believed for so long was wrong—

SCULLY: Is that what you really want? ("The Red and the Black," 5x14)

At the time, Mulder is uncertain what he wants, standing on the unstable ground of doubt. But by the end of the episode, he once again encounters potential evidence of UFOs and alien life, and his faith to keep looking is restored.

In the series finale, Mulder faces a new kind of faith crisis. Before, the problem had always been that the truth was kept out of his reach or he couldn't distinguish between the truth and the lies. The finale presents him with a new challenge: what happens when he finally does find the truth and it's something he doesn't want to hear? The truth he discovers is that the aliens are coming; a date for their invasion and colonization has long been set. The future is written, and it is bleak. Upon learning this, Mulder seems to give up all hope. It is his despair that prompts Scully to ask, "If this is the truth that you've been looking for, then what is left to believe in?" The question causes Mulder to realize that the Truth has to be something more than merely the truth about aliens. The truth he declares is that there is "something greater than us," something that can give us hope. When Scully tells him that the two of them believe the same thing, he responds by touching her cross.

A Truth beyond Our Own

Even though aliens are a predominant topic of X-Files cases, they are certainly not the only type of truth that Mulder pursues. His investigations include liver-eating mutants, fat-sucking vampires, lake monsters, sewer monsters—causing Scully to wonder, "Is there anything that you don't believe in, Mulder?" ("The Post-Modern Prometheus," 5x06). Although the question is rhetorical, it can readily be answered by anyone who has seen episodes such as "Revelations" and "All Souls": Mulder doesn't believe in God. However, this statement should be qualified: in a world where the innocent are allowed to suffer, Mulder does not believe in a God who is actively involved in people's lives. As Mulder succinctly describes his belief, "God is a spectator ... He just reads the box scores" ("Orison," 7x07). But does Mulder *want* to believe? In "Revelations" (3x11), Mulder tells his partner, "I wait for a miracle every day." The miracle he speaks of is the return of Samantha, or at least the truth about her fate. The statement itself shows that Mulder is once again looking for evidence. He is like the people described by the Grand Inquisitor (see chapter 1, above): his faith will be earned with miracles. As with Ivan Karamazov, the brother who tells the story of the Grand Inquisitor, the major obstacle to Mulder's faith in God is his struggle with the fact that the innocent suffer—innocents like his sister.

While Mulder's relationship with God is an understated theme of the series, mostly used to provide a foil for Scully's reemerging faith, a progression can be seen in Mulder's willingness to believe. The scene in "Conduit" with Mulder sitting in a church might seem surprising to viewers who know Mulder best from further into the show's run. In that scene, as he begins to cry over the photo of his sister, he folds his hands and slips to his knees. Is Mulder praying? If he really believes that God only reads the box scores, is he pleading for God's intervention? Or is it the fact that his prayers for Samantha's safe return are not immediately answered that leads him to believe God is distant? Set against Mulder's later negative reactions to faith in God, this scene from "Conduit" raises interesting questions about his religious background. Nothing is said definitively about it on the show, but the image of him kneeling in a church suggests he may have some childhood foundation for turning to God, or that he at least considers God to be an extreme possibility worth consideration.

It is clear from "Miracle Man" (1x17), another early episode, that Samantha's abduction is a point of vulnerability for Mulder. Just as his desire to believe in aliens leaves him open to the fault of gullibility and the ability to be manipulated, his desire to believe that Samantha is alive and well makes him susceptible to believing anyone who offers him information about her. (This is true also in later episodes, when it is suggested that Samantha was taken by a serial killer ["Paper Hearts," 4x08], or that she was saved from a horrible fate by spirits called "walk-ins" ["Sein und Zeit," 7x10]). In "Miracle Man," Mulder's eagerness to believe is provoked by a faith healer whose gift has apparently been tainted so that his hands perform murders instead of miracles. As soon as this young man, Samuel, says he senses Mulder's pain over losing a sister, Mulder's ears perk up. He wants to believe that Samuel is the real deal. Samuel has a message specifically for him: "I'll tell you, Mr. Mulder, God watches over his flock. He gives us signs every day. Open your heart. He might just open your eyes." Mulder later sees visions of a young girl who looks like Samantha. When Scully realizes what is happening and Mulder admits to her that he keeps seeing the girl, Scully tries to provide a rational explanation: "Maybe you just want to see her." He retorts, "I'm not delusional, Scully." She replies, "Mulder, don't discount the power of suggestion. A healer's greatest magic lies in the patient's willingness to believe. Imagine a miracle and you're halfway there." At the end of the episode, Scully asks him what he thinks about Samuel and the case. Mulder says, "I think people are looking hard for miracles, so hard that maybe they make themselves see what they want to see." Clearly, these words describe what he thinks about himself, that he's looking so hard for Samantha that he sees signs of her wherever he turns. As if to prove the point, just at that moment he again sees the young girl, reflected in the car window, but when he spins around no one is there. Mulder shakes off the experience and gets in the car, choosing to leave rather than to pursue. In Season 1, Mulder is willing to believe in such signs from God, but his turning away from the final vision of his sister may also be symbolic of him turning his back toward God. If God will provide a miracle—*the* miracle—then Mulder may again be willing to believe.

In the following seasons, Mulder fills his more familiar role of the religious skeptic. One example is in "All Souls" (5x17). In this story, the theme of sight arises, as it does in "Miracle Man" and many other episodes where seeing and believing are compared. When girls are found with their eyes burned out, Mulder suspects that Father Gregory is responsible and interrogates him with hostility: "Did they see you for who you are, like I do?" Yet Mulder does not see the same things that Scully does, including the true identity of another, demonic character. Father Gregory earlier has told the agents, "your secular prejudices blind you from seeing what's really happening here," but by the end of the episode, only Scully's eyes have been opened to what he was talking about. By Season 7, however, Mulder begins to have an awakening of sorts; he shifts away from staunch opposition to Scully's faith in God to a more median position. In "Signs & Wonders" (7x09), sight again emerges as a metaphor for spiritual enlightenment. Mulder begins the episode from the same negative position, believing that the conservative and fanatical Reverend O'Connor is responsible for the murders. During his interrogation, O'Connor tells Mulder, "Satan is near, and you don't even have eyes." But in the final confrontation, Mulder's eyes are opened. He listens to the words of O'Connor and puts the pieces together, telling the real murderer, "I'm just beginning to see it now." Mulder also challenges the suspect with a line echoing what he had said to Father Gregory; referring to the first victim, Mulder asks, "Did he . . . see you for who you really are?" A similar enlightenment occurs for Mulder in "Orison," the same episode in which he comments that God only reads the box scores. Throughout their investigation, Scully has been encountering clues, which she believes may be signs from God, including a song that she keeps hearing. Despite Mulder's skepticism, when he later hears the same song it is obvious that he finally takes it seriously, and thus the clue leads him to Scully's apartment just as she's being attacked. Six years after "Miracle Man," Mulder may finally be heeding the words of Samuel: "Open your heart. He might just open your eyes."

Further into Season 7, in "Closure" (7x11; the title refers to closure about his sister's abduction), it appears that Mulder may now be more receptive to the possibility of God's intervention. In the opening voiceover, over the scene of multiple graves of children being unearthed, Mulder explains more fully his belief in God's role: "These fates seemed too cruel, even for God to allow . . . I want to believe so badly, in a truth beyond our own, hidden and obscured from all but the most sensitive eyes . . . I want to believe we are unaware of God's eternal recompense and sadness. That we cannot see his truth. That that which is born still lives and cannot be buried in the cold earth, but only waits to be born again at God's behest." Mulder's belief in God, as always, revolves around his beliefs about his sister's fate, and the fate of others like her. He wants to believe that if God is real and benevolent, those who are lost from this earth live on in some other way. What Mulder finds in this episode is not only closure but peace. He has one final vision of Samantha and believes that she's "in a better place." At the end of the series, his response to Scully in "The Truth" reflects much the same idea: "I want to believe that the dead are not lost to us. That they speak to us, as part of something greater than us." When he then touches her cross necklace, it is both an inquiry and a confirmation of what they now hold in common—just as she has become more open to the truths about aliens, he has become more open to the truths about God. Yet even for this middle ground, it is on the critical issue of the fate of the innocent where they may still disagree. The peace that Mulder has found continues to elude his partner. This becomes most apparent in *I Want to Believe* and Scully's own struggle with why the innocent suffer.

SCULLY'S FAITH JOURNEY

While Mulder wants to believe, Scully does believe, and her beliefs are constantly tested by what she experiences while working on the X-Files. Unlike Mulder, Scully does not begin from the position of one life-changing event. Instead, she starts with a foundation of the religion she was raised in, the science she was trained in, and her trust in justice and authority. The extreme possibilities she encounters shake her foundations, challenging everything she holds to be true. The question for her in the long run is, Which beliefs have crumbled, which have strengthened, and which have adapted? By the seventh season, she realizes that she is not the same person she was when she began this journey, but she has been changed by it in positive ways ("all things," 7x17). However, is it true, as she tells Mulder in the finale, that "we believe the same thing"?

Full Circle to Find the Truth

One major foundation that is tested for Scully is the Catholic faith of her childhood and her understanding of God. Scully's religious beliefs are not truly addressed or challenged until the third season, when she returns to confession for the first time in six years ("Revelations"), but we do get hints of her religious background at the inception of the series. The symbol of Scully's cross necklace is present from the pilot episode. The cross is not directly explained until a year later, when Mulder tells Scully's mother, "That's something I never considered about her. If she was such a skeptic, why did she wear that?" ("Ascension," 2x06). Mrs. Scully relates that the necklace was a gift from mother to daughter, but the cross clearly comes to mean more to Scully, and to the show, than merely a family keepsake. Early on, the cross may be simply a relic of Scully's past, but even she, as she comes to confront her faith, must ask what it really means to her ("Redux II").

In "Miracle Man," Scully offers a glimpse of her religious upbringing and the beliefs it has imbedded in her. She tells Mulder, "I was raised a Catholic, and I have a certain familiarity with the Scripture. And God never lets the devil steal the show." Scully's Catholic beliefs especially begin to emerge in "Revelations," when she is confronted by paranormal evidence that may actually point to the divine and by Mulder's refusal to accept the divine as an explanation. While she examines the corpse of Owen Jarvis, certain anomalies, such as the lack of decomposition and the faint odor of flowers, remind Scully of stories she once heard about incorruptible saints. Seeing these childhood teachings become reality makes Scully question whether Owen was right, that God's hand is at work here, and that God has called her to help save the boy, Kevin Kryder. In the end, Scully is left struggling to understand what she has witnessed, especially since Mulder doesn't share her interpretation of events. Because of this, she doesn't feel comfortable discussing her struggle with Mulder, so she visits a confessional in the closing scene to talk matters through with a priest. She admits that she has seen things that defy explanation, "but now I wonder if I saw them at all, if I didn't just imagine them." She has doubts because Mulder didn't see the same things; "he didn't believe them, and usually he believes without question." The priest suggests,

"Maybe they weren't meant for him to see. Maybe they were only meant for you . . . Perhaps you saw these things because you needed to." "To find my way back?" she asks. The priest replies, "Sometimes we must come full circle to find the truth." This statement itself is another sign, echoing what was said to her earlier by Kevin Kryder's father. But hearing these words again, Scully states that it makes her afraid—"Afraid that God is speaking, but that no one's listening."

While "Revelations" marks Scully's return to church and to her faith, it is clear when she faces cancer in Season 4 that the return is not complete. In the three-episode story arc at the end of this season and the beginning of Season 5, Scully moves from a rejection of Father McCue's attempts to minister to her faith, to a faith crisis and then an openness to seek God's help. It is during this arc that Scully says of her cross, "Why do I wear this, Mom? I put something that I don't even know or understand under the skin of my neck. I will subject myself to these crazy treatments, and I keep telling myself that I'm doing everything I can, but it's a lie" ("Redux II"). Scully realizes that she has put faith in alien technology, and in medical science, but the one place she has not yet turned to look for a miracle is God. Later, Scully prays the rosary with Father McCue, symbolizing her return to the Church and her willingness to believe not only in science and extreme possibilities but in God as well. Yet that's certainly not the end of Scully's faith journey or of the challenges she will face. In fact, a new challenge arises in Season 5.

Just before the next Christmas, Scully meets Emily, a young girl with a potentially terminal disease, who Scully soon learns is her own biological daughter. But Emily was created to be little more than a lab rat. The girl's future becomes bleak when her adoptive parents are killed, and then her health also takes a downturn. As a doctor and a mother, Scully must face the difficult decision to let Emily die peacefully rather than to prolong her suffering through further tests and experimental procedures. Scully asks about Emily's creators, "Who are the men who would create a life whose only hope is to die?" ("Emily," 5x07). It later becomes clear that Scully struggles with this same question with respect to God.

A few episodes later, "All Souls" recalls themes from "Revelations": Mulder and Scully are again at odds over religion, and Scully's religious convictions provide the driving force for the story. She once more visits a confessional to discuss her experiences with a priest, these scenes providing a framework for the episode. Scully is first brought into the case by Father McCue on Easter Sunday; she tells him that she has been trying to attend church more regularly, evidencing a renewal of her faith and religious commitment since the remission of her cancer. The couple that Father McCue asks Scully to help has just lost their daughter to a mysterious death. The wife, Mrs. Kernof, explains that her husband is angry at God; "He'll never understand how God could forsake the life of an innocent girl. How God, in his mercy, could let this happen." As Scully admits to the priest in the confessional, "Mrs. Kernof was talking about her husband, but she might as well have been talking about me." Scully quite literally identifies Emily with the Kernofs' daughter and the other girls who are dying and struggles to understand how this could happen—how God could allow this to happen. In the story's climax, Scully is faced with the same decision she had to make with Emily: to allow the girl's physical death in order to preserve her soul. But Scully feels incredible guilt over this choice, as she discusses with the priest in the closing scene:

> PRIEST: You believed you were releasing her soul to heaven.
>
> SCULLY: I felt sure of it.
>
> PRIEST: But you still can't reconcile this belief with the physical fact of her death?
>
> SCULLY: No. I thought I could, Father, but I can't.
>
> PRIEST: Do you believe there is a life after this one?
>
> SCULLY: Yes.
>
> PRIEST: Are you sure? Has it occurred to you that maybe this, too, is part of what you were meant to understand?
>
> SCULLY: You mean, accepting my loss?
>
> PRIEST: Can you accept it?
>
> SCULLY: Maybe that's what faith is.

Even ten years later, in *I Want to Believe*, it is apparent that Scully still struggles with this same issue. In fact, if anything she has only become more angry toward God. When her patient, Christian Fearon, is faced with a terminal diagnosis, Scully can't accept the idea of giving up on his treatment and letting him die. She tells Mulder, "Even the experts say there's nothing to be done. Nothing but let him die. So I'm lying here cursing God for all his cruelties." She applies to God the same type of question that she asked about Emily's creators: "Why bring a kid into the world just to make him suffer?" While William, the son she gave up for adoption, is mentioned in this context rather than Emily, the loss of both children from Scully's life has left her with the same dilemma that was earlier an obstacle for Mulder: Why must the innocent suffer? Always providing a counterpoint to her beliefs, Mulder exhibits the peace that Scully lacks. He is willing to accept that his sister is in a better place, but although Scully tells the priest in "All Souls" that she does believe in an afterlife, there is no indication that she even considers this in *I Want to Believe*. Later in the movie, she admits that she has put Christian through hell in an effort to keep him alive (thereby making him suffer, the same thing of which she has accused God); she never expresses the possibility that releasing him from life might instead allow him to go to heaven.

This is not the only faith crisis Scully faces in the second *X-Files* movie. She is obviously in conflict with Father Ybarra, a hospital administrator, which may reflect either a problem with authority or a problem with the Catholic Church. But Scully has even greater conflict with another priest, the defrocked Father Joe, a convicted pedophile. She is livid at his very existence, let alone that he has the gall to pray for God's forgiveness. Yet when Scully—who in two previous episodes has turned to a priest in the confessional in order to understand her religious struggles—faces a crisis of faith, she turns not to an active priest but to one who is disgraced, the man she despises.[3] In a "confessional" scene, she uneasily approaches Father Joe alone, admits in anger that she is living in sin, and demands answers about the visions he is receiving. Rather than coming to this "confessional" to seek forgiveness, she comes to pass judgment. She spits at him, "You can ask for His pity, but don't expect mine." Scully's main difficulty is that Father Joe claims to be hearing from God, and that she actually believes these messages in spite of her own misgivings. She cannot accept that God would forgive so vile a sinner as Father Joe and would reward him by giving him visions and words from heaven. Presenting the opposite point of view, Mulder is willing to accept the possibility that God could forgive: "What if Father Joe's prayers were answered after all? What if he were forgiven, because he didn't give up?"

In her questioning of God's reasons and justice, Scully is much like two biblical figures: Job and Jonah. Job suffers the loss of his wealth and his children, and eventually his health, but through it all insists that he is a righteous man and does not deserve judgment. Scully too has suffered her share of losses: her career, her children, and for a period of time, her health. From the way she reacts to Father Joe it is clear that she associates herself with the righteous. Like Job, she wants to know why God would let the innocent suffer if he is a just God. The innocent she refers to are the children, like Christian, but the question also applies to herself. Why would God allow her to find Emily, only for Emily to die, or to have a miraculous conception of William, only to give William away? In some ways, though, Scully is more like Jonah, angry that God would show mercy to the guilty. Jonah reluctantly obeys God's command to warn the Ninevites, the enemies of God's people, that God is about to destroy them. Then he camps out, waiting to watch the fireworks God is about to rain down. Why is Jonah reluctant to tell his enemies that God's wrath is coming upon them? Because he knows God will be merciful if they repent. The punch line in Jonah's story is that he is more concerned about the plant God provides to give him shade than he is about human beings, while God cares about even their animals. Scully is Jonah railing at God, "How dare you be gracious and loving! How dare you forgive and spare my worst enemies!" She can't stomach the idea that God would forgive Father Joe and, moreover, bless him with divine messages. She wants to see God prove his justice in fire and brimstone, when he instead reveals it through his mercy.

At the end of *I Want to Believe*, Scully continues to act on Father Joe's message to her, "Don't give up." Does that mean she has accepted that God could forgive him? Has she finally come to peace with it? We don't know for certain, but we have reason to hope. Mulder repeats to her the same message, telling her that maybe that's the larger answer: "Don't give up." The slogan can be applied in any number of ways, but it may also apply to Scully's relationship with God. God never gave up on Father Joe, someone who didn't deserve mercy, so he would certainly not give up on Scully. She too should not give up on God. In Job's account, after everything he has lost, his wife and his friends want him to forsake God or simply accept his punishment. But Job never gives up on God. It is his faithfulness that gives him the right to ask the difficult questions. But to ask those questions, one must be willing to accept God's answers. Job receives answers, and he receives closure as God blesses him double for everything he has lost. For Jonah, though, his fate remains open—as does Scully's. But that is true to life. As Chris Carter described, faith is a struggle, and it is that honest struggle that Scully represents.

Science as Sacred

The other major foundation that is tested for Scully is her faith in science. In the pilot episode, Mulder asks his new partner, "Do you believe in the existence of extraterrestrials?" Scully replies, "Logically, I would have to say no." By the end of Season 7 she answers the same question with the careful declaration, "I've seen things that I cannot deny" ("Requiem," 7x22). Scully does not arrive easily at a belief in aliens, even though she herself comes to qualify as an abductee. While her foundation is shaken, it is not shattered, as she learns to adapt her understanding of the ends that science can achieve. For her, simply because science cannot explain certain things doesn't mean it will never be able to; she still believes in the methods and the principles, even if the evidence is beyond science's current abilities. As a cocky young scientist, she asserts in the pilot: "What I find fantastic is any notion that there are answers beyond the realm of science. The answers are there; you just have to know where to look." Years later, she may no longer be so certain where to look for the answers, but she still has confidence that the answers are there to be found.

Even in the first season, Scully begins to show some doubts about her scientific preconceptions. At the end of that season, in "The Erlenmeyer Flask," Scully encounters scientific evidence of DNA that can be described as nothing other than extraterrestrial. She tells Mulder, "I've always held science as sacred. I've always put my trust in the accepted facts. And what I saw last night, for the first time in my life, I don't know what to believe." But he has something even more extreme to show her: the human experiments being carried out with that DNA. He replies, "Whatever it is you do believe, Scully, when you walk into that room, nothing sacred will hold." Of course, the evidence has been cleared out and covered up, so Scully doesn't actually see it for herself, but she does later get to hold in her hands what looks very much like an alien fetus.

Paralleling Mulder's own beliefs, Scully's faith is not only challenged but also reinvigorated by the evidence she encounters. In "End Game," when Mulder turns up in Alaska nearly dead but with a newfound faith to keep looking for his sister, Scully's voiceover also affirms the renewal of her own convictions:

> Several aspects of this case remain unexplained, suggesting the possibility of paranormal phenomena, but I am convinced that to accept such conclusions is to abandon all hope of understanding the scientific events behind them. Many of the things I have seen have challenged my faith and my belief in an ordered universe, but this uncertainty has only strengthened my need to know, to understand, to apply reason to those things which seem to defy it. It was science that isolated the retrovirus Agent Mulder was exposed to, and science that allowed us to understand its behavior. And ultimately, it was science that saved Agent Mulder's life.

Scully knows that her partner depends on her scientific rationality, even as he bemoans it. At times such as this, her recourse to science literally saves his life; at others, it may save his sanity or his reputation. She recognizes throughout their partnership that her contribution is to hold his theories to a higher standard, to make them palatable to their FBI superiors and the justice system. In order to fulfill this part of her job, she refuses to compromise herself or her science. Her openness to Mulder's extreme possibilities, then, goes no further than what science will permit. As Scully tells him, "I'm willing to believe, but not in a lie and not in the opposite of what I can prove" ("The Beginning," 6x01).

There are also times when Scully is not as willing to believe. These usually revolve around her own personal experiences and her inability to assimilate them or to examine them objectively. For example, Scully doesn't contact Mulder right away when she learns that Emily is her daughter, "because I couldn't believe it" ("Emily").

Likewise, when she sees visions that suggest her own death is near as her cancer worsens, she doesn't tell Mulder at first because she doesn't want to believe what she has seen or what it could mean ("Elegy," 4x22). In Season 1, she admits to him, "I'm afraid to believe" ("Beyond the Sea," 1x12). That fear surfaces when something personal is at stake, when her scientific foundation feels shaky beneath her feet. But through the progression of the series, a shift occurs, so that by Season 8 Scully can then say that Mulder has given her the "courage to believe" ("Empedocles," 8x17). With understanding and openness to new possibilities, she has driven away the fear.

With "Requiem," and Scully's admission that she's seen things that she cannot deny, it is clear that she has already come a long way from the beginning of the series, yet an even more seismic shift occurs for her in Season 8. Mulder is gone, apparently abducted by aliens; their boss, Assistant Director Skinner, saw the UFO for himself and is willing to go on record as a believer; and Scully has a new partner, a skeptic, moving her to the position of the believer. Scully the scientist tries to play the role of Mulder. Yet, as a scientist, she still cannot compromise her beliefs in objectivity and evidence. It is an uncomfortable position for her, and leaves the audience uncomfortable as well, but the new perspective further expands her horizons. By the series finale, Scully is able to declare under oath, "I came to believe in the existence of extraterrestrial life," and to give a scientific narrative of the origins and perseverance of alien life on this planet. Yet, she has not abandoned her "need to know, to understand, to apply reason to those things which seem to defy it," as she described in "End Game." Her faith in science remains unshaken, even if her understanding of science has adapted to new experiences and data. When her tenure on the X-Files is over, it is her scientific roots to which she returns. Scully the FBI agent is packed away, yielding once more to Scully the doctor (*I Want to Believe*)—a doctor who is willing to take a chance on extreme possibilities.

SEEING IS BELIEVING—BELIEVING IS SEEING

In "Jose Chung's *From Outer Space*," a mysterious Man in Black lectures Roky Crikenson, "Your scientists have yet to discover how neural networks create self-consciousness, let alone how the human brain processes two-dimensional retinal images into the three-dimensional phenomenon known as perception. Yet you somehow brazenly declare, 'seeing is believing'?" The relationship between seeing and believing, or experience and faith, is explored in a number of ways throughout *The X-Files*. It is apparent in Mulder's spiritual awakening, when his eyes are opened along with his heart; it is also manifest in Scully's unwillingness to believe the things that she sees, and in her eventual acquiescence that she can no longer deny the proof before her own eyes. As the adage goes, "seeing is believing," which is another way of saying, "I'll believe it when I see it." But can you always rely on what your eyes see? If what you see challenges what you hold to be true, which will you choose to believe? And does belief itself sometimes shape perception, so that believing is seeing?

In the constant tension between the viewpoints of Mulder and Scully, *The X-Files* often plays with what Scully sees versus what Mulder sees in order to keep at bay Scully's ability to believe. For example, in "Shadows" (1x05), Mulder and another character are trapped in a room, caught up in a paper tornado brought on by a ghost—but by the time Scully is able to pry the door open, all motion has stopped. Or, in "Arcadia" (6x13), Scully is barricaded in a closet while a character battles a monster in the room just beyond; the same monster comes chasing after Mulder outside the house, but by the time Scully makes it to the front door the monster has disintegrated, so that all she sees is Mulder standing in a pile of dirt. By creatively preventing Scully from seeing what Mulder sees, the writers also prevent her from believing what Mulder believes.

Even when confronted by the "proof" of what she has seen for herself, Scully does not readily accept the same conclusions, or even trust her own eyes. To her, personal experience—even her own—is too subjective; instead, she needs quantifiable, reducible evidence. In "Nisei," Mulder challenges her, "Scully, after all you've seen, after all you've told me you've seen—the tunnel filled with medical files, the beings moving past you, the implant in your neck—why do you refuse to believe?" She answers, "Believing's the easy part, Mulder. I just need more than you. I need proof." Clearly, her own personal experience does not qualify as "proof" in her mind. The same issue emerges four seasons later in "Je Souhaite" (7x21) after she has encountered an invisible man; when the body disappears from the morgue—and thus the physical proof is gone—Scully is no longer sure what she experienced. Mulder tells her, "You saw it. It was real." But she replies, "I don't know what I saw, Mulder." In a later scene, she still expresses doubt. Mulder argues, "You examined an invisible body, remember?" Scully says, "I thought I did." (And Mulder groans in frustration.) Toward the end of the series, Scully can admit that she's seen things she can't deny, but it's still difficult for her to articulate exactly what her beliefs are, based on what she's seen.

Can one's eyes or personal experience always be trusted? For Scully, the answer is generally no. In fact, she would more readily declare herself temporarily insane or susceptible to suggestion than accept the conclusions of her own sight and memories. She especially doubts herself when she sees the same thing that Mulder has seen or described. This is illustrated most vividly in the episode titled "Folie à Deux" (5x19), a phrase that Scully translates for us as "a madness shared by two." This is how she is able to rationalize what she has encountered. The monster in the episode is one that can hide himself from the sight of others, so that only those whose eyes are properly opened can see what he really is. But those who claim they see this monster, instead of the kindly man that everyone else sees, are considered insane. This is true first of the workplace shooter, Gary Lambert, who claims that other people can't see the monster "because it hides in the light. I see it. I know where to look." But as Gary screams at Mulder to turn around and "Look at it!" Mulder too sees the creature that Gary has been ranting about. Acting on that new perception, Mulder is also judged to be insane. He tells Scully from his hospital bed, "*You* have to be willing to see." Her willingness doesn't come immediately, but later Scully also sees the zombies and then the creature that Mulder described. How does she reconcile these images with her perception of reality? A madness shared by two. It's easier for her to claim they were both temporarily "insane" (or shared the same misperception of reality) than to accept that what she saw could be true.

As with "Folie à Deux," there are a number of additional X-Files cases that revolve around the perpetrator influencing others' perceptions of reality, or causing them to see something that isn't really there and to act based on what they see. It is then the ability to discern what is a false vision and what is real that allows the investigator to solve the case or to bring the suspect to justice. In these situations, it is often true that believing is seeing. "Sleepless" (2x04) and "Pusher" (3x17)—along with "Kitsunegari" (5x08), the sequel to "Pusher"—both present similar scenarios, where the suspect is able to cause people to see certain things or to mistake one thing for another, such as seeing a Bible as a gun, or a baseball bat as a snake. In "Sleepless," the perceived reality is so strong that it can even kill—a man essentially burns to death, not because there was a fire, but because he believed there was. In "Kitsunegari," Mulder almost shoots Scully because the "pusher," Linda Bowman, wills Mulder to see Scully shooting herself, and then wills him to see Linda in place of the real Scully. Ready to take revenge on the woman who caused his partner's death, Mulder raises his gun to the woman he sees as Linda, when in reality he is holding a gun on Scully.

The ability to shape the perception of others is especially powerful in the conclusion to "Badlaa" (8x12). A Siddhi mystic causes others to see him as any number of other people, but in the final confrontation, he appears as a young boy. Scully knows logically that the image she's seeing is not the truth, and that in order to protect another child she may need to fire on the suspect. What her eyes see, though, in place of the suspect, is an innocent boy. She must make the difficult choice to fire at the boy, acting contrary to her own sight and her perception of reality. While she knows she made the right choice in the end, it is emotionally jarring because what she experienced was that "I shot a young boy." When Agent Doggett tells her that the good news is she's wrong, Scully replies, "But it's what I saw. With my eyes, anyway. Do you know what it's like not to be able to trust your own eyes?" By the next season, in "Scary Monsters" (9x12), Doggett has learned the lesson for himself. When a boy draws pictures that cause other people to see those things happening, Doggett understands that the things they're seeing aren't real, and that if they will refuse to believe these images, then the images can no longer do them harm. It is the belief itself that makes the false images "real." Once they are recognized as false, and no longer believed, they cease to be true.

These examples raise all sorts of questions, including: What is reality, and how is it related to perception? Can you believe your own eyes? Can belief itself create reality? One answer is that perception *is* reality for the person who perceives it—what you see is real to you. Another way of saying this is that one's understanding of reality is shaped by one's beliefs. What a person believes can or will happen shapes how that person interprets what does happen. As Mulder phrases it when discussing legends about monsters and inhuman creatures, such things are "true in the sense that they're believed to be true" ("The Post-Modern Prometheus"; see chapter 5, below). But these *X-Files* episodes also suggest that faith itself has a kind of power, or that willingness to see and believe opens a person up to a new realm of possibilities. (To modify Samuel's statement in "Miracle Man": Open your heart, and it might just open your eyes.) This is particularly true in episodes where Scully's eyes are opened to divine realities but Mulder's are not, such as in "Revelations" when Scully's ability to perceive the signs from God leads her to save Kevin Kryder's life. But is faith based on signs, or are signs the reward for faith? In other words, what is the relationship between faith and evidence?

One explanation of this relationship may be found in the Bible, with the signs and miracles that Jesus performs, why he does so, and how people respond to them. The Gospels present two different types of miracles, or two different relationships between miracles and faith. Particularly in the Gospel of John, miracles are signs, the evidence that gives people reason to believe in Jesus and his words. For those who demand a sign, seeing is believing. (See, for example, John 6:30: "What sign are you going to give us then, so that we may see it and believe you?") But, predominantly in the other three Gospels, the opposite is found: the miracle is a reward for faith—"Your faith has made you whole" (Matthew 9:22). For these people, believing is seeing.

Through the course of the Gospels, it is clear which category Jesus prefers, and which type of faith is more lasting. He condemns those who demand a sign from him (Matthew 16:1–4); he allows to go on their way others who have seen his signs but, once the show is over, refuse to believe or understand (John 6:66). Even Jesus's closest disciples struggle to believe without proof. Hence, doubting Thomas earns his infamy, saying after the resurrection, "Unless I see the marks of the nails in his hands . . . I will not believe" (John 20:25). In fact, it is often the people most removed from Jesus, both culturally and physically—a Roman centurion (Matthew 8:5-13), a woman who is ritually unclean and must fight her way through the crowd to get to Jesus (Matthew 9:20-22), a Canaanite woman who has to shout to be heard (Matthew 15:21-28)—who have the simplest faith and are rewarded for their belief with miracles. But the greatest reward is for those who will believe without signs or miracles; as Jesus tells doubting Thomas, "blessed are those who have not seen and yet believe" (John 20:29). The same point is made later in the New Testament, at the end of the great chapter on faith, Hebrews 11: the Old Testament figures named here are praised for their faith precisely because they did not see the fulfillment of everything that was promised to them, and yet they believed. The true and better fulfillment was yet to come with the arrival of Jesus Christ.

In their own way, Mulder and Scully exemplify the two relationships between faith and evidence depicted in the Gospels. When it comes to aliens, Mulder wants to believe, and has a kernel of belief, but he is ultimately seeking evidence to justify his faith and to prove to others the truth of his claims. On the subject of God, Mulder does not state so clearly that he wants to believe, but he does say that he waits for a miracle every day. He wants a sign to earn his faith. He challenges Scully to consider whether the existence of God could be proved or disproved. His final verdict awaits the empirical evidence. Scully, on the other hand, counters that God's existence is not something that can be disproved. To accept God's existence, then, requires faith. Her faith to follow the trail of things she cannot fully understand is rewarded by apparent divine intervention, to save a boy's life ("Revelations") and a girl's soul ("All Souls"). She takes a leap of faith to reimplant the microchip whose removal resulted in her cancer, and in faith she returns to her Catholic roots to pray for healing—as a result of one or the other (or both), her cancer goes into remission. Even in relation to science, Scully moves forward in faith and is rewarded with results. She believes that science holds the answers to the unexplained; if the answers don't seem to be there (if they remain unseen), it is only because science does not yet fully understand. But her faith is in the fact that science can, and will, provide the answers, even when proof of this does not yet exist. Ironically, then, Mulder the believer often requires evidence in order to believe, but Scully the skeptical scientist begins with faith and from that position seeks understanding.

BELIEVE TO UNDERSTAND

Scully's trust in science provides an example of faith seeking understanding, and perhaps also a paradigm for her returning faith in God. At the end of "Herrenvolk" (4x01), after another set of unbelievable experiences and proof that has once again slipped through their fingers, Mulder tells her, "You put such faith in your science, Scully. But, the things I've seen, science provides no place to start." In her reply, Scully states her conviction in science and its abilities: "Nothing happens in contradiction to nature, only in contradiction to what we know of it. And that's a place to start." That starting point is her faith in science, her surety that science ultimately can find the explanations it doesn't currently have. From that position of faith, Scully seeks the understanding that science can eventually bring. Faith provides a foundation from which to seek understanding, but faith can also open up one's mind to accept that understanding. It is Mulder's belief in the paranormal that allows him to reach conclusions Scully cannot; it is Scully's belief in God that allows her to perceive God's hand at work where Mulder cannot. Faith opens the doors to perception, which permits understanding.

The saying "faith seeking understanding" was the motto and guiding principle for the eleventh-century theologian St. Anselm. But the concept can be traced back at least seven centuries earlier, to St. Augustine. In *Sermon* 43, Augustine explains that to someone who would say, "Let me understand, in order to believe," he retorts, "On the contrary, believe in order to understand."[4] Anselm echoes the words of Augustine: "For I do not seek to understand in order to believe; I believe in order to understand."[5] Believe to understand—this expression means both that to know God (to understand) presumes one believes that God exists, and that faith drives one to desire a deeper understanding. This also describes the relationship between faith and reason, similar to the dynamic between faith and evidence. For both Anselm and Augustine, faith is not opposed to reason or a kind of blind acceptance that doesn't ask questions or dig too deep. Rather, reason is something that, as humans, we are meant to exercise. It is part of the way in which we were created in God's image. God gave us brains and wants us to use them. Yet Anselm considers it prideful to assume that reason alone is sufficient to allow him to "scale the heights" of God; "but I do long to understand your truth in some way, your truth which my heart believes and loves."[6] He starts with faith, the truth that he loves; his faith gives him the desire to understand the truth more fully.

While reason is the intellectual ability to understand, evidence is the data that reason weighs in its decision. What, then, is the relationship between faith and evidence? The bottom line is that we often interpret evidence, or we reason, based on what we believe or want to believe. Mulder and Scully prove this constantly: when confronted with the same information, they often interpret it in different ways based on their own preconceptions. Scully claims the existence of God can't be proved, but what would it take to prove God's existence to Mulder? Divine intervention? Signs? Miracles? And yet, when Scully believes she sees signs from God, Mulder doesn't see them, or refuses to see them, and tells her, "I wait for a miracle every day." What miracle is that? The return of his sister. The basis of his faith is narrowed to one specific issue, the one sign he wants to see. Once he understands his sister's fate, then he will believe. Even disbelief is a form of belief, just believing differently. We all have our preconceptions and our structures of how we want or expect reality to be, and this shapes how we will accept the "evidence" before us. In the end, though, can "evidence" alone ever be enough to prove, or disprove, that God exists? Should we understand to believe, or believe to understand? In terms of faith in God, Scully would say no, God's existence cannot be proved or disproved; therefore, you can't reason your way to faith. In this case, faith provides a basis for exercising reason—faith seeks understanding.

The expression "believe to understand" is also picked up by *The X-Files*; it occurs as the substituted tagline in the opening credits for "Closure." This phrase appears on the screen not long after Mulder's voiceover about the loss of so many innocents and God's role in such tragedy. In this monologue, Mulder states twice, "I want to believe."

The fact that his speech is followed by this tagline suggests that if Mulder will take the leap of faith, he will find enlightenment (if he will believe, he will understand). At the end of the episode, this is what he does find: a fulfillment of his desire stated in the opening voiceover ("that that which is born still lives and cannot be buried in the cold earth, but only waits to be born again at God's behest, where in ancient starlight we lay in repose") and closure of the gaping wound in his life—the fate of his sister. The foil to Mulder's faith in this episode is another character who has lost a loved one: Harold Piller. In the end, when Mulder believes he has discovered the fate of both his own sister and Harold's son, Harold refuses to believe what Mulder describes. Because Harold does not believe, he does not understand what Mulder understands, that the children are in a better place. Another negative example proves the point: when it comes to the paranormal, not only does Scully not believe, but she often refuses to believe. After she has seen a ghostly visitation in "Elegy," and Mulder asks her why she didn't tell him, she says, "Because I didn't want to believe it. Because I don't want to believe it." No amount of logic or personal experience will bring her to faith if she is not willing to believe. Belief must come first, and then understanding will follow.

FAITH THE SIZE OF A MUSTARD SEED

In the Gospel of Mark, there is an account of a father who brings his demon-possessed son to Jesus and pleads for his help, if Jesus is able to do anything for them. Jesus takes exception to the father's wording: "'If you are able'!—All things can be done for the one who believes." The father immediately says, "I believe," but then quickly qualifies it: "help my unbelief!" (Mark 9:23–24). It doesn't matter that some doubt lingers in the father's heart; Jesus rewards his willingness to believe by delivering his son, which gives him reason to believe as well. In Matthew, however, the same story is told with a different focus. Instead of noting the father's unbelief, Matthew highlights the weak belief of the disciples. Before coming to Jesus, the man first brought his son to Jesus's disciples, who had themselves been given authority over demons and the ability to heal. But they are confounded that they have not been able to cast the demon out of this boy. After Jesus is able to do so, the disciples ask him why they couldn't. He answers, "Because of your little faith. For truly I tell you, if you have faith the size of a mustard seed, you will say to this mountain, 'Move from here to there,' and it will move; and nothing will be impossible for you" (Matthew 17:20; cf. Luke 17:5–6). Faith, even in small amounts, is able to move mountains. It can result in miracles, or in understanding. Even when it is only the beginning of faith—the willingness to believe—and needs to be nurtured to grow into its full potential, faith is rewarded.

Hebrews 11:6 says, "Without faith it is impossible to please God." It is clear in the healing of this boy, and throughout the Gospels, that Jesus values faith. He rewards it with miracles, praises those who believe without seeing, and condemns those who demand a sign in order to believe. Why is faith so important to Jesus, and to God? The verse in Hebrews continues: "whoever would approach [God] must believe that he exists and that he rewards those who seek him." So this belief is twofold: that God is real, and that he interacts (positively) with his people. In *The X-Files*, the second part is the stumbling block for Mulder. He may accept that God exists, but not that God interacts with people if justice is not served. Scully is more accepting in her belief that God exists, and that he interacts with humans; although, like Job, she wants to hold him accountable for the fate of the innocent, and like Jonah, even more so for the fate of the guilty.

Faith is also important as a statement of trust. To trust is to believe in someone. Trust breeds intimacy, while the lack of trust is divisive. Mulder and Scully constantly exemplify this dynamic: it is their trust in each other, and each other alone, that binds them so closely together. A God who interacts with his people, who rewards those who seek him, is a God who desires relationship with them. He desires the intimacy and bond that comes through trust. Faith, therefore, entails not only acknowledging God's existence and his loving interaction with us, but also trusting his decisions in how to run the universe. We have to trust that he is God and, as Scully says, that "God has his reasons" ("All Souls"). This is the answer God gave when Job confronted him about the suffering of the innocent: I'm God, I created the universe, so trust me to take proper care of it (see Job 38–41). Faith is accepting that if God is just, then the injustice of this world will be balanced out by justice in the next. We may not always comprehend God's ways or his reasons, but from a position of faith, we can stand in dialogue with him and seek understanding.

There are always questions we continue to grapple with, but what Mulder represents for most of the series is the individual who asks those questions outside of a faith relationship: God, if you're up there, prove to me that you exist and that you are good, and then I will believe in you. Scully, on the other hand, represents Job or Jonah, someone who starts from a foundation of faith and asks the difficult questions within the faith relationship: God, it is because I believe you exist and you are good that I don't understand why there seems to be evidence that contradicts these truths. Mulder may want to believe, but Scully has faith seeking understanding. The person who is willing, like Mulder, to have at least a kernel of faith can cry out with the father in the Gospel, "Help my unbelief!" Faith, no matter how small, is still faith. The willingness to believe opens up a world of opportunities: with faith, anything is possible—even finding peace about the loss of a loved one or understanding about the things in the world that just don't make sense. Some of the answers to these challenging questions that plague believer and skeptic alike will be addressed in the chapters that follow, especially relating to love, fate, and the ultimate sacrifice.

NOTES

1. Frank Spotnitz, "Threads of the Mythology," *"The X-Files" Mythology: Black Oil*, DVD (Twentieth Century Fox Home Entertainment, 2005).

2. Chris Carter, "Threads of the Mythology," *"The X-Files" Mythology: Super Soldiers*, DVD (Twentieth Century Fox Home Entertainment, 2005).

3. There is another subtle connection between *I Want to Believe* and the confessional scenes from "All Souls." In a hospital administrative meeting during *I Want to Believe*, the camera spends a great deal of time on another priest seated next to Father Ybarra, a priest who never speaks a word and is given no name. This priest is played by J. P. Finn—the same actor who portrayed the anonymous priest in Scully's confessional during "All Souls."

4. Augustine, *Sermons on the Old Testament: 20–50*, trans. Edmund Hill, ed. John E. Rotelle, The Works of Saint Augustine: A Translation for the 21st Century 3/2 (Hyde Park, NY: New City, 1990), 240 (§7). (Cf. Augustine, *On Free Choice of the Will*.) This is based in part on his reading of Isaiah 7:9 (following the Greek [Septuagint]), which he quotes as "Unless you believe, you shall not understand." Following rather the Hebrew, English versions translate the verse: "If you do not stand firm in faith, you shall not stand at all" (NRSV).

5. Anselm, *Proslogion: With the Replies of Gaunilo and Anselm*, trans. Thomas Williams (Indianapolis: Hackett, 2001), 6 (chapter 1).

6. Anselm, *Proslogion* (trans. Williams), 6 (chapter 1).

3

Hope

"I Can't Give Up"

SCULLY: I've seen things too. But there are answers to be found now. We have hope that there's a place to start. That's what I believe.

MULDER: You put such faith in your science, Scully. But, the things I've seen, science provides no place to start.

SCULLY: Nothing happens in contradiction to nature, only in contradiction to what we know of it. And that's a place to start. That's where the hope is. ("Herrenvolk," 4x01)

The last episode of Season 1 ends with the X-Files being shut down by the powers that be. Mulder is distraught, but he vows to Scully, "I'm not going to give up. I can't give up, not as long as the truth is out there" ("The Erlenmeyer Flask," 1x23). This statement of determination and hope is one that resounds throughout the series. Mulder's hope that he can find both his sister and the truth surrounding her disappearance (therefore, the truth about aliens) is the driving force for the show. It is also the driving force for Mulder, what keeps him going, along with the others who have been drawn into his quest. By the end of the series, Scully echoes her partner's commitment: "I know you—you can't give up. It's what I saw in you when we first met. It's what made me follow you, and why I'd do it all over again" ("The Truth," 9x20).

In this persistent quest, Mulder represents the human need to have hope, something to look forward to so that we can push on in the face of adversity. Scully recognizes that sense of drive and purpose in him, and it propels her onward as well. Even when the future seems bleak and set in stone, Mulder is able to say, at the end of the series finale, "Maybe there's hope." It's hope that gives him reason to carry on every day, even when his work has been shut down, or when the truth he's learned is that he's already been defeated. Hope tells him that maybe the future isn't determined, maybe things can still change for the better, and it's worth pressing on and fighting the good fight in case it's still possible to win. Hope allows us as humans to thrive, to show our incredible resilience and tenacity, and to find meaning in every day. Hope allows us not to give up.

THE SUBSTANCE OF THINGS HOPED FOR

Hope is in many ways closely linked to faith. These two form part of the great triad of theological virtues: faith, hope, and love. Hebrews 11:1 even defines faith in terms of hope: "Faith is the substance of things hoped for" (KJV), or said differently, "faith is confidence in what we hope for" (NIV). Faith is a belief, a conviction, a sense of surety. Hope is not an assurance but a desire; it is less certain than faith, and is dependent on uncertainty. But having faith allows us to hope, and hope itself can grow into the certainty of faith. Mulder expresses his own hope in terms of faith: in "End Game" (2x17), after Mulder has faced doubts about his quest, he tells Scully that he has found "faith to keep looking." This is a statement of hope. It is another way of saying that he won't give up, because he has the conviction that the answers are there to be found and are worth pursuing. He believes the truth is still out there, which gives him hope to keep looking for it.

Scully also defines hope in relation to faith, but for her, it is in the context of science. In "Herrenvolk" (4x01), Mulder says that

Scully puts such faith in her science. For Scully, that faith gives her a reason to hope: "Nothing happens in contradiction to nature, only in contradiction to what we know of it. And that's a place to start. That's where the hope is." Her faith in science's ability to find answers gives her hope that the explanations she doesn't currently have can and will be found. Like Mulder, she believes the truth is out there, but where she pursues that truth is in science. Just as Mulder finds the faith to keep looking for his sister, Scully finds the faith to keep researching and applying the scientific method to unexplained phenomena. For her, that's the source of hope—she believes science will provide a reasonable explanation.

Hope in the Possibility

Hope and faith are also closely connected in that they are both related to the unseen. In a way, hope can even be defined as wanting to believe, or wanting that assurance. But while faith can apply to a number of things seen or unseen, known or unknown, the very nature of hope is entirely dependent on uncertainty and possibility. We hope for things that haven't happened yet or of which we don't know the outcome. We hope for the future, not the past. Another way this can be understood is by comparing hope and expectation, or anticipation. Both relate to what has not yet happened, but hope is a desire for what might happen, whereas anticipation is based on what we know will happen. It is the difference between hoping that the home team will win a game, and anticipating a concert for which you have tickets. Mulder expresses this regarding his pursuit of the lake monster Big Blue, but his words apply to his quest in general. After Scully asks, "You really expect to find this thing, don't you, Mulder?" he explains, "I know the difference between expectation and hope. Seek and ye shall find, Scully" ("Quagmire," 3x22). He continues to seek based on the hope that he will find. But while hope carries with it the possibility of success or fulfillment, it also carries the possibility of disappointment. Mulder is willing to accept this risk because he believes that his hope is justified and that the reward is worth it. In the end of this episode, Mulder *is* disappointed because instead of Big Blue, the creature he is chasing apparently turns out to be an alligator. Mulder tells his partner, "I guess I just wanted Big

Blue to be real. I guess I see hope in such a possibility." Scully replies, "Well, there's still hope. That's why these myths and stories have endured. People want to believe."

The reality that hope depends on the unknown also means that as humans we thrive on the uncertainties of life and on the fact that the future is not yet written. *The X-Files* uses negative examples to prove this point: if one can know the future, either through time travel ("Synchrony," 4x19) or through psychic abilities ("Clyde Bruckman's Final Repose," 3x04), all hope is lost. Mulder faces this type of emotional challenge in the series finale ("The Truth," 9x19–20): Is the future already set? Does that mean there is no longer hope? In such cases, a degree of faith is required—you must believe the message or trust the messenger to accept their description of the future. The same issues apply to the present for things that have already happened but the results are unknown to someone, such as discovering the fate of a loved one, a fate long sealed but only now learned. This is especially illustrated by Mulder and the truth about what happened to his sister. The hope and uncertainty of not knowing that truth are often reflected in parallel accounts of others who have lost children. In "Paper Hearts" (4x08), for example, Mulder and Scully visit a man whose daughter went missing back in the 1970s, to tell him that her body has been found. The words the father speaks cut directly to Mulder's heart: "I used to think that missing was worse than dead because you never knew what happened." But, the man says, he now counts his wife lucky because she passed away the previous summer without learning the horrible truth that their daughter was murdered. It was the uncertainty about what happened to the girl that allowed them to consider the possibilities, both for the best and for the worst. As long as there was a possibility for a good outcome, there was still hope. Once the truth is known, the possibility is removed, and, by definition, hope is gone. The question is, What replaces hope—peace or despair?

The contrast between these two choices is depicted in "Closure" (7x11), when Mulder finally does learn what happened to Samantha. When he realizes she is dead, that means there is no longer a possibility she is alive—there is no more hope. Instead, he is left with the peace that she is in a better place. For him to accept this peace, however, he must accept the truth; he must believe the answer he has found. This is made clear through the foil of a character who chooses not to believe: Harold Piller. Although Harold also seeks to learn what happened to the child he has lost, when Mulder claims that Harold's son is dead along with Samantha, Harold refuses to accept it. He would rather cling to the possibility that his son is still alive because the uncertainty allows him hope. The unbearable alternative that he is running from is clearly not the peace Mulder has achieved but despair. Yet is false hope, or hope built on a lie, better than no hope at all?

The notion of false hope is represented by Dostoyevsky's Grand Inquisitor, one who would offer "hope" to others by controlling their knowledge. Two different characters in *The X-Files* depict this facet of the Inquisitor. One is the Cigarette-Smoking Man (CSM) in "Talitha Cumi" (3x24; see chapter 1, above). Here, he asks Jeremiah Smith in regard to the miracles he has performed, "Have you any idea what the cost of your actions is? ... Who are you to give them hope?" CSM expresses his controlling tendencies even more directly in "Closure" when he and Scully discuss what really happened to Mulder's sister. CSM says that he has always believed Samantha to be dead. Scully says accusingly, "So you just let Mulder believe that she was alive for all these years." He replies, "Out of kindness, Agent Scully. Allow him his ignorance. It's what gives him hope." But in "The Truth," CSM makes it clear that keeping Mulder in ignorance was not an act of compassion or kindness but control. He was waiting for the right moment to tell Mulder the truth, to see him broken and afraid. It appears CSM has succeeded in this, as Mulder is defeated and despairing, until the end of the last scene when Scully helps him realize that "maybe there's hope."

A character similar to CSM appears in "Hell Money" (3x19). This story takes place in a Chinese immigrant community in San Francisco where Chinese men are discovered to be part of a secretive group that plays a kind of "game." It is a lottery: if they win, they will be rich; if they lose, they must donate a body part, such as an eye, a kidney, or even a heart. Each night, they go into the lottery drawing with high hopes of the money they could win and what that could mean to their families. The doctor who sponsors the lottery represents for them the great wealth and success that they can attain. What the men do not know, however, until it is revealed at the end of the story, is that the game is rigged. The game pieces are all the same, so that whoever draws will be guaranteed only one result: the sacrifice of a body part. When the doctor is arrested for running this scam, he comes across as a Chinese version of CSM, casually puffing away while Scully interrogates him. She charges him with preying on the men's hopelessness and desperation: "You cheated them out of life by promising them prosperity when the only possible reward was death." The doctor calmly tells her, "In my belief, death is nothing to be feared. It's merely a stage of transition. But life without hope—now, that's living hell. So, hope was my gift to these men." Like CSM, he declares that out of kindness he kept the men in ignorance so they would have the hope to keep living; in truth, though, he was the reason their future was hopeless. But the doctor's words do hit on a certain truth: life without hope is like a living hell. Humans need hope in order to thrive. While this does not have to mean ignorance is bliss, it does mean we need something to look forward to, something in the future that is positive and can give us a reason to carry on. Those who don't find that hope in this world look to it in the next. These negative examples highlight how at times people put their faith, and therefore their hope, in the wrong place.

Just as withholding knowledge can be negative, it can also be done for more positive reasons. Parents don't tell children what they are going to get for Christmas, to allow them the excitement and hope of awaiting their desired gifts on Christmas morning. The lack of full disclosure can lead to happy surprises. It can also lead to the joy of discovery, and the pride of searching and finding. This is why treasure hunts and puzzles are fun, and why mystery novels are a favorite genre; there is a pleasure in finding the result. "It is the glory of God to conceal a thing, but the honor of kings is to search out a matter" (Proverbs 25:2, KJV). This is the verse that Father Joe quotes to Scully in the second *X-Files* movie, *I Want to Believe*. In the context, it is a clue to help Scully find Mulder and save both his life and the life of a young woman. But in a broader sense, the verse talks about the mystery in life. God knows everything, but he doesn't reveal all of his knowledge to humans. At times, that is frustrating, but it can also lead to the enjoyment that comes with seeking and finding. Mystery allows us hope as well. It provides something for us to look forward to, something to press on toward. It teaches us faith so that we must accept the things we cannot see and find certainty in the things that we hope for. But hope also relies on the faith that answers do exist and may someday be found. For those who believe that God exists and that he has the answers, hope lies in seeking the answers from him with the faith that if we seek, we will find. That's where the hope is.

What Do You Hope to Find?

For Mulder, it is the hope that he will find his sister or the truth about her disappearance, combined with his determination not to give up, that fuels his quest and provides the main through line for the series. In contrast, there was once a time in Mulder's life when he had no hope of finding out the truth. In the pilot episode, he recounts to his new partner the story of Samantha's abduction and how it affected his family. "She just disappeared out of her bed one night. Just gone, vanished. No note, no phone calls, no evidence of anything . . . It tore the family apart. No one would talk about it. There were no facts to confront, nothing to offer any hope." The hope he finally found came during his regression-hypnosis session, when his recovered memories of an alien abduction gave him a place to start looking for her. That moment is what initiated his search and propels him on the passionate search that is his trademark.

At a few different points throughout the series, someone poses to Mulder a variation of the question, "What do you hope to find?" These are opportunities for him to restate his quest, to identify where his hope lies and the end goal of his perseverance. In Season 3, while the answer includes the truth about his sister, the list has expanded to include, "why they killed my father . . . and what they did to Agent Scully" during her own abduction ("Paper Clip," 3x02). By the end of the sixth season, some answers have been found, and some loose ends have been tied up; Scully says to Mulder, "After all you've uncovered—a conspiracy of men doing human experiments, men who are all now dead—you exposed their secrets. I mean, you've won. What more could you possibly hope to do or to find?" Mulder's answer is simple: "My sister" ("Biogenesis," 6x22). The mystery that started his quest is still what propels him—until midway through the seventh season, when he believes that he has found out the truth about his sister's fate. By the end of "Closure" Mulder is able to declare that Samantha is dead, that she's in a better place; he says, "I'm free." He is released from his quest.

But if the search for Samantha and uncertainty about her whereabouts is what has given Mulder hope, once the truth is discovered, to use Scully's words, what more could he hope to do or to find? One answer comes in the series finale ("The Truth"): Mulder has still been seeking the truth about extraterrestrial life and what plans the aliens have for our planet. In the course of the episode, he finds out the date for colonization is set, the future is already written. He seems to despair, until the final scene when he determines there is yet another place to look for hope: "I want to believe that if we listen to what's speaking, it can give us the power to save ourselves." Mulder no longer looks to aliens for the truth; he looks to "something greater than us," and he discovers that "maybe there's hope." In a sense, though, Mulder never stops looking for his sister, never gives up his hope of saving her. This is what Scully asserts in *I Want to Believe*—once Mulder is convinced his sister is dead, he looks for other "sisters." Just as he has done throughout the series, he continues trying to save other young women, especially those for whom all hope has been abandoned, because in each of them he sees Samantha. Thus, as long as there is uncertainty about their fate, he never gives up hope that these missing women can be found.

While not every person has one defining moment or one single purpose to send them on an all-consuming quest, as Mulder does, we can all identify with his need for hope about the future and the unknown. The question could also be posed to each of us: What do you hope to find? Or, what do you hope for in life? Where do you place your hope? What gives you the drive to carry on each day? The question can also be phrased in terms of faith: What do you want to believe? Mulder believes in the truth; he wants to believe that the truth can be found. What he wants to believe is also the source of his hope: he hopes to find the truth. That hope enables him to persevere. As for Scully, she puts faith in science, and finds hope that science can provide answers to the unexplained. Hope helps her to press on, to keep looking for the scientific explanations. In terms of her relationship with God, Scully believes that God intervenes in human life by providing signs to guide us. This faith gives her hope, for example, that she can save the life of Kevin Kryder ("Revelations," 3x11). When Mulder chooses to look beyond aliens for the truth and wants to believe in "something greater than us," that gives him hope in the future. For each of us as well, whatever we believe, or want to believe, about who we are as people, what our purpose is in life, whether there is something greater than us and how we relate to that, can give us hope for the present and for the future.

DON'T GIVE UP

If hope is tied to faith, then hope can also flag when faith wavers. Despite Mulder's declaration at the end of Season 1 that "I can't give up" even though the X-Files have been closed, as Season 2 opens, his determination is beginning to wane. The attempts to thwart his work are taking their toll, and his resolve is wearing down. Even his beliefs are starting to falter: he is having doubts about his own memories of his sister's abduction. Those memories are what have given him hope to keep looking, and as the doubts creep in, the hope fades. Scully senses the defeat in Mulder and tells him, "Don't give up." It is not only Mulder's hope, but also his tenacity, his perseverance, that makes him who he is and makes Scully want to follow him on his quest (as she says in "The Truth"). At times when his determination is failing, Scully steps in to bolster his faith and his hope, and to urge him on, not to give up.

The phrase "Don't give up" becomes a major theme in *I Want to Believe*. Rather than Scully being the one to speak it, it is said to her by Father Joe, presumably as a message from God. Throughout the movie, she struggles to understand the source and meaning of the words, but they apply to many different threads in the story. Despite her negative opinion of Father Joe and his visions, Scully heeds his words and takes them as a directive not to give up on the experimental treatment to save the life of her young patient, Christian. She admits at the end that she believed Father Joe, that she acted on her belief, and as a consequence has put Christian through painful procedures even though she still cannot be sure they are having a positive effect on his condition. But her persistence with his treatment also has other results: her research into the procedures leads her to information connected to the case Mulder is pursuing, and in the end provides the clues for her to find Mulder in time to save his life. It is possible that Father Joe's message, although given to Scully, was meant for Mulder as well, telling him not to give up on the case. She recognizes that Mulder has never given up on rescuing his sister; even now he persists by looking for the missing women.

"Don't give up" also epitomizes Father Joe's relationship with God: Father Joe has not stopped praying for forgiveness and the salvation of his soul, and if the visions are any indication, God has not given up on Father Joe or the possibility of his redemption. This serves as a model for Scully, both in her relationship with Mulder and ultimately in her relationship with God. When Scully is unhappy that Mulder won't give up on the case, she appears ready to give up their relationship, but the fact that they are still together at the end of the movie means that she has not. But it is still open ended whether Scully has learned the same lesson in her relationship with God. She clearly is struggling with her faith and is angry with God "for all his cruelties," but has she decided, like Father Joe, not to give up on God? God certainly will not give up on her any more than he has given up on redeeming Father Joe.

The irony in all of this is that Scully, who more than once in the past encouraged Mulder not to give up, is now the one telling him to stop looking for the missing women (and his sister), to stop pursuing the case, while a man that she despises must be the one to exhort her, "Don't give up." There are larger, unspoken—and unaddressed—questions about Mulder and Scully and their lives after the series finale. That episode ends with their determination that maybe there's hope, that maybe they will have the power to save themselves in the face of the coming invasion. But no hint of that is found in *I Want to Believe*. Mulder is essentially a recluse, tucked away in their isolated house. Scully wants nothing to do with the FBI or paranormal investigations. Have they lost hope? Have they given up on fighting the future? Have they given in to fate? If so, Father Joe's message may also speak to this situation, telling them to renew their hope for the future and return to the fight. The final conversation between Mulder and Scully seems to acknowledge as much, that they can't hide from the darkness because it is a part of the tapestry of their lives. This too is left open at the end of the movie, whether the partners will decide to reengage in the struggle against the scheduled alien colonization.

"Don't give up" is a wonderful encouragement to persevere, to hope put into action—but is there a point at which perseverance becomes obsession? To a certain extent, Scully deals with this in the matter of Christian's treatment. The procedures are painful, and not guaranteed to work, and Scully's actions are based on the words of a convicted pedophile. Scully is uncertain whether she has made the wrong choice and is perhaps giving his family false hope. But Scully is not ready to abandon hope herself. The issue between Scully and the hospital administrator, Father Ybarra, is: At what point do you accept that it is time to give up on a course of action and make other plans? Father Ybarra may be abandoning hope for Christian's physical life, but Christian's very name is a reminder that he still has an eternal hope.

The same decision that Scully faces with Christian, she also once faced with her own daughter ("Emily," 5x07) and with four girls she was trying to help save ("All Souls," 5x17). In those scenarios, Scully did give up her efforts because she believed it was the best choice, to release the girls from the pain and sorrow of this life into a better place. But in *I Want to Believe*, Scully grapples with the opposite decision, and especially with trying to understand whether God is telling her not to give up treatment, while in the case of the girls God was apparently asking her to let them go.

The question of at what point one should give up also arises between Mulder and Scully in "Quagmire." Mulder's pursuit of the lake monster prompts Scully to compare him to Ahab from Herman Melville's novel *Moby Dick*. "That's funny," she says, "I just realized something . . . How much you're like Ahab. You're so consumed by your personal vengeance against life, whether it be its inherent cruelties or its mysteries, that everything takes on a warped significance to fit your megalomaniacal cosmology . . . The truth or a white whale—what difference does it make? I mean, both obsessions are impossible to capture, and trying to do so will only leave you dead along with everyone else you bring with you. You know, Mulder, you *are* Ahab." The similarity Scully sees between Mulder and Ahab is their determination not to give up in pursuit of the ultimate goal. The question behind this is, to what end or at what cost? When do you realize that the sacrifice required to maintain the hunt is too great, give up, and cut your losses?

Early in *Moby Dick*, before Ahab's true nature and obsession have become apparent, a sermon is delivered by Father Mapple on the biblical story of Jonah and the whale. This sermon invites readers to evaluate Ahab and his own whale in light of Jonah. There are clearly some key differences between the two figures. While both set out on a ship, on a selfish pursuit and in rebellion against God, where the two differ is in their reaction to the circumstances. When caught up in a storm, Jonah recognizes that God is trying to get his attention, and he sacrifices himself, offering to be thrown into the raging waters in order to save the lives of his innocent shipmates. In doing so, he saves both their lives and their souls, since the crew witnesses the immediate stilling of the storm once Jonah is off the ship, and they come to believe in Jonah's God. The whale, then, becomes Jonah's salvation, a symbol of God's mercy and forgiveness and his willingness to give Jonah a second chance. The whale brings Jonah's redemption. Ahab, however, chooses another course. He clings tightly to his single purpose, pursuing vengeance against the whale, and insists that his crew do likewise. In his selfishness and refusal to repent, not only does he sacrifice his own life, but the final maelstrom that encompasses his ship claims the lives of all but one of his men. Ahab's whale is therefore a symbol of judgment. Jonah knew when it was time to give up; Ahab did not.

If Mulder is like Ahab, the danger is that at some point the cost of Mulder's quest will be too great. Mulder is always willing to sacrifice his own life, since he sees it as a sacrifice for his sister. He never intends to cause the sacrifice of others, but at times it is an unavoidable consequence. Scully in particular pays the price. Her older brother, Bill, confronts Mulder about the risks and losses while Scully is battling cancer. He tells Mulder, "I've already lost one sister to this quest you're on, now I'm losing another. Has it been worth it? . . . Have you found what you've been looking for?" Mulder replies, "No . . . I lost someone very close to me. I lost a sister, I lost my father, all because of this thing I'm looking for" ("Redux II," 5x03). As the costs for this quest mount, so do the motivations to continue it. The leg Ahab lost to the whale is no longer the only thing being avenged. With each new loss—of father, sisters, children—Mulder becomes only more determined to find the truth in order to obtain justice for each of them. But he does finally realize that the cost may be too high for Scully. In "Requiem" (7x22), he tells her that "there has to be an end," meaning that it may be time for her to give up on the quest because the personal costs are too high. It's time for her to cut her losses.

In *I Want to Believe*, Scully also questions whether the cost of her persistence in Christian's treatment is too high. She is in danger of becoming an Ahab, but in a way she is also a Jonah. She is rebelling against religious authority and against God's mercy for Father Joe. The tempest in which she is caught up rages in her own soul: she is clearly in turmoil, especially whenever she encounters Father Joe, in contrast to the peace that Mulder has found. (Father Ybarra also encourages Scully to "let the boy go in peace," as though Christian too is ensnared in her tumult.) In *Moby Dick*, Father Mapple describes the bowels of the ship in which Jonah slept as a foretaste of the bowels of the whale that would later contain him. Scully too must enter a putrid and stifling place, the "vile box of monsters" where Father Joe lives, as the vehicle that will carry her back toward God. For Father Joe, this is his own whale, the place from which he continually cries out for God's forgiveness. When Scully is spit back onto dry land after the case is over, reeling from the experience, she must decide whether God really did answer Father Joe's prayers for redemption and in that redemption sent a message to Scully that would help her save both Mulder's and Christian's lives.

Another issue raised through the example of Father Joe is persistence in prayer. Mulder wonders, "What if Father Joe's prayers were answered after all? What if he were forgiven, because he didn't give up?"[1] Does prayer work that way? Do prayers get answered simply because you say them enough times? There is a story told by Jesus that suggests as much. Luke 18 introduces the narrative this way: "Then Jesus told his disciples a parable to show them that they should always pray and not give up" (NIV; the NCV reads, "and never lose hope"). The account Jesus tells is of a widow and an unjust judge. The widow went to the judge, over and over again, pleading for justice. At first, the judge refused. Eventually, however, her persistence wore down his resolve. He finally gave her what she asked for, simply so she would leave him alone. The point Jesus makes is that if even an unjust person would grant justice in the face of perseverance, then surely God will do the same for his children who call out to him day and night (Luke 18:1–8). The Apostle Paul likewise encourages his audience to "pray without ceasing" (1 Thessalonians 5:17). Why? Persistence in prayer is an act of faith, based on the belief that God hears and answers prayers, or that "he rewards those who seek him" (Hebrews 11:6). This is also the context for "seek and ye shall find" (see Matthew 7:7–11). It is an exhortation to pray, and to believe that God will answer and that as a good Father he wants to give good gifts to his children. Persistence in prayer is also a statement of hope. As Jesus tells his disciples, don't give up; pray and never lose hope. That is what Father Joe does: he never gives up praying for salvation and God's forgiveness. If the visions he receives are any indication, God has forgiven him and has offered him a way of undoing some of the consequences of his actions.

The other question that accompanies prayer and persisting in the same request is whether, as with the unjust judge, God's mind can be changed. The Bible speaks of God repenting or relenting—in other words, changing his mind. One example comes from the story of Jonah. God sends Jonah to proclaim the destruction of the Ninevites, but when the people repent, so does God. This is the very hope of the king of Nineveh when he tells the people to fast and pray: "Who knows? God may relent and change his mind; he may turn from his fierce anger, so that we do not perish" (Jonah 3:9). That is exactly what happens. But is this description of God simply anthropomorphism (applying to God human characteristics), or is it a literal description of what happens when we pray? The answer is also connected to the subject of whether God is truly all knowing (does he know not only everything that has happened but everything that will happen?), or whether he has chosen to limit his knowledge of and control over the future in order to allow our prayers to be effective. (In good *X-Files* fashion, these probing questions will only be posed here, not completely answered.)² The related dilemma is whether the future is already set, so that our prayers make no difference, or can our prayers change the course of the future? If the future is written, does prayer still offer us hope?

WHO HOPES FOR WHAT IS SEEN?

The concept of hope—whether in prayer, in pursuit of a truth, or in planning for tomorrow—is inextricably connected to knowledge of the future and whether the future is set in stone. The Apostle Paul states, "Now hope that is seen is not hope. For who hopes for what is seen?" (Romans 8:24). Hope is based on the unknown, especially the unknown future. There are two different contexts found both in science fiction in general and in *The X-Files* where the issue of knowing the future is often addressed: time travel and foretelling the future (through prophecy or paranormal abilities).³ *The X-Files* addresses these subjects, respectively, in "Synchrony" and "Clyde Bruckman's Final Repose." Such situations also lead to larger discussions of determinism, or to what extent we have control over our lives and the future.

A World without Hope

Clyde Bruckman is a man with a unique gift: he can see how people are going to die. This gift (which he laments is nonreturnable) helps him sell life insurance, but it doesn't seem to allow him much pleasure in life. Mulder argues with Bruckman whether the future can be changed, and whether we should try to change it. Bruckman is willing to help Mulder and Scully find the bodies of the victims, but because of his visions he is sure that he can't help them catch the killer before more people die—and even if he could, he's not sure that he should.

> CLYDE BRUCKMAN: How could I see the future if it didn't already exist?
>
> MULDER: But if the future is written, then why bother to do anything?
>
> CLYDE BRUCKMAN: Now you're catching on.

> MULDER: Mr. Bruckman, I believe in your ability but not your attitude. I can't stand by and watch people die without doing everything in my, albeit unsupernatural, power to interfere with that fate.
>
> CLYDE BRUCKMAN: Well, you see, that's another reason I can't help you catch this guy. I might adversely affect the fate of the future.

Mulder's position speaks also to the matter of whether prayers are effective. If the future is already written, even if it is unknown to us, should we make an effort to change fate by petitioning God? Mulder has hope that he can do something—he at least has to try.

While most people in "Clyde Bruckman's Final Repose" die the way Bruckman has predicted (including Bruckman himself), he has one vision that does not happen exactly the way he describes it. What Bruckman narrates is a vision by the killer (who also sees himself as a psychic); in describing the vision to Mulder, Bruckman influences Mulder's later reactions when Mulder finds himself in that exact scenario. Even though Mulder reacts differently than seen in the vision, it appears the outcome will be the same, until Scully interferes. The killer says, "Hey, that's not the way it's supposed to happen." Does the fact that Mulder and Scully have prior knowledge about this scenario allow them to change it, thereby altering fate? Mulder may assume as much, asking his partner, "How'd you know where to find us?" But Scully answers, "I didn't. I got on the service elevator by mistake." "Thank heaven for happenstance," Mulder replies. That the situation played out differently from how it was predicted does not seem to be impacted by their foreknowledge of it. Perhaps it was Scully's fate to intervene all along—and perhaps they *should* thank heaven for that happenstance. Whether or not the future can be intentionally changed, though, one thing is clear: Clyde Bruckman seems to have a rather hopeless life because of his ability to see what is to come. As Scully says, "By thinking he can see the future, he's taken all the joy out of his life."[4]

The same type of issue is addressed in "Synchrony." Jason Nichols, a scientist responsible for making time travel possible, comes back from the future to kill off all his fellow scientists who contributed to the discovery and to destroy his own research. He wants to prevent time travel from becoming a reality. He describes to the younger version of himself what they created: "A world without history, without hope. Where anyone can know everything that will ever happen." If people can travel through time, they can see the future; if the future is known, hope is gone, because hope depends on uncertainty and mystery. What Nichols has seen is a world in which people have lost hope and therefore have lost meaning. But this interpretation of the world and the implications of time travel is based on the assumption that the future is fixed and cannot be changed; if the future could be changed, there would still be uncertainty, and therefore there would still be hope. This is the debate that emerges between Mulder and Scully. Interestingly, Scully's senior thesis from college touched on the subject of time travel (Einstein's twin paradox), so Mulder smugly quotes her own words back at her: "'Although multidimensionality suggests infinite outcomes in an infinite number of universes, each universe can produce only one outcome.' . . . I take that to mean that you were suggesting that the future can't be altered. Which means that the elder Jason Nichols's attempts to stop his own research will fail, and that eventually his compound, and time travel, will be discovered." Although we don't know for sure what happens, the end of the episode suggests that time travel may occur anyway: Nichols's research partner, whom he tried to kill, has survived and continued their research based on what she now knows because of his return from the future. The question this leaves is, Can the future be changed by our free will, or do all choices and all roads lead to the same fate?

Fate versus Free Will

This larger matter of fate versus free will comes up a number of times in *The X-Files*. Although Mulder and Scully are not necessarily strictly associated with one view or the other, they often take opposing sides in the debate simply for the sake of discussion. One episode where this is a major theme is "Monday" (6x15). The world seems to be caught in a time loop, reliving the same day over and over again, but only one woman is aware of this. For her, it is a living hell. She tries changing every variable she can think of to alter the day and end the loop, but nothing works. The outcome is always the same:

her boyfriend goes into the bank to rob it, Mulder and Scully end up inside, and her boyfriend detonates the explosives strapped to his chest, blowing up the bank. In each loop, before they go to the bank Mulder and Scully end up in the X-Files office having a discussion about good intentions and circumstances beyond our control.

> MULDER: Scully, did you ever have one of those days you wish you could just rewind and start all over again from the beginning?
>
> SCULLY: Yes. Frequently. But, I mean, who's to say that if you did rewind it and start over again that it wouldn't end up exactly the same way?
>
> MULDER: So you think it's all just fate? We have no free will?
>
> SCULLY: No, I think that we're free to be the people that we are, good, bad, or indifferent. I think that it's our character that determines our fate.
>
> MULDER: And all the rest is just preordained? I don't buy that. There's too many variables, too many forks in the road . . . Free will. With every choice, you change your fate.

At first, it appears that Scully is right, because no matter how many different ways the two of them play out the day, they both end up inside the bank. It seems fated to happen. But eventually the scenario does change. Mulder does the one thing that hasn't happened yet: he brings the girlfriend, Pam, inside the bank. Her presence affects her boyfriend's actions, and he doesn't blow up the bank. They have changed fate. But it isn't merely by chance. Mulder is able to carry a memory of the bomb from one time loop into the next, so he essentially knows the future. He is able to use that knowledge in order to change what happens. Until that final day, when they break out of the loop, Pam has been living a hopeless existence. Her release actually comes in the form of her death, which is the variable that finally changes fate for everyone.

The topic Mulder and Scully debate is how much control we have over our own lives based on the choices we make, and how much is predetermined for us. Does every choice change our fate, as Mulder argues? Or, as Scully stated in her thesis, is there only one possible outcome? A similar dialogue occurs in "all things" (7x17).

Scully is reflecting on what her life would have been like if she had followed a different path when she was younger. Mulder says, "I don't think you can know. I mean, how many different lives would we be leading if we made different choices?" Scully asks, "What if there was only one choice and all the other ones were wrong, and there were signs along the way to pay attention to?" Mulder replies, "All the choices would then lead to this very moment." In this view, taken together with the conversation from "Monday," people are free to make choices based on their character; but the same type of character will always incline toward the same type of choices, which makes a specific outcome more likely, if not guaranteed. Scully also refers to there being signs along the way. There are clearly other times when she believes she has encountered signs that point her in a particular direction ("Revelations," "All Souls," "Orison"), which she generally interprets as signs from God. This begs the question: How involved is God in the universe, and therefore in the course of our lives? To put the question about fate versus free will more pointedly, How much freedom of choice does God allow us, and how much of our lives are guided or predetermined by him?

There are at least three different answers to this question. The first view would be to side entirely with predestination or determinism: our lives are predetermined by God (or fate, or another force external to ourselves). A visual depiction of this scenario is found in a Rube Goldberg machine, as seen in "The Goldberg Variation" (7x02). In such a world, we are all caught up in an elaborate chain of cause and effect where, for example, one man's choice to play poker with mobsters to earn easy cash eventually leads to one of the mobsters becoming an a organ donor for a boy with a rare blood type. From inside the "machine," we can only see parts of the whole, not how they all fit together. But from an outsider point of view—or from the perspective of the creator—every movement within the complex machine has purpose and contributes to the final result. Every action and reaction is a part of the intricate, predetermined plan.

The second option is the opposite extreme, that nothing is predetermined; rather, life is entirely guided by human choices and free will. While in this view there may be a Creator, he simply wound the clock and let it run but is not directly involved in the daily workings of the universe. This is Mulder's view expressed in "Orison" (7x07): "God is a spectator, Scully. He just reads the box scores." For Mulder, as for many other people, this perspective is connected to theodicy, or the problem of evil. In "All Souls," Mulder tosses out the questions: "Why would God allow this to happen? Why do bad things happen to good people?" The other essential question, for both Mulder and Scully, is, Why do the innocent suffer? Mulder's reasoning may be that if God is all-powerful, benevolent, and just, *and* he is involved in our lives, then God is culpable for the evil and suffering in the world when he does not step in to stop it. In the face of this reality of wickedness and pain, one may arrive at the conclusion either that God is guilty for allowing evil (and therefore is not truly just), or that he is not all-powerful (because he is apparently unable to overcome evil). Another solution, which Mulder prefers, is that God is not involved; in this case, the course of the world is left entirely up to our own choices.

A third option for the relationship between fate and free will is a middle road. In terms of God's involvement in the world and the problem of evil, this view states that while God is all-powerful, his intervention in our lives is necessarily limited by our free will. This also serves to answer the questions of why bad things happen to good people and why the innocent suffer, and ultimately where the blame lies for allowing injustice. *The X-Files* explores at least two potential answers to these questions. One is that the struggles or bad things we face are part of the maturing process for human beings—we have lessons to learn through these experiences. Mulder discovers this the hard way through his encounter with a genie in "Je Souhaite" (7x21). When Mulder is given the opportunity to have three wishes granted, his intention is to establish peace on earth. As with all of the wishes this warped genie grants, however, the wish goes awry: everyone disappears from the face of the earth. Mulder complains, "You don't have to wipe out the entire population of the whole planet just to effect a little peace on earth and goodwill towards men." The genie counters, "You didn't say, 'goodwill towards men.' So you expect me to change the hearts of six billion people? No religion in history has been able to pull that off. Not Allah or Buddha or Christ. But you'd like me to do that in your name? So, what? You can feel real good about yourself?"

Later in the episode, Scully drives home the point. Mulder tells her how he intends to use his final wish: "It's going to be a safer world, a happier world. There's going to be food for everyone, freedom for everyone, the end of the tyranny of the powerful over the weak. Am I leaving anything out?" But Scully explains to him why, as wonderful as that sounds, creating such a world might not be a good thing. "Maybe it's the whole point of our lives here, Mulder, to achieve that. Maybe it's a process that one man shouldn't try and circumvent with a single wish." As the genie has pointed out less gently, Mulder is essentially trying to play God. He's doing what he thinks an all-powerful God should do: end suffering. But if the world is made perfect for us by no effort of our own, something is lost. We become the equivalent of spoiled brats, children of God who are given everything we could want or imagine without learning about the hard work that goes into providing those things. Part of the lesson of life is how to overcome adversity, because adversity makes us stronger. "Suffering produces endurance, and endurance produces character, and character produces hope" (Romans 5:3b–4). The challenges in life teach us perseverance, and through perseverance we learn what it means to hope. This, then, is one explanation for why God allows bad things to happen: to help us grow and mature.

A second answer *The X-Files* proposes for why bad things happen to good people relates directly to free will and its implications. In simple terms, bad things happen because God allows people to choose to make bad things happen. God grants us free will, but for free will to truly be free, God's ability to intervene must be restricted by our freedom. The account of Adam and Eve in the garden of Eden is a basic illustration of free will and its repercussions. God tells them not to eat the fruit of one tree in the middle of the garden, but he grants them the free will to choose whether to eat from that tree. They choose wrongly, rebelling against him, and face the consequences (Genesis 3). The punishment has brought suffering not only upon themselves but upon all of their descendants. This is the current reality of the world: God gives us guidelines, and we are free to obey or disobey. When we disobey, however, the consequences may affect both ourselves and others. Much of the suffering in the world is the result of wrong choices made by other people.

This type of tension between God's involvement and the consequences of free will is illustrated especially in "Improbable" (9x14). The story is primarily about a serial-murder case: a character referred to as Wayno (or Mad Wayne) is killing women in patterns of threes; Agent Reyes, along with Agents Scully and Doggett, is investigating the crimes. Outside of the case, there is another figure who appears in many of the scenes, representing God ("Mr. Burt," played by Burt Reynolds). Throughout most of the episode, Mr. Burt persistently shadows Wayne, talking to him, giving him clues, trying to persuade him that he can choose to stop killing. Mr. Burt states his philosophy to Wayne at the very beginning, using the deck of cards in his hand as a metaphor: "You know your problem, my friend? It's not the cards. It's playing the hand you were dealt. Plenty of guys get a bad deal. It's all in what you do with it." Fate, or what is predetermined, is the hand we were dealt in life, but our free choice decides what we do with it. While Mr. Burt constantly steps into Wayne's path, he never physically tries to stop Wayne from killing. Why? Because Wayne has the freedom to make that choice, as wrong as it may be, and Mr. Burt (or God) by his own choice is limited by that freedom. Does that mean God doesn't intervene? On the contrary, Mr. Burt is continually meddling throughout the episode. He never gives up on convincing Wayne to make a different choice; he sets up clues and signs for Doggett, Reyes, and Scully to find. He provides the means to stop the murders, but he doesn't directly interfere to stop them himself.

This is the portrait of God that we often see in *The X-Files*, especially through Scully's eyes. In "Revelations" and "All Souls," God provides signs that help her save the lives, or souls, of children. In "Orison," the signs lead to her own life being saved. As these episodes suggest, God gives us clues to help us succeed, but we have to pay attention in order to see them. Mr. Burt tells Wayne (in reference to the investigators, but with relevance also for Wayne), "Can't show them what they can't see." Our hearts have to be open so that our eyes can see the signs. We have to seek in order to find. What Scully says of science can also be applied to God: "the answers are there; you just have to know where to look." God conceals things so that we will search them out (Proverbs 25:2). He speaks in riddles so that we will have to listen carefully in order to understand. As "Improbable" depicts, those clues are even built into the very fabric of creation. God provides the tools we need to find our way. For some people, it seems the deck is stacked against them. But there are more cards available in the deck than simply the hand you're dealt; and you have a choice how to play it.

These episodes give another indication of how God intervenes in the world: not through a single divine hand, but through hundreds, thousands, millions of human hands. Scully encounters this in the signs that she sees as God uses her as his hands to help save the lives or souls of children. This role for humans is also implied in her words to Mulder when he uses his three wishes to "play God": the very purpose of our lives is to become part of the solution—to feed the hungry, to do justice, to teach truth in the face of oppressive lies. "Improbable" shows the same thing, but from God's point of view. Mr. Burt does eventually stop Wayne from killing—through Scully and Reyes, and Doggett. The numbers and games represent the signs that God uses to point us in the right direction, if only we'll pay attention. We can ignore him if we choose, like Wayne does. We can pretend that the patterns are only coincidences or aren't really there. But if we look closely, if we ask what the patterns mean, we can find arrows to point us in the right direction. To echo Scully's haunting statement from "Revelations": What if God is speaking, but no one's listening?

By allowing us free choice, and allowing us to participate in the daily upkeep of the world, God gives us both privilege and responsibility. God does intervene in the world, but he doesn't simply take action *for* us, he acts *through* us. This means we have the responsibility to act rightly, and that we are responsible for when we act wrongly or fail to act at all. These are the privileges and the consequences of free will. In this case, when God speaks, we must listen. But what of the reciprocal? When we speak, does God listen? This returns to the question of whether our prayers are effective. In a world where God limits himself to permit us free will, our prayers are part of the will to choose rightly. We are free to ask for God's intervention, so that God can act for us and through us as far as we will allow. That doesn't mean that the answer to prayer will always be exactly what we ask for or expect, but the fact that God answers differently doesn't mean that he doesn't answer (see chapter 6, below). If we believe he hears and he answers, that gives us hope to pray and to persist. But if we want God to listen to us, it goes both ways: God also wants us to listen to him. When we pay attention, we may find that the answers are already right before our eyes.

Another question related to free will is raised by Dostoyevsky's story of the Grand Inquisitor, and alluded to in "Talitha Cumi" (see chapter 1, above): Is free will such a good idea? If freedom leads to suffering and human culpability for doing or permitting evil, should God have granted us free will in the first place? The Inquisitor determines that free will was a mistake, one that he will graciously undo by offering people clear consciences in exchange for their freedom. The Cigarette-Smoking Man (CSM) states, echoing the Inquisitor, "We appease their conscience. Anyone who can appease a man's conscience can take his freedom away from him." The Inquisitor's logic is that choosing between right and wrong is too great a burden for humans to bear, and being weighed down by the choice also piles on guilt when wrong choices are made. "There is nothing more seductive for man than the freedom of his conscience, but there is nothing more tormenting for him, either."[5] If there is no choice, then there is no guilt. We can live happily and free of concern if we have no responsibility for our actions—but to have no responsibility means to do exactly as another tells us to do. The Inquisitor chastises Jesus that instead of going this route and making people obey him, Jesus burdened them with freedom of choice, all because he wanted them to love him freely. This is essentially where the Grand Inquisitor's accusations begin and the parallel in "Talitha Cumi" concludes: love. God permitted humans free will so they would love and serve him by choice, not out of compulsion or obligation. In return, it is our ability to love freely that characterizes us as humans. As Jeremiah Smith answers CSM, "And if you can't appease their conscience, you kill them. But you can't kill them all. You can't kill their love, which is what makes them who they are, makes them better than us—better than you."

Free will means freedom to love, freedom to hope; freedom to listen to God or freedom to reject him. But free will also means responsibility. Why do bad things happen to good people? Because humans are free to do bad things, and to allow each other to do so as well. But humans are also free to be part of the solution, to live out God's image in us as loving, just creatures, and to participate in God's plan. If there is so much free will, though, and if God has chosen to limit his intervention so as not to violate our free will, does he still have a plan? What place is there for fate? To return to the conversation between Mulder and Scully in "Monday" may be to find a middle ground here too. Arguing in favor of fate, Scully says, "We're free to be the people that we are . . . It's our character that determines our fate." In this view, we still have freedom of choice, but we tend toward certain choices based on who we are. Our fates may be established because of the type of choices we make. In the example of the Goldberg device, we can be placed in certain positions or serve certain functions within the machine based on our character and the choices we tend toward. Both fate and free will, then, have a place. Free will gives us hope because our prayers and choices matter; the future is not simply written independent of our involvement. But there is hope to be found even in fate, because it gives us a sense of purpose in God's plan and the bigger picture. Also, fate often refers to one's ultimate end, and therefore to justice. For many people, their hope is founded on the belief that the injustice in this world—due to free will—will eventually be rectified.

A FUTURE WITH HOPE

In "Millennium" (7x05), Mike Johnson, a taxidermist who moonlights as a necromancer (someone who raises the dead), expresses his despair about the current world and his hope for its end: "There's no justice in this world. But there will be in the next . . . You know what the world is. Evil goes unpunished. The good suffer. There's no future here but uncertainty and pain. Let the judgment come!" Johnson's statement represents, in one form, a belief held by many people that true justice will only be found beyond this world. That the suffering and evil prospering now will one day receive their due punishment, and good will be rewarded. In the midst of a world where there is suffering and pain, looking toward a time or place in which wrong will be set right gives people hope to endure the present in order to arrive at that future. Yet as Johnson shows, these ideas can also be taken to a negative extreme, so that beliefs that should offer hope for the present seem only to result in the opposite: hopelessness about our current existence, and determination to do whatever is necessary to bring the present reality to an end.

Apocalypticism: The End Is Near

When *The X-Files* premiered on television, the world was counting down the final years of the millennium. Whether because of Y2K-bug warnings or religious prophecies, there was a feeling in the air that the end could be near. The year 2000 came and went, but *The X-Files* set its sights on a new date, the next big target for doomsday prophecies: December 22, 2012. The apocalyptic or doomsday atmosphere sparked by these dates clearly appealed to Chris Carter since he created another television series, aptly named *Millennium*, based on such ideas. Similar themes also surfaced in *The X-Files*, most blatantly with the episode "Millennium" (a crossover with Carter's series of that name), which takes place in the days leading up to January 1, 2000.

As Frank Black (the ex-FBI agent and consultant from the series *Millennium*) describes to Mulder and Scully in this episode, the views of the Millennium Group, as with many other apocalyptic adherents, are based primarily on the book of Revelation. Black explains, "The book of Revelation describes the end of the physical world in a battle between heaven and hell: good against evil. The Millennium Group believed that that time was upon us." In general, the group is concerned with being aware of the signs of the times and with preparing themselves for this final battle. But the characters in this particular episode are a splinter group. Black says, "They believe that for the end time to come as it must, man must take an active hand in bringing that about." To this end, four members of this splinter group kill themselves so they can be resurrected as the Four Horsemen of the Apocalypse and in this way fulfill Revelation 6. They believe the world's fate is predetermined, but they're trying to help fate along by making it happen themselves. Another group focused on the book of Revelation is depicted in "The Field Where I Died" (4x05). This story features a cult that named themselves the Temple of the Seven Stars in reference to Revelation 1:16 and the seven churches in Revelation 1–3. The group sees their current existence as the final battle between good and evil, and the FBI and ATF agents who are raiding the compound as the foretold enemy (the dragon of Revelation 12:17).

A key verse in both of these episodes, and for both of these apocalyptic groups, is Revelation 1:18: "I am he that liveth, and was dead; and, behold, I am alive for evermore, Amen; and have the keys of hell and of death" (KJV). The verse is used to foreshadow the death of the Seven Stars members and the resurrection of an officer killed by one of the wannabe Four Horsemen. With the misapplication of this verse also seems to come a perverse fulfillment. Another scriptural text that the necromancer, Mike Johnson, repeatedly quotes is John 11:25–26: "I am the resurrection, and the life: he that believeth in me, though he were dead, yet shall he live. And whosoever liveth and believeth in me shall never die" (KJV). Both passages, from Revelation and John, were spoken by Jesus and refer to eternal life. Yet, in taking this resurrection and life too literally, the cultists and the Millennium Group members seem to have doomed themselves to a repeated cycle in *this* life rather than escape into the next. The main theme for "The Field Where I Died" is reincarnation, and the cult leader, Vernon Ephesian, apparently believes that he has been alive on earth in previous eras. The Millennium members who kill themselves are resurrected as zombies. Instead of entering the eternal, spiritual life that Jesus has spoken of, they have only trapped themselves in this physical life by abusing Jesus's words to take their fate into their own hands.

Another example of such misuse of Scripture is found in the episode "3" (2x07) among a group of vampires, or aspiring vampires. They quote (or misquote, using the wrong verse number) John 6:54: "He who eats of my flesh and drinks of my blood shall have eternal life and I will raise him up on the last day." But the "Son" in their unholy trinity (John) makes it clear that they don't believe in eternal life or resurrection in the last day. John tells Mulder, "What nobody realizes is that there is no afterlife . . . There's no heaven. There's no soul. There's just rot, and there's just decay. And I will never, ever, ever, ever have to face that." In defiance of death, then, and out of fear of what may come after it, John and his companions willingly cause the death of others in an attempt to help themselves live forever—but on this earth, which is their version of eternal life. Like the Seven Stars cult and the Millennium Group extremists, this unholy trinity has also misunderstood and misappropriated the Bible, therefore missing its hopeful message. The irony of their misinterpretation is found in John's very words: in this life, and these bodies, there is truly only rot and decay. The zombies raised by the Millennium Group's necromancer are a vivid depiction of that. The promise of true eternal life transcends the current reality. Mike Johnson has it right when he says that in the next world there will be justice. Yet he misses the fact that such belief is supposed to provide hope—hope to endure the "uncertainty and pain" of the present—not despair.

There is one verse that is notably not quoted by either the Millennium Group extremists or the Temple of the Seven Stars: "But about that day and hour no one knows, . . . only the Father" (Matthew 24:36). Throughout Matthew 24, Jesus is telling his disciples about the end times before his return to earth, what those days will be like and the signs leading up to that time. However, in the midst of this, he tells them that no one but God knows exactly when this will happen. After Jesus's death and resurrection, when he is about to ascend to heaven, his followers again make a point of asking him when he will accomplish what was expected of the Jewish messiah: to restore the kingdom of Israel. Jesus tells them, "It is not for you to know the times or periods that the Father has set by his own authority" (Acts 1:7). God's predetermined future isn't for us to know or figure out. Yet, symbolic of many people who believe the end times are near, the Millennium Group tries to calculate exactly when the end will come. When some of the Group members don't see the end arriving on their schedule, they try to help it along. But hope is based on the unknown. "For who hopes for what is seen? But if we hope for what we do not see, we wait for it with patience" (Romans 8:24–25). The Millennium Group extremists certainly do not come across as patient, nor do the cult members of the Seven Stars, who kill themselves to hasten their own end. Although they have beliefs that should offer them hope, these groups instead seem to represent despair because they can't persevere in the here and now or accept the uncertainty of when the future will arrive. They try to take the easy way out, only to find they've missed the correct exit.

A Living Hope

In contrast to the impatience and despair of Mike Johnson and the Millennium Group, Mulder at the end of the final season represents an image of hope in the face of a predetermined date of possible doom. His last words in the series finale are, "Maybe there's hope." But that hope for the future, a hope based on "something greater than us—greater than any alien force," does not cause him to hasten the end or to give up on the present; instead, it enables him to carry on. The hope that Mulder finds may be based, at least in part, on the truth he has discovered about his sister and her fate. If he truly believes she is in a better place, then he believes that there is such a thing as a better place, and that the good or innocent are taken to the better place where they can no longer be harmed by suffering or evil. He has hope that "the dead are not lost to us," that there is something beyond merely this life, and the hope he finds for his future gives him hope to live in the present. Scully, on the other hand, struggles to find peace about the afterlife and about final justice, but she still finds the determination, the hope, not to give up, based on the possibility of God's mercy and interaction in our lives.

If Mike Johnson and others like him have missed the point, and the hope, of eternal life, then what is the truth they have missed? The place where they have tried to find answers is in apocalyptic texts, but interpreted through their own radical views. Jewish apocalypticism, found in books like Daniel, was birthed long before Christ in an era when the Jews yearned for the full restoration of their land and the twelve tribes, culminating in the sovereign reign of King David's heir. This heir they called the Messiah, the anointed one. As reflected by the question Jesus's followers asked before his ascension—"Lord, is this the time when you will restore the kingdom of Israel?" (Acts 1:6)—the hope of the Jews, even those who accepted Jesus as Messiah, was for a renewed kingdom on this earth. This is the hope promised to them by prophets like Jeremiah: "For surely I know the plans I have for you, says the Lord, plans for your welfare and not for harm, to give you a future with hope. Then when you call upon me and come and pray to me, I will hear you. When you search for me, you will find me; if you seek me with all your heart, I will let you find me, says the Lord" (Jeremiah 29:11–14a). These were God's words to his people, telling of the hope that would await them when they returned from exile. But in the New Testament, through Jesus the future hope is extended beyond the Jews, to all people. In the letter to the Romans,

Paul quotes the Greek version of Isaiah 11:10: "The root of Jesse shall come, the one who rises to rule the Gentiles; in him the Gentiles shall hope." Paul continues with this benediction: "May the God of hope fill you with all joy and peace in believing, so that you may abound in hope by the power of the Holy Spirit" (Romans 15:12–13).

The hope God promised to the Jews was a future in their homeland; what Jesus's disciples did not immediately understand is that the hope Jesus brings for all people is a future in a heavenly homeland (cf. Hebrews 11:13–16). This is the true hope found in the book of Revelation and contained in the promises of resurrection and eternal life. When Jesus says, "I am he that liveth, and was dead and, behold, I am alive for evermore" (Revelation 1:18) and "I am the resurrection and the life" (John 11:25), he is referring to his own death and resurrection (not to vampires or zombies) and the future resurrection of all people. Some of the Jews already believed in a resurrection of all people in the end time to face the judgment day (evident in Martha's statement about her brother Lazarus in John 11:24, prompting Jesus's declaration). But Jesus brought the hope of something more—resurrection to eternal life, not in the earthly kingdom, but in the kingdom of God. The book of Revelation ends with a description of this kingdom, where God "will wipe every tear from their eyes" and "Death will be no more" (Revelation 21:4), and with an invitation issued to "everyone who is thirsty" and "wishes to take the water of life as a gift," which flows from the heavenly city (Revelation 22:17).

With this eternal kingdom also comes justice. Such everlasting joy and prosperity is only possible because death and evil have finally received their due and been vanquished. This kingdom is a return to the Eden that God intended for his children before they exercised their free will to disobey. For those who choose to obey instead, Eden and the tree of life at its center are waiting. That is the hope at the end of this life and the end of this world. "By his great mercy [God] has given us a new birth into a living hope through the resurrection of Jesus Christ from the dead, and into an inheritance that is imperishable, undefiled, and unfading, kept in heaven for you, who are being protected by the power of God through faith for a salvation ready to be revealed in the last time" (1 Peter 1:3b–5). By faith, we accept that this is the true fate of the world, which gives us hope for the future and for today. But though we know, through faith, that this is the future already written, we still have the uncertainty of when it will happen, or how life will play out in the meantime. Our free will allows us to choose whether we will accept the invitation to drink the water of life and join God's kingdom. And we have the choice to participate in God's good work in the here and now.

While Mulder's conclusion that "maybe there's hope" does not describe such a detailed faith or vision of the future, he does express a desire to believe—a hope—that the answers for the present lie beyond the barrier of death and beyond our own abilities. Mulder's very act of touching Scully's cross after he has expressed this desire is itself a statement of hope that he has found a place to start looking. Perhaps this is Mulder's new quest, to seek the truth about our fate beyond this life, about that better place where he believes he will truly find his sister. But it is a quest he does not travel alone. Together, he and Scully grapple with issues of faith and perseverance to find the answers about God's mercy and justice. Together, they find the hope not to give up. In so doing, they exemplify the truth that surfaces in the narrative of the Grand Inquisitor: while free will may be a source of suffering, it also makes us free to love. For, while faith and hope are essential to life, love is the greatest of all.

NOTES

1. In the novelization of the movie, Scully speaks in between Mulder's two questions. Thus, to his first question, she replies, "Why would they have been? So many prayers go unanswered . . . Why would God choose a sinner like Father Joe?" Mulder then answers, "Maybe because . . . he didn't give up . . . ?" (Max Allan Collins, *The X-Files: I Want to Believe*, based on the screenplay by Frank Spotnitz and Chris Carter [New York: HarperEntertainment, 2008], 232 [ellipses original]). This version of the dialogue emphasizes even more the idea that Father Joe was heard specifically because of his persistent prayers.

2. The Bible does offer an answer to whether God changes his mind. Speaking of God's promises, Naaman prophesies, "God is not a human being, that he should lie, or a mortal, that he should change his mind" (Numbers 23:19; cf. 1 Samuel 15:29). To ask whether God knows the future, and if he does whether that means our prayers have no impact, is to assume that God exists within linear time in the same way that we do. If God exists outside of our timeline, from his perspective he can see everything that happens regardless of when, whereas from our position inside the timeline we can only see those same things in terms of past, present, and future. For both sides of the recent debate about the subject of God's knowledge

and whether he can change his mind, see Millard J. Erickson, *What Does God Know and When Does He Know It? The Current Controversy over Divine Foreknowledge* (Grand Rapids: Zondervan, 2003).

3. For other examples from science fiction, see Gabriel McKee, "In the Fullness of Time: Free Will and Divine Providence," chapter 4 of *The Gospel according to Science Fiction: From the Twilight Zone to the Final Frontier* (Louisville: Westminster John Knox, 2007), 63–96. Describing an illustration from *Star Trek: Deep Space Nine*, McKee states, "The mystery of the future is what makes life worthwhile" (75). This is a depiction of hope: mystery is necessary for hope, and hope gives life a sense of purpose.

4. For a discussion of this episode and the issues of freedom and foreknowledge from a philosophical point of view, see Dean A. Kowalski, "'Clyde Bruckman's Final Repose' Reprised 2009," in *The Philosophy of "The X-Files,"* ed. Dean A. Kowalski, updated ed., The Philosophy of Popular Culture (Lexington: University Press of Kentucky, 2009), 189–208.

5. Fyodor Dostoyevsky, *The Brothers Karamazov*, trans. David McDuff, rev. ed. (London: Penguin, 2003), 332.

4

Love

"My Constant, My Touchstone"

MULDER: I love you.

SCULLY: Oh, brother. ("Triangle," 6x03)

While faith, trust, hope, truth, and fate are all regularly discussed on *The X-Files*, love is a theme that remains tacit but pervasive. "Love" is not a word often tossed around on the show, especially between the main characters. Instead, they express the emotion with terms like "constant," "touchstone," "trust," "perfect opposite," "one in five billion." Mulder and Scully live out the exhortation of 1 John 3:18: "let us love, not in word or speech, but in truth and action." They act out their love through partnership and respect, through trust and loyalty, protecting one another at all costs and literally going to the ends of the earth for each other. Even when, late in the series, the pair could be called lovers, they are first of all partners and friends. They form two halves of a whole, two contrasting elements working in tension and in harmony to create an effective synergy. The characters, and the show itself, are noticeably lacking when one half of the pair is missing. Together, however, they are formidable, and more than the sum of their parts.

The reflection of love in action on *The X-Files* goes beyond merely the relationship between Mulder and Scully, though. As in life, every human relationship reveals elements of the ways in which we love: as family (parent, child, or sibling), as friends, as lovers, and as beloved or lovers of God. These four categories are *The Four Loves* enumerated by C. S. Lewis and provide a helpful framework for discussing the various types of love and relationships.[1] Lewis refers to the four as affection (familial relationships), friendship, eros (romantic love), and charity (divine love). These categories will serve here as a paradigm for examining the different ways in which humans care for one another, what that tells us about ourselves, and ultimately what those interactions tell us about our relationship with God and how we can live out his two greatest commandments: to love God and to love one another.

THE GREATEST OF THESE IS LOVE

Before a discussion of these various relationships can begin, there is one other important relationship that should be considered: the relationship of love to faith and hope. The three virtues are often grouped together, as they are in the closing scene of *The X-Files'* series finale: faith and hope are major topics of Mulder and Scully's discussion, while as always they exhibit rather than speak of love. But when these three are grouped together at the conclusion of 1 Corinthians 13, one is clearly seen to surpass the others: "And now faith, hope, and love abide, these three: and the greatest of these is love" (13:13). Why is love superior to faith and hope, and in what way?

First of all, the context for this verse is important. It comes at the end of the "love hymn," which discusses the characteristics of love: "Love is patient, love is kind. It does not envy, it does not boast, it is not proud. It does not dishonor others, it is not self-seeking, it is not easily angered, it keeps no record of wrongs. Love does not delight in evil but rejoices with the truth. It always protects, always trusts, always hopes, always perseveres. Love never fails" (1 Corinthians 13:4–8a, NIV). The verses before and after this, such as verse 2, focus essentially on what faith can accomplish: "And if I have prophetic powers, and understand all mysteries and all knowledge, and if I have all faith, so as to remove mountains, but do not have love, I am nothing." Throughout this letter by the Apostle Paul, he has been emphasizing to the Corinthian church that they need to function as a unified body and to start putting others first rather than thinking only of themselves. He sees their faith, and commends hope (see 1 Corinthians 15), but love is one thing they especially lack. Yet love is the most important.

While faith, even as small as a mustard seed, can move mountains (see Matthew 17:20), and hope can empower us to persevere against all odds, love has the greatest power of all: love can make us more like God. How? God is not faith or hope, but "God is love" (1 John 4:8). Faith and hope are valuable human qualities, and they can draw us closer to the divine, but both are based on the unseen and the unknown. God does not need faith or hope because he knows all. But love is at the very heart of God's character. As humans, when we love we act out the image of God inside us, and we fulfill one of the reasons for which we were created. Faith and hope are virtues that we can exhibit on our own as individuals, such as by believing in a principle or hoping for an event. But love extends us beyond ourselves and makes us consider the good of others. As Paul tries to teach the Corinthians, "love builds up" (1 Corinthians 8:1; cf. 10:23). Love is constructive and creative. It unifies and strengthens. It builds families and communities. Faith and hope have their place and are to be commended, but without love, they are incomplete. Love in word only, however, is equally as empty; love must be put into action in order to be true.

The love hymn in 1 Corinthians 13 waxes poetic on love and elaborates the many ways it can be recognized and acted out. But love can be described simply in this way: "in humility regard others as better than yourselves" (Philippians 2:3; cf. 1 Corinthians 10:24). This is the Golden Rule: do unto others as you would have them do unto you (Matthew 7:12). Put other people first, and treat them with the same respect that you desire for yourself. Notice that it's not a description of how you should feel about another person, but how you should treat them. Love requires action. That action takes place in the various relationships in our lives, which are sometimes easy, sometimes challenging, sometimes rewarding, sometimes heartbreaking. In each human interaction, we learn what it means to act in love, even at times when we lack the emotion of love. Love as a virtue takes action even when love is the last thing that we feel. Yet through the action, our hearts can be transformed, and so can we.

AFFECTION AND FAMILY

Affection is the description of love between family members. It includes the reciprocal relationships between parent and child and between siblings. The family unit, whether the socially ideal form or totally fractured, is the first context in which we learn about love, caring, and relationships. Affection is what C. S. Lewis calls the most natural of loves, but it is also the least optional, since by and large family is formed not through personal choice or common interests but simply through biology.[2] This situation can create both beautiful harmony between people who have nothing in common other than genetics and residence, and extreme conflict between those forced into a lifelong connection. Family can bring out the best and worst in people; either way, it remains a fundamental part of what forms our character and influences all other relationships in our lives.

Affection can also describe the connection that emerges in other types of community relationships, such as situations in which people are put together as neighbors or coworkers. While friendships and deeper relationships can develop in these circumstances, often there is simply a kindness or caring that extends no further than the connection itself— for example, neighbors who smile at each other across the street or pick up the other's mail while one is on vacation, but fail to keep in touch when one of them moves away; or coworkers who form cordial relationships because they are assigned to the same office or project, but never contact each other outside the workplace. Affection may also describe the bond formed in a social group, where the members may have one main interest in common but still differ in many other respects. All these types of community may mimic the family unit, and family affection, in the sense of either brotherly love or sibling rivalry, or as genuine care between a boss and those under his or her responsibility. (An illustration of this occurs in the episode

"Shadows" [1x05]: a secretary and her boss become like a daughter and father to each other, a connection that extends even beyond his death.) In this sense, then, affection may also apply to the initial relationship between Mulder and Scully, who were assigned to be partners by no choice of their own, and whose businesslike affection later grew into friendship.

While various aspects of functional and dysfunctional families are represented in *X-Files* episodes, two familial relationships are especially important: Mulder as brother and Scully as mother.

Brotherly Love

One of the most essential relationships to *The X-Files'* plot and mythology is Mulder's role as a brother. In the very first episode and his first case with Scully, he describes the disappearance of his sister and how that has impacted his life. Even fifteen years later, in the second movie, Mulder's sister is invoked as a primary motivation for his choices and actions. Although he only knew her and interacted with her for the eight years prior to her abduction, this relationship shaped the rest of his life. Rather than an ongoing, evolving interaction, then, the relationship is in many ways symbolic and one-dimensional. The lost sister motif is only compounded when Scully is herself abducted, becoming a representative of all the "lost sisters" and their ordeals, and then her own sister is killed (in Scully's place). As a result, both partners have the same motivation: finding truth and justice for their sisters. As members of law enforcement, Mulder and Scully are committed to sacrificing their lives for others, but it is the loss of their sisters and the need to find justice for those who have equally been wronged that makes both agents personally invested. The personal loss is what turns a career into a quest.

The family dynamic between siblings is the crucible in which people initially learn how to get along with others. It is where we first learn how to share, or how to compete; how to respect the rights and feelings of another, or how to cultivate jealousy and envy; how to resolve conflicts, or how to complain that life isn't fair. This family crucible generates both brotherly love and sibling rivalry. Brothers and sisters may be completely alike, or they may have nothing else in common besides the people who birthed or raised them. But even if siblings have no common ground they may still develop affection, and thus learn to love one another, for no other reasons than that the other person exists and that they share the same parents, who love them both. In this way, then, the relationship with a brother or sister (or other extended family members living in the same household) is the forerunner for affection, friendship, and love for the neighbor. It is even the forerunner for romantic love, as we learn to get along under the same roof and respect people for their differences.

Loving our brother or sister—both literally and metaphorically—is also essential to our lives and faith. First John 4:20 states, "Those who say, 'I love God,' and hate their brothers or sisters, are liars; for those who do not love a brother or sister whom they have seen, cannot love God whom they have not seen." If we can't love those we are closest to, how can we claim to love anyone else? A verse earlier in the same letter provides a reminder of why love for the brother or sister is so important: "We must not be like Cain who . . . murdered his brother" (1 John 3:12). Cain and Abel, the first siblings, didn't set a very good example of brotherly love. In many ways, their story is familiar. Abel does what is pleasing to his Father God, while Cain does not. God says to Cain, "Why are you angry . . . ? If you do well, will you not be accepted? And if you do not do well, sin is lurking at the door; its desire is for you, but you must master it" (Genesis 4:6–7). Cain is jealous of his brother for being the favorite son, although the Father tells Cain that if he will be obedient, he will win the same favor. Either Cain can set aside his anger, follow Abel's example, and receive the same praise; or he can foster his anger and sense of injustice and let them get the better of him. Unfortunately, Cain decides that the best solution is to get Abel out of the way. As a result, Abel's innocent blood cries out from the ground, and Cain forever pays the price. This story highlights how challenging sibling relationships can be, how difficult it is to vie for the attention and praise of parents, and yet how important it is to learn love in those early relationships so that we can show equal respect for neighbors, coworkers, strangers—and even enemies. Sibling and family relationships are the testing ground for all other forms of love.

In *The X-Files*, we don't learn much about the children Fox and Samantha and how well they got along, but we do see a glimpse of their interaction through Mulder's memories of her abduction. In "Little Green Men" (2x01), he relives the scene. Twelve-year-old Fox is in charge while the two are home alone. He wants to watch one television show, and she wants to watch another. When she calls him a name and tries to change the channel, he yells at her, "Hey! Get out of my life!" and she screams back. Not an unusual exchange for a brother and sister. But when Samantha is taken from the room only moments later, under the watch of young Fox, who is powerless to prevent it, he has no chance to retract his unfortunate words. They become an eerie prophecy that will forever ring in his ears. While Mulder is not responsible for his sister's absence, he certainly takes that responsibility upon himself and carries it with him throughout his life. The love that he couldn't express to Samantha in their time together, he instead expresses through his self-sacrifice by putting her life and welfare before his own. And that same sacrifice that he learned toward Samantha, he applies to numerous other situations, involving other young women who need someone to save them.

Motherly Love

While loss and sacrifice are certainly not the only or even primary elements of family life for most people, they are a main focus in *The X-Files*. The self-sacrifice illustrated in Mulder's role as a brother is central to Scully's role as a mother as well. Sacrifice also arises in the story of Mulder's own mother, the mother of the show's original lost little girl. In fact, it is this sacrifice that initiates Mulder's quest. His mother, Teena Mulder, was faced with an impossible Sophie's choice—to choose the life of one child and sacrifice the other. Whether she took part in this choice or it was left up to others, the result was that Samantha was abducted, while Fox was left behind. Although Scully is not forced to make the same type of choice, there are other difficult decisions she must make in the role of mother, to decide what is best for her child regardless of the cost to herself.

Of all the loves, a mother's love for her child truly is the most natural and the most basic. It is the first relationship into which we are born, one that develops even as we develop in the womb. A mother's love is the love for the one to whom she gave life, to whom she has given of her time and her health and her body, one created both through pleasure and through pain, who is a part of her and perhaps even like her. A mother's love also represents the basic human desire to create and nurture new life, and to pass on a part of oneself in another being. It is the instinct to participate in creation, and in that way to mirror the role and affection of God. God is often depicted as a parent, at times particularly as a mother. When God's people (symbolized here through Mount Zion) cry out, "The Lord has forsaken me, my Lord has forgotten me," God replies, "Can a woman forget her nursing child, or show no compassion for the child of her womb? Even these may forget, yet I will not forget you" (Isaiah 49:14–15; cf. 66:13). In the same way that a mother loves her own child, God loves the people he has created. By becoming parents, humans participate in the divine act of creation.

Along with the desire to create also comes responsibility for that life and acceptance that the new creature is his or her own person and must eventually be allowed to live a separate life—symbolized in the act of cutting the umbilical cord. Maternal love requires both holding on tight and knowing when to let go. In many ways, Scully's relationship with her daughter, Emily, illustrates these aspects of parental love. Although Scully does not conceive, carry, or give birth to Emily, she feels an immediate connection to the girl simply because Emily is her own flesh and blood. Scully also, then, represents the love of a father—one who has not borne the child but feels an intense bond simply based on genetics. Scully feels this connection even before she learns that Emily is her daughter, when Scully at first thinks the child belongs to her own lost sister, Melissa. Regardless of the exact relationship, Scully quickly steps in to adopt Emily, to assume the role of her mother. Over a very short period of time, Scully both feels the responsibility for this life that is part of her and faces the difficult decision of when to let go. While maternal love is filled with pride and joy, it also requires sacrifice.

For a mother, or any parent, it is easy to sacrifice herself for her child. Most parents would do this in a heartbeat without even pausing to think about it. But the more difficult choice—the impossible choice—is when sacrificing yourself is not an option. The decision that Teena Mulder was given is an extreme case: to give up one child for the sake of another. But the dilemmas with which Scully must grapple are more common: to give up the fight for a child's life (Emily's), or to release a child to be raised by someone else in a better situation (William). In both scenarios, Scully must also sacrifice her right and desire to be a mother. But ultimately such choices, made correctly, can only be made out of love.

When Scully first meets Emily, the girl is already battling a terminal disease, held in check only by the experimental treatment she is receiving. The very reason Scully encounters the girl is that her home life is beginning to fall apart, with the death of her adoptive mother, all because of the controversial treatment. Even as Emily's life is already starting to unravel, her health quickly takes a downturn. Much of Scully's interaction with the girl happens after Emily is hospitalized. This is Scully's abbreviated first experience as a mother; she is already thrust into a difficult situation before she's had a chance to discover the joys and pleasures meant to accompany parenthood. Without even a legal right to do so, Scully feels the responsibility for Emily's well-being and her future. Scully recognizes that there is little medical science can do for the girl, and even what little it can will only prolong Emily's pain and inevitable death. Scully must make the excruciating decision of when to end the treatment and let Emily die. It is a choice that no parent wants to make, but one that can only be made out of love and selflessness, because in ending Emily's pain Scully is contributing to her own. Yet out of love, Scully will gratefully take on the burden of loss if it means Emily will no longer suffer. In the end, as Scully struggles to find meaning in Emily's creation and death, Mulder tells her, "But that you found her, and you had a chance to love her—maybe she was meant for that too" ("Emily," 5x07).

In some ways, Scully's story imitates that of several mothers in the Bible, women who yearn for motherhood and face the challenges of loving and losing a child. One woman whose story is similar to Scully's is Hannah. Like Scully, Hannah thinks she might never become a mother. For years, Hannah has endured sorrow and ridicule for her barrenness. She weeps before God, pleading for a child, and God answers her prayers. But with her pleas, Hannah also makes a promise: if God will give her a baby, she will give the child back to God to serve him. The son she desperately wants and prays for she thus has with her for only a short time. When the boy is weaned, she takes him to the temple and returns him to God, to be raised there and serve with the priests (1 Samuel 1:1—2:11). What Hannah does in a physical sense, Scully also has to do more metaphorically: take the child she has desperately wanted and thought she could never have, whom she has known for only a short time, and release the girl into God's hands. This is the supreme sacrifice of a mother, to return the child God has given her back to God.

There are two other respects in which Scully is like Hannah: Hannah is blessed with additional children, and Hannah's child is given up to be raised by others. For Scully, these both come true with her son, William, the child she herself bears. Scully's pregnancy seems to be a miraculous conception, echoing Hannah and many other women in the Bible who are barren or unlikely to conceive. While Scully surely loved Emily, her affection for William must be all the deeper for the experience of bearing and nursing him and caring for him for so many months. But with William too Scully is forced to make a choice. It is perhaps all the more wrenching because it is entirely on her own initiative. William's life is endangered even at his birth; later he is almost murdered, then he is kidnapped, and subsequently he is injected with an unknown substance. Scully finally realizes that she is not able to give her son the safe and normal life that he deserves. She comes to the difficult conclusion that he would be better off raised by other parents. In a situation where she feels so many choices have been taken away from her and her son, she realizes there is one thing still in her control: "I do have a choice about the life my son will have" ("William," 9x17). Out of love, she sacrifices her own happiness so her son may have a better life, even at the risk that he may never know her or what she has done for him.

This difficult decision puts Scully in the good company of yet another biblical figure, the mother of Moses. Her account is a short one, in which she goes unnamed, but her story is compelling. At the time when Moses is born, the pharaoh fears the might and numbers of the Hebrew slaves, so he orders the male infants to be killed. Moses's mother hides her son for as long as she can. While he remains with her, though, his life is in danger. One day, she takes the risk of bundling him into a basket and setting him afloat on the river. The baby drifts into the pharaoh's own household. While this could, and should, mean the child's certain death, instead he is raised as royalty. Even though Moses's mother is granted the privilege of being his nursemaid, she gives up all rights to be known as his mother (Exodus 2:1–10). She makes the hard choice to let go of her son and allow him to be raised by another woman in order to save his life and give him a better future. Like Hannah's son Samuel, Moses will grow up to become a great man for his people, so that the mother's sacrifice and the love behind it pay off in the son's life, whether he ever fully understands or appreciates the choice that she has made.

But perhaps the most moving story of a mother's sacrificial love is the account of two mothers who come before Solomon in a dispute over a child. The child of one has died, while the other infant still lives. The mother of the living infant claims that the other woman switched the dead baby for her living one while she herself slept, but the other woman says it is a lie. To resolve the disagreement, Solomon calls for a sword so that the surviving baby can be divided and each woman can have half. The true mother cries out to stop him; she would rather the other woman have the child than the baby be harmed. Solomon immediately recognizes that she is the baby's real mother and returns her child (1 Kings 3:16–28). While this account is lauded as a show of Solomon's wisdom, it is also a depiction of a mother's love. She would sooner give up her own rights and happiness than see any harm come to her child. This is the choice that Scully makes: she gives up William to be raised by another family, yielding her own rights and joy, so that he will no longer be in harm's way.

Two other *X-Files* stories bookend and provide a foil for Scully's experiences as a mother. The first is in "Home" (4x03). This episode features the ultimate dysfunctional family, the inbred Peacocks, whose physical deformities reflect their malformed sense of love and loyalty. The death of an infant with multiple birth defects leads Scully to reflect on motherhood. Her words, in retrospect, would one day take on a whole new meaning for her: "Imagine all a woman's hopes and dreams for her child, and then nature turns so cruel. What must a mother go through?" At the end of this conversation, Mulder tells her, "I never saw you as a mother before." Up to this point in the series, Scully has not been portrayed as a mother, nor has it been revealed that a consequence of her own abduction is the removal of her ova, and thus of her ability to become a mother. But this episode foreshadows her in that role. Later in the narrative, Scully appeals to Mrs. Peacock to protect her sons from harm by turning them in for the murder they have committed, but Mrs. Peacock says, "I can tell you don't have no children. Maybe one day you'll learn the pride, the love, when you know your boy will do anything for his mother." Of course, her sense of pride and love are as twisted as her mangled body, but this macabre example presents a foil for Scully's own experience as a mother, when she will discover the love of a mother who will do anything for her son.

On the other end of the timeline stands the second movie, *I Want to Believe*. In this story Scully's patient, Christian, is a young boy with whom she feels a strong connection, and Mulder recognizes she may be identifying him with William. When, in a staff meeting about her controversial course of treatment for Christian, Scully challenges, "Would you do it if it was your son?" it is clear she is thinking as a mother, not as a doctor. It is thus like a slap in the face when the boy's mother, Mrs. Fearon, later tells Scully, "If you were a mother, you'd understand." Scully does not correct the woman's statement, but the audience knows just how wrong it really is. The precise problem is that Scully *does* understand, all too well. It is because of her own losses that she is so determined not to give up another child. But the Fearons, as the boy's true parents, also realize something that Scully once understood and related to, even if she doesn't at the moment: as voiced by the husband, "We think that Christian's been through enough." This is a decision Scully has already had to make twice as a parent, releasing one child to death and another to a better life. But she is still coming to terms with when it is time to let go. Although Scully may no longer have a child in her care, she still has a mother's heart.

FRIENDSHIP

While love sometimes involves loss and sacrifice, that is certainly not its only feature. What makes love worthwhile is the other side, the joy of companionship. Humans were not created to be alone (Genesis 2:18; in chapter 1, above, see the section titled "We Are Not Alone"). We were created to live in relationship with each other, to work together, to play together, and to enjoy one another's company. Even before the first family existed, before there was a mother and father or brothers, there were simply two people, male and female, living together as companions. It was the two of them, together, who were made in the image of God (Genesis 1:27). In this same sense, it is Mulder and Scully, together as companions, who represent everything *The X-Files* is about. Their partnership is the cornerstone of the entire series, and really what generated its popularity and longevity. Mulder and Scully epitomize what's best about human friendship, loyalty, and love.

Love Rejoices in the Truth

In the Aristotelian model, true friendship only occurs between equals.[3] C. S. Lewis describes the difference between friendship and romance in this way: lovers stand face to face, turned toward each other, while friends stand side by side, turned toward a common interest or goal. He phrases this common goal as, "Do you care about the same truth?" While it is vital to friendship for people to agree that some question or issue is of great importance, they need not agree on the answer to that question.[4] This description is very apt for Mulder and Scully. Their mutual commitment is perhaps best referred to as a search for the truth—they may disagree on what the truth is, or how to arrive at it, but they agree that truth, and justice, is the ultimate goal. To this end, they travel together side by side, focused forward on the same path. This, in fact, is where their relationship begins. Assigned to work together as partners, Mulder and Scully are acquaintances who develop an affection for each other. Before long, that affection blossoms into friendship.

If Mulder and Scully's friendship is based on a common pursuit of truth and justice through their role as federal agents, this begs the question: What is left when you remove the common goal? If Mulder and Scully no longer have the X-Files, or the FBI, in common, what then do they have? It is actually as this question is posed and answered several times throughout the series that the true nature of their friendship is brought to light.

As Season 1 ends, the X-Files are shut down. Mulder and Scully are reassigned, to separate areas. Season 2 opens with Scully teaching pathology at Quantico and Mulder working menial wiretapping duty. Their only contact is clandestine. As the two meet secretively in a parking garage, it is clear where their relationship stands: Mulder sees their contact as a way of continuing their pursuit of the truth, in defiance of the FBI; Scully, however, has no new information to report—she simply wants to make sure that he's okay ("Little Green Men"). They still hold a common goal, but their common interest is evolving into a concern for each other.

The personal attachment, and friendship, between the partners becomes more apparent through the losses that they both face over the seasons. During Scully's abduction (Season 2) and her cancer (Season 4), Mulder copes with first the reality and then the possibility of her absence. The common goal also becomes more personal so that it is no longer an abstract pursuit of justice, but a search to find justice for Scully herself. The vehicle for that pursuit remains the X-Files division. At the end of Season 5, however, going into the movie *Fight the Future* and Season 6, the X-Files are once again shut down. While Mulder and Scully are still partners, this setback doesn't seem to daunt them. But when the FBI decides to separate them (in *Fight the Future*) and Scully responds by handing in her resignation, their relationship once again stands at a crossroads. As Scully comes to deliver the news, she says to Mulder, "I debated whether or not even to tell you in person." One wonders, what was the alternative? Was she going to leave a message on his answering machine, "Oh, by the way, I quit. Have a nice life"? When she begins to walk away, Mulder may fear that she's leaving not only his apartment but his life. He pleads with her not to quit, because he can't continue the quest alone. Then he leans in to kiss her—until they are interrupted by a bee. But the question lingers: What is their relationship without the FBI or the X-Files?

In Season 6, that very issue arises. Mulder and Scully have remained partners, but not on the X-Files. When they defy the rules one too many times, they are suspended. They continue their search for the truth anyway because they are both personally invested. But their partnership is fracturing, and it is not clear if their friendship is enough to hold it together. As they argue over data and loyalties, Mulder accuses, "Scully, you're making this personal." She tells him,

"Because it is personal, Mulder. Because, without the FBI, personal interest is all that I have. And if you take that away then there is no reason for me to continue" ("One Son," 6x12). After everything they've been through, it still appears that the FBI, and their common work, is the glue holding their relationship together. They get the X-Files back shortly thereafter, and continue to work together. But a fundamental shift clearly takes place before they are separated once again. Somewhere in Season 7, it appears that their friendship is no longer focused outward but inward. In the end, personal interest is exactly what they have left. So, at the end of the series, when they no longer have the X-Files or the FBI, what they do have is each other, and that's all they need to keep them together.

Love Always Protects, Always Trusts

Exactly when and how Mulder and Scully's relationship may have shifted from friendship to something more the audience is left to wonder. There are no "I love you's" exchanged (just a stray one from Mulder when he is possibly hopped up on painkillers), no hot-and-heavy bedroom scenes. Merely, as always, gentle touches, forehead kisses, and a lot of meaningful looks. Does this mean that their mutual affection can't be termed love? On the contrary; around Season 5 creator Chris Carter admitted, "Scully loves Mulder, and Mulder loves Scully. It's a wonderful romance. It's just not a sexual romance. It's not a physical romance. It is a caring, tender, respectful relationship. It's an ideal."[5] Eventually, of course, the relationship would cross that line, but even when the romance did become physical, it was entirely offscreen. In front of the camera, their relationship is trademark for being remarkably chaste—especially compared with most other shows on television.[6] Because of this, their partnership has never been characterized by lust or physical passion, but by respect, loyalty, and trust.

Any number of terms could be used to describe friendship, but for Mulder and Scully these three—"respect," "trust," and "loyalty"—are perhaps the most important. All three elements can be seen developing even in the first season, beginning as early as the pilot episode. Respect is the earliest ingredient, and foundational for the other two. In fact, before the new partners first meet, there is clearly a professional respect emerging. Scully acknowledges Mulder's reputation as a brilliant criminal profiler, and Mulder realizes he has met his match in Scully's scientific prowess. When they meet, it is a meeting of minds. The intellectual parry and thrust of their initial conversation sets the tone for the case and their partnership. In the third episode, Mulder recognizes, "In our investigations, you may not always agree with me, but at least you respect the journey" ("Squeeze," 1x02). For all of their disagreements, the one thing the partners always have is respect for each other's abilities and ideas. They take one another seriously and give one another the benefit of the doubt. They may dismiss each other's theories, but they don't dismiss each other.

With each character, this respect comes across in a slightly different way. Scully's respect for Mulder is primarily that she does not write him off as a lunatic as so many others would. She may not believe in aliens or the paranormal, but she believes in Mulder and regards what he says as worth listening to and worth refuting. If she didn't respect his theories, she wouldn't waste her time debunking them. While she admits that "Mulder's ideas may be a bit out there," she defends him as "a great agent" ("Squeeze"). She is even willing to give him the benefit of the doubt when he is committed to a psych ward and strapped down to a bed for his bizarre behavior on a case ("Folie à Deux," 5x19). She respects his intellect, and his sanity, and is willing to take him seriously when no one else will.

While Mulder's respect for Scully is equally intellectual, his main show of respect for her is also based on (or in spite of) her gender. This is best highlighted by comparing two episodes, one with Mulder as her partner, and another when she is newly partnered with Agent Doggett. In Scully's first case with Doggett, they run into a chauvinistic detective who is quite condescending toward Scully. Doggett "resolves" the situation by pulling the detective aside to have a little man-to-man talk so that he will follow through with what Scully has requested ("Patience," 8x04). It could not be clearer in this moment that Agent Doggett is not Mulder and that Scully's partnership with Doggett will be very different. Mulder, in fact, not only would but did do completely the opposite. In "D.P.O." (3x03), when Mulder and Scully meet a chauvinistic sheriff who turns his attention solely to Mulder as the man, Mulder steps away from the conversation entirely, deferring to Scully and letting her handle the sheriff. Mulder respects Scully as an agent, a scientist, and a woman, and he never treats her as though she can't defend herself, and him, or hold her own. Although Mulder does have a reputation for ditching her, it isn't because of her gender—Mulder is an equal-opportunity ditcher. This is apparent when he does the same thing to Agent Krycek on their first case together. Early on, Mulder ditches Scully because he doesn't yet fully trust her (the same reason he ditches Krycek), or simply doesn't want to be held back. But later, he ditches her because he recognizes the sacrifices she has made for his quest and doesn't want to drag her down any further for his personal agenda. While his actions are misguided, considering that she always has to come rescue him anyway (in "Deep Throat," "Colony," "Triangle," and so on), even here there's an element of respect, since he respects her too much as a human being and a person of integrity to let her or her career suffer the same losses that he does.

Out of that foundation of respect, Mulder and Scully are able to overcome his initial doubts and build a solid trust. In fact, the term "trust" may be to the partners what the word "love" would mean to anyone else. Instead of declaring, "I love you," they affirm, "I trust you." Their trust is mutual and exclusive, and when that exclusivity is in jeopardy, so is their partnership. The initial signs of trust blossom in the pilot episode, on their first case, and illustrate how their trust is built on respect. In their opening conversation, Mulder shows her slides of strange bumps on the backs of several individuals. He claims they're related to alien abductions. While Scully doesn't accept this theory, she does believe that he knows something about what's happening to the victims. She respects his opinion—so much so that when she finds bumps on her own back, she rushes to his motel room and drops her robe to let him see her bare back so he can tell her what the marks are. To her relief, he declares they are merely mosquito bites. But the fact that she is able to be physically vulnerable in front of him, and that she believes he can genuinely explain the marks, is a show of trust in him as a man and an agent and a show of respect for his ideas. Mulder, in turn, makes himself emotionally vulnerable to her, trusting her with the account of his sister's abduction and his motivation for pursuing the X-Files. While trust is not complete in that moment and still has to be earned over time, that incident of mutual vulnerability allows the two to begin constructing a firm and lasting trust.

The character of Deep Throat, Mulder's informant throughout the first season, also helps to illustrate the growing trust between the partners. Mulder first meets Deep Throat in the second episode (aptly titled "Deep Throat," 1x01), but he doesn't include Scully in their encounters. In fact, even midway through the season ("Eve," 1x10), Mulder rushes her from his motel room so he can secretly meet with his informant, who asks him, "Are you certain she hasn't followed you?" It is not until late in the season that Mulder shows enough trust in Scully to let her in on this relationship with Deep Throat, and then she finally meets the man for herself. Mulder even begins to listen to Scully's advice, trusting her over Deep Throat when she questions the informant's motives and honesty. But soon thereafter, Deep Throat meets his demise, gasping to Scully with his last breath, "Trust no one" ("The Erlenmeyer Flask," 1x23). His words become a motto through the rest of the series, a warning to consider whom or what you trust. When trust is so rare a commodity, then, the absolute trust that Mulder and Scully establish with each other stands out that much more starkly.

Despite their declarations to each other, "You are the only one I trust" (Scully to Mulder in "E.B.E." [1x16], and Mulder to Scully in "Wetwired" [3x23]), there are still times that their trust is put to the test or seems compromised by a show of trust in someone outside the two of them. On a smaller scale, this occurs in episodes like "Colony," when it seems that Mulder will gullibly believe (and therefore trust) anyone who tells him a story he wants to hear. But more significantly, their trust is strained through the appearance of Mulder's former "chickadee," Diana Fowley. Even after Mulder's declarations of need for Scully and his near-kiss in *Fight the Future*, by the very next episode he seems to be ignoring these things and siding with Diana over Scully. Scully tells him, "It comes down to a matter of trust. I guess it always has." The problem is that he won't accept her scientific conclusions, but she takes his rejection of her science as a denial of her request to "trust my judgment—to trust me" ("The Beginning," 6x01). Although they seem to shelve the conversation for a while, it returns in full force by the middle of Season 6. Scully has uncovered what she believes is evidence of Diana's duplicity, but Mulder dismisses it. Scully says to him, "You ask me to trust no one, and yet you trust her on simple faith" ("One Son"). Both his trust in Diana and his lack of trust in Scully's judgment about Diana cause a rift in their relationship. It is immediately following this that they talk about Scully "making this personal." The Diana issue is obviously very personal and threatens to undermine the trust that is so essential to any friendship, but especially for these two who trust each other as they trust no other—or at least, that's what Scully believed until Diana came along. When Diana is removed from the equation (first by her reassignment, then by her death), so is the threat, and Mulder and Scully's trust emerges intact and apparently as strong as ever. But any willingness to believe or trust another person over each other will always be a sore spot for the two of them.

One episode in particular reflects the importance of trust to friendship. In "Redux II" (5x03), three different characters offer to "befriend" Mulder, but the motives and sincerity of all three are in question. One of these, Assistant Director Skinner, summarizes the bottom line: "You don't want to forget who your friends are, Agent Mulder. To remember who you can trust." That is the essential issue with each of these three "friends"—which of them Mulder can trust, and which of them may be the mole in the FBI who has been betraying him from the beginning. What remains unstated throughout the episode is the true standard of friendship, the one to which all others are compared: the friendship of Scully. She is the one who remains trustworthy, who at that moment is in a hospital bed paying the price for her friendship with him, and even yet is willing to sacrifice her reputation and possibly even her freedom for his sake. She doesn't need to claim to be his friend, as the others do—she declares it daily by living it out.

Out of this trust, then, grows loyalty. Loyalty is a commitment and a devotion, but it is often given freely only when the other person is found worthy. Respect makes the person worthy in the friend's eyes, and with trust comes acceptance that the loyalty goes both ways. Loyalty is something that Mulder and Scully develop first of all because of their FBI partnership—partners can't function together without a certain amount of trust and loyalty. But what emerges between these two goes beyond mere workplace requirements. Late in Season 1, Scully makes an admission that is apparently surprising to Mulder: "I wouldn't put myself on the line for anybody but you" ("Tooms," 1x20). It is one thing to risk her life for him—that goes with the job—but another thing entirely to risk her career and reputation. Later in that episode, she's even willing to lie to their superiors on his behalf, setting up a pattern that speaks volumes about her loyalty.

Scully is known for her honesty, perhaps to a fault. She doesn't mince words when passing along that someone has died, or when telling Mulder that his mother committed suicide. Because of this honesty, she doesn't make a very good liar. Their boss, Skinner, seems especially perceptive about when she's lying. He better than anyone knows how often these two will cover for each other. Even when Scully completely disagrees with Mulder's actions, she will protect him rather than concede any doubts in front of others (e.g., "Grotesque" [3x14], "Folie à Deux"). She'll go to prison to protect Mulder ("Terma," 4x10), and even lie point-blank to an FBI committee to temporarily cover up his crime ("Redux," 5x02). In Mulder's estimation, however, her willingness to lie for him is a show of her integrity because she is committed to the Truth and the greater good. This loyalty, then, is both a commitment to each other and a common commitment to the same goal, based on the same values.

While Mulder would certainly compromise his own reputation or even his life for Scully's sake, he does not value these things highly, so their loss would not reflect great sacrifice on his part. But there is one instance that serves as a prime example of his loyalty to Scully: his willingness to sacrifice his own sister. In "End Game" (2x17), Scully is held hostage, and the requested trade is for Mulder to hand over the woman who has come to him claiming to be his long-lost sister. It is clear from the subsequent scenes that Mulder is fully convinced this woman is Samantha. Even so, he is willing to risk her life and safety in order to have Scully released. His loyalty to Scully supersedes all others, so that for her sake he would jeopardize what he values most.

One story arc that summarizes well the loyalty and friendship between this pair is the finale for Season 6 ("Biogenesis") and the two-part premier for Season 7 ("The Sixth Extinction" and "The Sixth Extinction II: Amor Fati"). Showing again the lengths they will go for each other, Scully travels to Africa to follow evidence that Mulder would want to pursue, and that may help save him as he lies incapacitated in a hospital bed back in Washington, DC. Diana has reappeared, once again providing a source of tension and a foil for Scully's relationship with Mulder. The third of these episodes is largely a dream sequence of Mulder's, showing him a life where he buries his head in the sand about the coming apocalypse and therefore blissfully receives everything he could ever want. Diana's part in this beautiful deception parallels her deceptive role in the waking world. But Scully intrudes on the dream, telling Mulder the truth about the real world outside that he's chosen to ignore. At the end of the episode, back in reality, they share their experiences. Scully admits that her beliefs have been shaken, not least by the discovery that Diana helped provide the information to save Mulder's life and has since been killed for this last act of friendship. Scully tells him, "I don't know what the truth is. I don't know who to listen to. I don't know who to trust." But Mulder reassures her: "Scully, I was like you once—I didn't know who to trust. And I chose another path, another life, another fate, where I found my sister. And even though my world was unrecognizable and upside down, there was one thing that remained the same: You were my friend, and you told me the truth. Even when the world was falling apart, you were my constant, my touchstone." She confesses to him, "And you are mine."

Rather than declaring, "I love you," Mulder and Scully use other words that bear the same meaning for them: "trust," "truth," "constant," "touchstone." "Amor Fati" also aptly depicts the proverb: "Well meant are the wounds a friend inflicts, but profuse are the kisses of an enemy" (Proverbs 27:6). The words that Scully speaks to Mulder in the dream are harsh, especially in contrast to the wonderful things that have been given to him by his enemies (including the kisses of Diana), but the sharp arrows of Scully's words are necessary to goad him out of complacency. It's her honesty, although painful at the time, that is a true show of friendship. For Mulder, whose faith is in the Truth, the supreme act of friendship is to tell him the truth at all times, regardless of what he wants to hear. That confidence in each other's honesty, that dependability that comes with trust and loyalty, provides a solid ground on which the two of them may stand. Then, even when the world around them may be topsy-turvy, shaking the foundations of their faith or making them question their choices and commitments, they can reach out to each other as a constant and touchstone, knowing their friendship is the one thing that stands strong.

Perfect Other, Perfect Opposite

"TrustNo1" (9x08) opens with a voiceover by Scully, addressed to her son. She describes her relationship with Mulder, in part to explain the miracle of William's birth. "Chance meeting your perfect other, your perfect opposite, your protector and endangerer. Chance embarking with this other on the greatest of journeys—a search for truths fugitive and imponderable." On the road that Mulder and Scully travel together, this is how she comes to view their voyage, as the meeting of "other" and "opposite." Their differences function not as a dividing line but as a synthesis, integrating two halves into a whole. Their opposing points of view and approaches develop into their greatest asset. Their partnership is the essence of teamwork.[7]

While this symbiosis may be apparent to the audience, it is something that Mulder and Scully must grow to understand. The first movie, *Fight the Future*, presents a key point at which they recognize that their partnership is truly a combined effort, not merely Mulder's work that Scully is trying to inhibit.

> MULDER: I need you on this, Scully.
>
> SCULLY: You don't need me, Mulder. You never have. I've just held you back . . .
>
> MULDER: If you want to tell yourself that so you can quit with a clear conscience, you can, but you're wrong.
>
> SCULLY: Why did they assign me to you in the first place, Mulder? To debunk your work, to rein you in, to shut you down.

> MULDER: But you saved me! As difficult and as frustrating as it's been sometimes, your . . . strict rationalism and science have saved me a thousand times over. You've kept me honest. You've made me a whole person . . . I don't know if I want to do this alone. I don't even know if I can. And if I quit now, they win.

For Mulder to recognize and express how much he values Scully's contribution to the quest appears to be a huge step forward for him. This is the same man who has a reputation for ditching her when he prefers to go it alone, who never bothers to get her a nameplate for the office door, or a separate desk. By all outward appearances, he sees the X-Files as his work and passion alone, something to which she was simply assigned as an auxiliary (see "Never Again," 4x13). But here he finally comes to understand, and lets her know, that she has become indispensable.

The second movie echoes this theme, especially to highlight the evolution of their relationship. Mulder says to Scully regarding the case, "I need you on this with me." He tells one of the agents that he is only half the team, on what was once the X-Files. He constantly keeps Scully in the loop on the case, seeking her input despite her refusals to get involved. What Mulder first articulated in *Fight the Future*, that the work is no longer his alone and is incomplete without her by his side, is clearly how he remembers their partnership. In fact, in *I Want to Believe* when the FBI requests his involvement on the case, Mulder's one condition to say yes is that Scully accompany him. As he once told her, he doesn't want to do this alone. She fights against participating in the investigation because she is trying to leave other aspects of her old life behind, only to realize that she can't. In the end, it is together, with her contribution, that they solve the case.

Although Scully is initially assigned to the X-Files to debunk them, she instead provides the scientific basis that justifies and legitimizes many of Mulder's outlandish claims. The fact that they function best as a team is apparent whenever one of them tries to work cases without the other (Mulder in "3," Scully in Season 8). What they represent is two poles, two opposites, that in pulling against each other achieve a balance. They are yin and yang, anima and animus. They represent the male-female divide and dynamic built into creation. But it is not strictly that Mulder is the masculine and Scully is the feminine. In fact, quite often their gender roles are reversed. Scully is logical while Mulder is intuitive; Scully is more stoic while Mulder is emotive. Scully stands in for the hard sciences, reason, and authority (often deemed masculine), while Mulder depicts the social sciences, perception, and mystery (more feminine stereotypes).[8] In combination they represent the tug and pull of opposites attracting. It is *together* that they symbolize male and female, the two halves of humanity in creative tension—just as together it is male and female that reflect the image of God.

The dynamic between Mulder and Scully of opposites attracting, or more important, of working in conflict and yet in harmony, is not just an aspect of romantic love, where the male-female pairing is most often emphasized. This is an element of their friendship and partnership, and therefore reflects both what the two genders can contribute to one another beyond simply procreation or a sexual relationship, and also what any two human beings can contribute to each other through their differences. Mulder and Scully each bring something to the partnership that the other lacks. Scully contributes coolheadedness to his impulsivity; Mulder adds spontaneity to her reticence. She provides a foundation of weighing evidence and establishing provable facts, while he has the imagination to think outside the box and make intuitive leaps. Although their differences lead to many arguments, the pair uses this in the positive sense of arguing one side of a case and thereby reinforcing it, rather than allowing their disagreements to become merely fights. They let their differences and their contradictions combine to become their greatest strength.

What Mulder and Scully come to represent, then, is not merely what each gender contributes to the other, but what other people contribute to our lives to make up for our own weaknesses. Where there is potential for conflict, through our oppositions and our differences, balance and completion can arise instead. While each of us has a divine spark within and the image of God imprinted on us, only by combining the best of humanity—all of humanity—can we together represent God's character. Nothing illustrates this better than love. God *is* love, but love cannot exist in isolation. Love requires the presence of another. We must love each other in order to love at all. By loving the other, by working together in companionship with people who are unlike us but who will walk alongside us on the same journey, we reflect God's character. Humans were not made to function alone. We need other people in order to be complete and to achieve our full potential.

On the other hand, though, it cannot be overlooked that friendship between male and female presents a unique situation. This too is embodied by Mulder and Scully. While their relationship in its early years is incredibly chaste, there always remains what is often dubbed unresolved sexual tension. As C. S. Lewis states, "When the two people who thus discover that they are on the same secret road are of different sexes, the friendship which arises between them will very easily pass . . . into erotic love. Indeed, unless they are physically repulsive to each other or unless one or both already loves elsewhere, it is almost certain to do so sooner or later."[9] In a negative sense, there is clearly potential for betrayal and affairs in such a situation when one or both in the friendship *do* already love elsewhere and yet the two of them still allow the platonic friendship to develop into something more. But on the positive side, a friendship between an unattached male and female can lay hardy roots for a romance to blossom and flourish. Scully recognizes as much when she gives advice to another woman on her love life: "It seems to me that the best relationships, the ones that last, are frequently the ones that are rooted in friendship. You know, one day you look at the person and you see something more than you did the night before. Like a switch has been flicked somewhere. And the person who was just a friend is suddenly the only person you can ever imagine yourself with" ("The Rain King," 6x07). Of course, as Scully says this, we wonder if she is reflecting on her feelings about Mulder. Although the audience never knows precisely how and when, we do know that eventually that switch has been flicked. Friends have become lovers, but lovers remain friends.

EROS: ROMANTIC LOVE

As Mulder and Scully move from friends to lovers, they add on to their friendship another form of love: eros, or romantic love. While this is the category of love that includes sexual relationships (hence, common usage of the term "erotic"), Lewis makes a distinction between sex and eros: "Sexual desire, without Eros, wants *it*, the *thing in itself* [i.e., bodily pleasure]; Eros wants the Beloved."[10] The fact that in the early years Mulder's and Scully's individual sexuality never involves the other, and even after they become romantically involved their sexual relationship is never depicted onscreen, reinforces that what the couple shares is true eros—desire for the beloved, not merely sexuality in itself. Partnership and friendship, respect and loyalty come first; the sexual relationship is only secondary and kept private. This too is one of the many ways their relationship stands out as an anomaly on television.

The ideal for which erotic love was created, and where sexuality comes into play, is when "a man leaves his father and his mother and clings to his wife, and they become one flesh" (Genesis 2:24). In this joining, the divine elements that were separated into male and female at creation are reunified, giving us the ability to participate in creation by creating new life. Hence, in the procreation that results from sexual union, male and female quite literally become "one flesh" by comingling parts of themselves in a new human life. This is yet another way in which humans cannot exist alone; the very continuation of the human species requires the collaboration of male and female. While such creation can also be represented emotionally or symbolically by a couple pairing their talents to create a "brainchild" or partnering to create a family through adoption, Mulder and Scully do share in physical parenthood, however briefly, and become one flesh through their son, William. Although his conception in some ways remains an enigma, the fact that he exists is physical evidence of their sexual relationship with each other, their erotic love. He remains a part of the connection that holds them together, even though the loss of their son could easily tear them apart (as such a loss has done for Agent Doggett and his wife). Instead, they find their solace in each other, which provides them strength to endure their loss.

With the shift into eros, Mulder and Scully also make the shift from facing forward toward the same goal to facing each other. This is illustrated in a very literal sense in a pose that has become famous for them: leaning their foreheads against each other's (fondly referred to by fans as "forehead sex," which is the only sex the couple ever has onscreen). In these moments standing face to face, they reinforce their mutual commitment and draw strength from one another. The first time we see them in this pose is in *Fight the Future*, just as their partnership has been dissolved—when they are no longer paired side by side, and therefore turn to renew their commitment face to face. The same pose is mirrored toward the end of *I Want to Believe*, accompanied by a kiss; the kiss that was interrupted in *Fight the Future* is thus fulfilled in the second movie, illustrating how their relationship has changed over the years.

The question that is explored during the series—If Mulder and Scully no longer have the FBI to hold them together, then what do they have?—is brought to light in a different way in the second movie. As work partners, it is the pair's orientation toward the same goal that binds their lives and fates together. Without the X-Files or the FBI, all that is left to keep them together is personal interest, which is exactly their situation for the six years between the series finale and *I Want to Believe*. During that time, they are also tied together by living as fugitives, the same thing that prevents them from legally making their bond strictly about each other by getting married. In the movie, however, they finally emerge from life in hiding and so are released from that bond that made their companionship essential for survival. While before, the FBI was their common link, now it threatens to pull them apart as they lean in opposite directions. Is personal interest enough to keep them together anymore? Is there enough of a bond left between them to necessitate that they stay together?

This is what the pair must decide in the course of *I Want to Believe*. The chains of life on the run that bound them have been loosed, and they have been set free—but free from each other? The movie's refrain, "Don't give up," applies to their relationship as well. What Mulder and Scully have left, without the FBI or their mutual fugitive status, is their commitment to each other. "Don't give up" is the essence of commitment: refusing to give up on a person or a relationship even when common ground has fallen away, even when the individuals have changed or grown apart, even when there are disagreements, when the only reason to stay is the commitment itself. This is the true constancy of love, not in the persistence of an emotion, but in the choice to make and honor a commitment. For Mulder and Scully, the end of *I Want to Believe* is a renewal of their commitment to one another, the decision to move forward together to face whatever may come. Their connection to each other, face to face (or forehead to forehead), is alone what now defines them—friendship has become eros.

CHARITY: DIVINE LOVE

The King James Version of 1 Corinthians 13 translates love as "charity": "And now abideth faith, hope, charity, these three; but the greatest of these is charity" (v. 13). This is an English rendering of the Latin *caritas*, a translation of the Greek *agapē*. It is a distinct kind of love from the Greek *eros* (romantic love) or *philia* (friendship or brotherly love). Charity represents God's love of humanity, and so also the ways that humans reciprocate love to God and love another as God loves each of us. Therefore, charity, as we have come to think of it in modern English—giving to the needy or underprivileged—is a reflection of the original Charity, God's nurturing love for his creation. Charity, in this modern sense, is loving people as God loves them, not for what they can do for us or give to us in return, but simply because they are human.

Charity, or divine love, goes beyond the natural loves. It is in our nature to have affection for a parent or child, to care for our friends, or to cherish a lover, but divine love embraces the unlovable as well. It is unconditional and often unreciprocated. This is the love that calls us not only to love our neighbor, but to love our enemy. This kind of love, therefore, is not merely an emotion (since at times it may run contrary to our emotions) but a virtue. Divine love both calls and enables us to love the people we have no reason to love, and even those we have reason *not* to love. It is love freely lavished upon us, with the request that, in return, we pass that love on to others. Charity is then the original and supreme form of love. It is the summation and fulfillment of all other loves. Affection, friendship, and eros are thus merely facets of divine love. Each offers a glimpse of how God loves us, so that when they are considered together, we might understand divine love more fully. God exemplifies for us affection, friendship, and eros, so that he is not only Creator but also Father, Friend, and Lover.

Love Never Ends

Before we consider God in each of these roles, one other aspect of divine love should be noted. Divine love is the only form of love that is eternal. As 1 Corinthians 13:8 says, "Love"—or charity—"never ends." In the Song of Solomon, love (here more likely erotic love) is described as powerful and enduring: "for love is strong as death, passion fierce as the grave. Its flashes are flashes of fire, a raging flame. Many waters cannot quench love, neither can floods drown it" (8:6–7). But truly, such love can only last as long as does the beloved. The finiteness of love is depicted vividly in "Kaddish" (4x12), the story of a Jewish couple whose love proves to be as strong as death, and yet not strong enough to vanquish it completely. When Ariel's betrothed, Isaac, is murdered before their wedding day, she turns to a myth from Jewish mysticism that enables her to resurrect him as a golem. She isn't ready to let go of love, but in her attempt to prolong it, she only manages to create a false approximation of her lover. The golem is little more than a monster, a body without a soul. Ariel must come to the hard realization that what she has brought to life is not Isaac. Her true beloved is already gone, and she must bid him a final farewell. What she learns firsthand is that love for a finite creature always carries the risk of heartache because sooner or later the beloved will be lost. The emotion of love may be stronger than death, but love cannot prevent the death of a loved one.

Even when a couple is blessed with many years together, it is inevitable that someday the time will come to an end. Scully is told as much by Alfred Fellig, a man who has cheated death and now seemingly cannot die ("Tithonus," 6x09). He has become a lonely, miserable man who spends his days chasing down Death, longing for the one thing that everyone else has but which continues to elude him. He has lost all meaning in his life. When Scully asks him, "What about love?" he says, "What, does that last forever?" He tells the sad account of how one day, after living for so many decades beyond his natural life, he had to go look up his wife's name because he could no longer remember it. "Love lasts seventy-five years, if you're lucky," he tells Scully. "You don't want to be around when it's gone." All good things, and relationships, must come to an end. This is why Scully has such a hard time allowing people to get close, as she admits to a social worker regarding her petition to adopt Emily ("Christmas Carol," 5x05): "Ever since I was a child, I've never allowed myself to get too close to people. I've avoided emotional attachments. Perhaps I've been so afraid of death and dying that any connection just seemed like a bad thing, something that wouldn't last." Her words ring true for what will soon happen to Emily, whose funeral closes out the next episode.

The only love, then, that cannot disappoint, that cannot fail and never ends, is love grounded in the one who is eternal. In book 4 of his *Confessions*, St. Augustine tells the story of a dear friend who died and how he himself was left heartbroken at the loss. Eventually Augustine comes to realize that the only love that will not involve loss and heartache is love for the one who cannot be lost: "No one can lose you, my God, unless he forsakes you."[11] But love for friends and family may likewise endure if we have hope for their eternal life. Lewis describes this: "Only those into which Love Himself has entered will ascend to Love Himself . . . Natural loves can hope for eternity only in so far as they have allowed themselves to be taken into the eternity of Charity."[12] Everything in this life, in this timeline, is transient. Love may last, but the things and people that we love won't, at least in this lifetime. Augustine says, therefore, that the only true happiness is found in the love that is eternal because every other love will eventually be lost and bring sorrow and grief. Yet people can find joy even in death when they have hope that they will see their loved one again and be reunited for eternity. This is the lesson Scully continues to grapple with, accepting that Emily has been released to a life beyond this one where Scully may someday see her again. Here, faith, hope, and love are once again intertwined: faith in the source of eternal love allows us to hope that those we love will be restored to us in eternity.

Dio Ti Ama

God is often referred to or portrayed as a father, especially in the Gospels. One parable in particular gives a poignant account of the type of father that God is and the way he loves humanity. The story is best known as the Prodigal Son (Luke 15:11–32). The youngest of a father's two sons asks to receive his inheritance immediately and then leaves home to squander his money, earning himself the title "prodigal." Once the money is gone, the son is destitute and realizes that even his father's slaves are better off, eating well while he has less to eat than do the pigs he is feeding. He decides to return home, but as a slave, since he feels he has lost his right to be his father's son. Yet as the son approaches home, his father runs to him, throws his arms around him, and kisses him. The father prepares a celebration to welcome home his son, "for," he says, "this son of mine was dead and is alive again; he was lost and is found!" (v. 24). The father does not care where the son has been or what he has done; the father only cares that the son who was once lost to him has returned, and that reason alone is cause for celebration. In Luke, this story is preceded by a similar one to drive home the same point: "Which one of you, having a hundred sheep and losing one of them, does not leave the ninety-nine in the wilderness and go after the one that is lost until he finds it? . . . Just so, I tell you, there will be more joy in heaven over one sinner who repents than over ninety-nine righteous persons who need no repentance" (Luke 15:4, 7). God is the shepherd who cares enough about an individual sheep to chase after it when it has wandered away; like the prodigal's father, he celebrates when the one who was lost returns to the fold.

This aspect of God's character is also reflected in the *X-Files* episode "Improbable" (9x14). Mr. Burt, representing God, hounds Mad Wayne by following him around and constantly trying to influence his choices away from evil (the serial murders Wayne is committing) and toward the good. Mr. Burt tries to convince Wayne that he has a choice about his actions, but Wayne won't hear it. Mr. Burt tells him, "You know, there's a secret to this game, Wayno, and I'm going to tell you what the secret is: Choose better." But Wayne snaps, "You got something to say to me, you say it." Mr. Burt replies, "Son, I just did." This reference to Wayne as "son" illustrates the type of parental care that God feels toward humanity, even the worst of humanity. Wayne is a lost sheep, and Mr. Burt is pursuing him to bring him back into the fold. Later, Mr. Burt tells Wayne, "You're a card. You really are a card, but I love you." This unconditional love that Mr. Burt, or God, has for his creation is the theme of the episode, emphasized at the beginning with the tagline, "Dio ti ama"—God loves you. God loves Wayne in spite of everything the man has done and goes to great lengths to restore Wayne to the right path. But God also allows Wayne to choose his own way, even if he consistently makes the wrong choices, choices that grieve God.

Another prodigal who eventually does choose better is Father Joe in *I Want to Believe.* Like the prodigal, Father Joe has recognized his wrongs and returned to God repentantly, hoping not necessarily for full sonship but for even the scraps from the table. The visions he receives appear to be a sign of God's forgiveness and offer him the opportunity to atone for some of his wrongs. How others respond to this apparent redemption also reflects the rest of the story about the prodigal son. While the parable is primarily about the son and his father, the prodigal also has an older brother, who has remained obedient to his father and stayed by the father's side. One day, the brother comes in from the field to hear a celebration going on. When he learns that the prodigal son's return is being celebrated with a lavish party, the older brother is furious. He has never received such a celebration in spite of his loyalty, while the other son is being rewarded for his irresponsibility. The father tells the older brother, "Son, you are always with me, and all that is mine is yours. But we had to celebrate and rejoice, because this brother of yours was dead and has come to life; he was lost and has been found" (Luke 15:31–32). In this exchange, one could easily see Scully having such a conversation with God. She doesn't hide her animosity toward Father Joe or her rejection of the idea that God could forgive or redeem him. She feels that she is righteous while he is not, and she can't accept that God would reward him with visions for his disobedience. Her anger reflects that of the prodigal's older brother and the indignation that many of us feel when we see the wicked prospering or receiving blessings that we feel we deserve instead.

Such stories, and Scully's understandable frustration, beg the question, Does God love the wicked more than he loves the good? Does he love Wayne more than he loves Wayne's victims? Does he love Father Joe more than he loves Scully? No—but it may seem so to us because we have a harder time accepting that he loves the bad than accepting that he loves the good. This is the God who will chase down one lost sheep out of a hundred. He throws a grand party to celebrate the return of one lost son. And when we're part of the ninety-nine, or we're the dutiful older brother, we have a problem accepting that our Shepherd and Father would go to such extremes out of love for those we see as less worthy than ourselves. What we often fail to see is that the message isn't just for the unworthy: if God can love even the worst criminal, then his love is big enough to embrace us on days when we're less than kind, when we're uncharitable if not downright mean, when we put someone else down to elevate ourselves—on days when we're not so lovable. And we all have those days. We all fail. We all make mistakes. And yet, like a parent who graciously understands that children aren't always perfect, God loves us unconditionally. On our good days, we're the spitting image of our Father, and he beams with pride in our accomplishments. On our not-so-good days, he's disappointed, and sometimes heartbroken, but he's still waiting to celebrate when we'll come back to him and ask for a second chance. He wants us to be children he can be proud of, but he'll love us even when we're not.

This, then, is charity, the unconditional love of a father who can love even his most unlovable child. But love requires action, so God's love for us has gone one step further: "What is love? It is not that we loved God. It is that he loved us and sent his Son to give his life to pay for our sins" (1 John 4:10, NIrV). God was willing to give up what was dearest to him, his own and only Son, so that by Jesus's death the rest of us could have eternal life. This sacrificial love echoes the sacrifice seen in Scully's maternal love, to let go of a beloved child. In the same way, God let go of his only begotten Son, the Son of his own nature and being; but that loss led to gain, opening the way for the rest of us to be adopted into the same divine family (see Romans 8). God released his Son not merely to die but to do battle with death, knowing that Jesus would emerge victorious. By the Father handing his Son over to death, not only did the Son himself pass over into eternity, but the rest of us may too. The resurrection of Jesus paved the way for the resurrection of us all into a better life—into life everlasting.

No Greater Love

Through this sacrificial love, in addition to being a divine Parent, God also plays the roles of Brother and Friend. Jesus, as God, loved us by sacrificing himself. In this, he is contrasted with Cain, the first and worst brother: "We must not be like Cain who . . . murdered his brother . . . We know love by this, that [Jesus] laid down his life for us" (1 John 3:12, 16). While Cain sacrificed his brother, Jesus is our Brother who sacrificed himself. Jesus is also the antithesis of the prodigal son. Instead of demanding his inheritance prematurely and squandering it on his own fleeting pleasure, Jesus forfeited his rights as Son of God to become human, as lowly as the slave that the prodigal was forced to become; "And being found in human form, [Jesus] humbled himself and became obedient to the point of death—even death on a cross" (Philippians 2:7b–8). Jesus relinquished his rights to his inheritance so that we could become part of God's family and thus coheirs with him (Romans 8:15–17). He took on a human body and called us his brothers and sisters, becoming like us in every respect, even dying like we die, in order to gain victory over death for us all (Hebrews 2:10–18).

In *The X-Files* this sacrificial love of a brother is familiar from Mulder's commitment to his sister, Samantha. He has devoted his life and career to saving her, disregarding his own health and reputation for the single-minded pursuit of her well-being. In the same way, Jesus is the brother who devoted his life, to the point of losing it, for the sole pursuit of saving us. He gave up both his heavenly rights to the throne of God and his earthly rights to a normal life and committed his human career to seeking our eternal well-being. This type of love that Mulder shows for Samantha he later transfers also to Scully. As Scully's partner and friend, he is willing to risk both life and reputation for her safety, which she reciprocates. According to Jesus, such a willingness to sacrifice oneself is the mark of true friendship: "No one has greater love than this, to lay down one's life for one's friends" (John 15:13). Jesus here speaks of himself. He became our true Friend through his willingness to lay down his life for our sakes. His request in return is that we "love one another as I have loved you" (John 15:12), that we too should be willing to set aside our own rights for the sake of others.

Another aspect of friendship that is highlighted in our relationship to God as friend is trust. It is clear from the trust between Mulder and Scully just how essential this quality is to friendship, and how a relationship can be damaged when trust is lacking. The role of trust in our interaction with God is especially seen in the life of one man who is referred to as God's friend: "'Abraham believed God . . . ' [Genesis 15:6] and he was called the friend of God" (James 2:23; see also Isaiah 41:8). To believe someone, or believe *in* them, is to trust them. God asks Abraham to trust him, first in the promise that God will provide a son and heir to Abraham, and later that God will spare that son when God asks Abraham to put the son's life in danger (see chapter 6, below). On both counts, God comes through: he provides a miraculous pregnancy to Abraham and his wife in their old age (Genesis 21), and he provides a ram in the bushes as a means to spare the son's life (Genesis 22). Because Abraham trusts God, and God proves his loyalty by fulfilling his promises, Abraham becomes known as God's friend.

Jesus likewise asks his friends to trust him, or to believe in him. One place where Jesus makes such a request of a friend is in the account of his raising Lazarus from the dead. Jesus refers to Lazarus as his friend (John 11:11), and we are told that Jesus loved Lazarus and his sisters (11:5). Lazarus has been dead and buried for four days when Jesus comes to the family, reassuring them that Lazarus will live. Jesus tells Martha, one of the sisters, "I am the resurrection and the life. Those who believe in me, even though they die, will live, and everyone who lives and believes in me will never die" (11:25–26). He is essentially saying to Martha, "Trust me." He asks for the same trust from anyone who, like Lazarus or Martha, would be his friend. What he offers in return is eternal life. Jesus does resurrect Lazarus, as a sign of the new life that he wishes to give all who would trust him as a friend. Jesus is the friend and brother who has already proved his loyalty and trustworthiness by laying down his own life, and so has shown us how great is his love.

I Am My Beloved's and My Beloved Is Mine

Beyond a Father, Brother, and Friend, God is also depicted as a Lover. The love poetry in Song of Solomon is often read as an allegory of God's love for his people. The beloved declares of her lover, "I am my beloved's and my beloved is mine" (Song of Solomon 6:3). This verse is used in Jewish wedding ceremonies, and Ariel can be heard reciting these words to her betrothed in "Kaddish." The image is applied to God and the people of Israel, especially in prophetic writings such as the book of Isaiah. On the negative side, God charges that his people have become like an adulterous wife by pursuing other gods. God isn't a swinger—he wants a monogamous relationship with his people. But on the positive side, God has made a commitment to his beloved, and in spite of her unfaithfulness and the hurt she has caused to their relationship, he will not abandon her so easily.

> For your Maker is your husband, the Lord of hosts is his name; the Holy One of Israel is your Redeemer, the God of the whole earth he is called. For the Lord has called you like a wife forsaken and grieved in spirit . . . In overflowing wrath for a moment I hid my face from you, but with everlasting love I will have compassion on you, says the Lord, your Redeemer. This is like the days of Noah to me: Just as I swore that the waters of Noah would never again go over the earth, so I have sworn that I will not be angry with you and will not rebuke you. For the mountains may depart and the hills be removed, but my steadfast love shall not depart from you, and my covenant of peace shall not be removed, says the Lord, who has compassion on you. (Isaiah 54:5–10)

With compassion and care God wishes to restore his wife's beauty and renew his vows with her. Against all odds, his love for her will never fail.

In the New Testament, this same image of lover and beloved is applied to Jesus Christ, who is the bridegroom, and his betrothed, the church worldwide. The Apostle Paul uses this metaphor in his instructions to households as an example of how husbands should treat their wives.

> Husbands, love your wives, just as Christ loved the church and gave himself up for her, in order to make her holy by cleansing her with the washing of water by the word, so as to present the church to himself in splendor, without a spot or wrinkle or anything of the kind—yes, so that she may be holy and without blemish. In the same way, husbands should love their wives as they do their own bodies. He who loves his wife loves himself. For no one ever hates his own body, but he nourishes and tenderly cares for it, just as Christ does

for the church, because we are members of his body. "For this reason a man will leave his father and mother and be joined to his wife, and the two will become one flesh" [Genesis 2:24]. This is a great mystery, and I am applying it to Christ and the church. (Ephesians 5:25–32)

Just as in marriage a husband and wife join together to become one flesh, so Jesus Christ is depicted as joining together with his people to become united as one. Therefore, Christ cares for his people in the same way that any of us would care for our own bodies. He lived out this love for his betrothed by sacrificing himself for her. He gave up his divinity, his royal throne, even his life for her sake, so great was his love (Philippians 2:3–11).

The cleansing brought by Jesus's sacrifice, which presents his beloved "without a spot or wrinkle," is depicted in the book of Revelation through the pure, bright gown of the bride. The story of Revelation—the story of the end of this world and the beginning of the next—culminates in the wedding of the Lamb, the triumphant Jesus Christ returning for his bride. "'The marriage of the Lamb has come, and his bride has made herself ready; to her it has been granted to be clothed with fine linen, bright and pure' . . . 'Blessed are those who are invited to the marriage supper of the Lamb'" (Revelation 19:7–9; cf. Matthew 22:1–14). In the meantime, the here and now, the universal church awaits the return of the bridegroom. Just as in "Kaddish" Ariel and Isaac are referred to as married but have not yet had the official wedding ceremony, so we are living in those in-between days when the bride is fully committed to her husband but the wedding and celebration have not yet taken place. The bridegroom has gone away for a time to prepare a home for his beloved (John 14:2–3), and when he returns, there will be a wonderful time of feasting and celebration.

This waiting period may also be seen in the relationship of Mulder and Scully. Through Seasons 7 and 8, several Christ-like or messianic images are applied to Mulder (see chapter 6, below). In "Requiem," he is the central figure in a "Last Supper" before he heads into an outdoor setting (like the garden of Gethsemane) and is carried off to his doom by his enemies. In Season 8, Mulder undergoes his "crucifixion," then he is returned dead, is buried, and is resurrected three months later. After a period of a few weeks, Mulder leaves for an extended time, one day to return. To carry through the messianic imagery to its logical conclusion, Mulder's departure at the end of Season 8 is his "ascension," which means that Season 9 is the time when his beloved, Scully, is promised to him but the wedding has not yet taken place. Like the church, she awaits her lover's return, not knowing the exact day or hour (see Matthew 25:1–13). But the hope and expectation is that when he returns, the two will be reunited with a great celebration, culminating in their marriage.

This wedding celebration is the counterpart to the Last Supper, when Jesus tells his followers, "I will never again drink of this fruit of the vine until that day when I drink it new with you in my Father's kingdom" (Matthew 26:29). The day he refers to is the Lamb's triumphant return and the celebratory wedding feast when he will finally be united with his bride. That day will be the consummation of the kingdom of heaven, when God and his people will finally and eternally be united as one. In *The X-Files*, of course, Mulder's last supper has not yet seen its fulfillment with his friends reunited at his wedding feast. However, the hope remains that there is a wedding still to come (or perhaps the rowboat scene at the end of *I Want to Believe* hints at a honeymoon?). On that wedding day, Scully—along with the beloved in Song of Solomon and the universal church awaiting her bridegroom—will be able to say, "He brought me to the banqueting house, and his intention toward me was love . . . My beloved is mine and I am his" (Song of Solomon 2:4, 16).

THE TWO GREATEST COMMANDMENTS

For all the complex laws in the Old Testament, and the Ten Commandments given to Moses, the entirety of God's law can be simplified into two basic principles: love God and love others. But both these principles are founded on another simple fact: "We love because he first loved us" (1 John 4:19). In asking us to love, God isn't requesting anything that he hasn't already done himself. He loved first, and out of that example we can learn how to love. How has God loved us? As a father who must let us make our own choices and mistakes but awaits our return with open arms. As a mother who will give up even what's dearest to her to give us the best life possible. As a brother and a friend who would lay down his life for us. As a lover and husband who is committed to us, even if we are unfaithful, and takes care of us as though we, the beloved, were his own body. In the same way that he has set these examples, God asks us to love him in return and to love others with the same love.

Some kinds of love are easy for us. As parents and family, it is second nature to love our own flesh and blood or those whom we consider to be like family. For our friends who are our closest companions and the most loyal to us we would readily give anything. And it goes without mention the lengths to which lovers will go out of their passion and compassion for one another. But those closest to us can also rub us the wrong way the most easily, so that sometimes they present the greatest challenges to love. This concern arises in Dostoyevsky's *Brothers Karamazov*: one of the issues that prompts Ivan to tell his story of the Grand Inquisitor is his difficulty in accepting God's charge for us to love others. Ivan admits to his brother Alyosha, "I have never been able to understand how it is possible to love one's neighbor. In my opinion the people it is impossible to love are precisely those near to one, while one can really love only those who are far away."[13]

Anyone who has a difficult relationship with a family member can certainly sympathize with Ivan's statement (for example, think of Scully's strained relationship with her brother Bill). But family, friendship, and marriage—situations where love should be the most natural—teach us how to love the other so that we can expand that same love to occasions where love does not come naturally. The relationship between siblings is especially significant, which is why 1 John says that someone who doesn't love a brother or sister can't claim to love at all. With siblings we learn to share with others and to respect their feelings, to apologize when we have hurt them, to tolerate their quirks and their intrusion on our own space and time. If we can learn to love those who are closest to us and who therefore know best how to provoke us, then we can apply that same love to others who seemingly have nothing else in common with us than the fact that we are children of the same Father God. By recognizing our common humanity, we can treat all people with the same respect we would give to our own family. Showing this kind of love, in fact, brings out the best in all of us. As Jeremiah Smith points out in the Grand Inquisitor dialogue of "Talitha Cumi" (3x24), it is our ability to love that is one of humanity's best qualities and greatest strengths.

The love command that Ivan finds so difficult is considered by the Jewish law, and affirmed by Jesus, to be one of the two greatest commandments. In the Gospel of Luke, a lawyer who questions Jesus summarizes the law in these two commands: "You shall love the Lord your God with all your heart, and with all your soul, and with all your strength, and with all your mind; and your neighbor as yourself" (Luke 10:27; see also Deuteronomy 6:5; Leviticus 19:18). When the lawyer then asks, "And who is my neighbor?" Jesus responds with a parable: the story of the Good Samaritan (Luke 10:29–37). Because of this story and its spread throughout Western culture, the term "Samaritan" has taken on a positive meaning. But the true impact of the story emerges when we understand that to the Jews of Jesus's day, "Samaritan" was like a dirty word. Jews and Samaritans truly exemplified what Ivan meant when he said that those closest to us are hardest to love. Because of their proximity to one another and their long history, as with estranged brothers there was no love lost between the two people groups (similar to any two antagonistic groups that share a boundary or have been divided by a civil war). Thus, when Jesus answers the question "Who is my neighbor?" with a story about a Samaritan who shows compassion to a Jew, he is essentially saying, "Love your enemy" (cf. Luke 6:27). Even more than that, the story is an example of your enemy loving you—the one who is hated is held up as the model for fulfilling God's commandment.

Elsewhere, Jesus expands on this same teaching. It is in the context of "love your enemies" that we get the expression "turn the other cheek" and a reiteration of the Golden Rule (Luke 6:29, 31). Jesus elaborates, "If you love those who love you, what credit is that to you? . . . If you do good to those who do good to you, what credit is that to you? . . . If you lend to those from whom you hope to receive, what credit is that to you? . . . But love your enemies, do good, and lend, expecting nothing in return. Your reward will be great, and you will be children of the Most High; for he is kind to the ungrateful and the wicked. Be merciful, just as your Father is merciful" (Luke 6:32–36). It's not much of a stretch for us to love those who love us or do nice things for us. The real challenge is loving the people who hate us. Even more of a challenge is loving them through our actions: turning the other cheek and giving to them without expecting anything good in return. Why should we do this? Because this is exactly what God does for us. "He makes his sun rise on the evil and on the good, and sends rain on the righteous and the unrighteous" (Matthew 5:45). God has created a wonderful world full of good things, and he offers those good things for our use whether we deserve them or not. He sends rain to water the crops of people who never acknowledge him as the maker of the rain. He sends the same sun to rise both for the people who thank him for its warmth and for the people who curse him all the way to their graves. God asks us to love not only him but others, because he first loved us.

In *I Want to Believe*, loving in this way, and accepting the fact of God's mercy, is certainly a challenge for Scully. To the question, "Who is my neighbor?" the answer for her is, Father Joe. He is clearly an example for her of the person who least deserves to be loved. Her hostility toward Father Joe from the first moment she meets him is glaring in comparison with how he is treated by Mulder and the FBI agents. There is no indication that these others approve of Father Joe's crimes, but none of them shows sheer loathing toward him as does Scully. Why? The gaping wounds she feels likely run deep for a number of reasons. First, Scully is now a doctor and works primarily with children. Father Joe represents a danger to the very group she has chosen to serve. But that alone does not seem enough to explain Scully's reaction. A second reason may be especially unique to her among these other characters: she is Catholic. When Father Joe molested the altar boys, he not only violated and betrayed them, but he betrayed God, the Catholic Church, and all the people he had vowed to serve—people like Scully.[14] She takes his betrayal very personally. But more than that, Scully has likely felt the burden of the impact that such betrayals have on the reputation of Catholics. Those outside the Church may tend to lump together the sinners and saints. Scully herself may have faced the prejudice of others who look down on Catholicism because of the public scandals over pedophile priests. Perhaps a third reason could be added to Scully's list as well. She too has been victimized, having undergone what amounts to medical rape. On several levels, then, she can identify with those who have been violated or betrayed by the likes of Father Joe. It is no wonder that she feels no need to hide her contempt.

In contrast to Scully's animosity, the implied love and mercy shown to Father Joe by God stands out in sharp relief. How could she possibly love someone like Father Joe, someone who represents everything that she hates, the very evil that she has fought against as an FBI agent, as a doctor, as a Catholic, and as a victim? Clearly, she cannot love Father Joe on his own merits because it seems he has none. And yet God wants us to love the Father Joes of the world. How is this possible? The answer is twofold. First, God himself loves such people. Father Joe points out to Scully that she has come to judge him, yet she clearly does not qualify as someone without any faults of her own (as she has just admitted that she's living with a man she's not married to) who has a right to cast the first stone (cf. John 8:7; also John 4:17–18). She tells him that he's in no position to judge, and yet neither is she. However, there is one who is in a position to judge—the Judge himself, who has been directly wronged by Father Joe's violation of his priestly vows. If the heavenly Judge, the only one who truly has a right to condemn Father Joe, has chosen to show him mercy, then shouldn't we? After all, it's the same mercy that we ourselves need to appeal to when we're the ones at fault.

But there is a second answer to how Scully can come to love Father Joe, hinted at by his very name: Joe *Cris*sman—J. C. Father Joe cannot be loved on his own merits; instead, we are to love his kind on the merits of the other J. C., Jesus *Christ*. Jesus himself depicts this through his story of the sheep and the goats. At the end time when he will return, Jesus explains, everyone will be gathered for final judgment, and he will "separate people one from another as a shepherd separates the sheep from the goats." To those on the right hand (the sheep) he will say, "Come, you that are blessed by my Father, inherit the kingdom prepared for you from the foundation of the world; for I was hungry and you gave me food, I was thirsty and you gave me something to drink, I was a stranger and you welcomed me, I was naked and you gave me clothing, I was sick and you took care of me, I was in prison and you visited me." These people will ask when it was that they did all these things for him. He will answer, "Truly I tell you, just as you did it to one of the least of these who are members of my family, you did it to me." Those on Jesus's left hand (the goats) will be charged with failing to do any of these things. They likewise will ask, "Lord, when was it that we saw you hungry or thirsty or a stranger or naked or sick or in prison, and did not take care of you?" And he will answer, "Truly I tell you, just as you did not do it to one of the least of these, you did not do it to me" (Matthew 25:31–46).

We are to do charity in response to the Charity that was given to us. We love our enemies, not because of their own worth, but because we are to see in each one of them God's own imprint, his divine image built into every person. Yet even more than this, we are to love them because Jesus loved them enough to be the friend who would lay down his life for them. We are to love them as we would love the one who gave his life for each of us. "In this is love, not that we loved God but that he loved us . . . Beloved, since God loved us so much, we also ought to love one another" (1 John 4:10–11). This may be a tall order, asking Scully to love Father Joe, or asking us to love the most vile of criminals. But the task should at least be easier if instead of focusing on them and their faults, we can focus on the great love that has already been lavished on us.

If this second reason, to love others as God first loved us, is not enough to love the likes of Father Joe, there is a third answer that may be added: the second of the two love commandments is phrased, "love your neighbor *as yourself*" (Matthew 22:39; see also Leviticus 19:18). The same principle is phrased in the Golden Rule, "Do to others *as you would have them do to you*" (Matthew 7:12). Jesus Christ exemplified this for us by loving his church as he would love his own body (Ephesians 5:25–30). If we know how to feed ourselves, how to clothe ourselves, how to take care of our bodies when we're unwell, then we know how to do the same for other people. After all, love isn't (just) a warm, fuzzy feeling. Love is a verb. "How does God's love abide in anyone who has the world's goods and sees a brother or sister in need and yet refuses help? Little children, let us love, not in word or speech, but in truth and action" (1 John 3:17–18). Love takes action. If we act out love, based on the love that was acted out on our behalf, the positive feelings that are initially absent may then follow. By fulfilling her oath as a doctor and caring for Father Joe's physical needs when he has a seizure, Scully has already taken a step in the right direction. In this way, her own act of mercy to spare Father Joe's life imitates the mercy that God has shown him, the same mercy that God extends to Scully, and to us all.

Part of loving others, then, is to delight in God's mercy for them. When the prodigal son returned, the father threw a party. We can choose to be either the older brother, complaining that it isn't deserved, or the guests at the party, who join in the celebration. When it comes to the prodigal Father Joe, Scully identifies more with the older brother. But there's a party going on, and she, along with all of us, is invited to join in. The difficulty that the older brother has in loving properly stands out clearly against the description of love in 1 Corinthians 13: "It does not envy, it does not boast, it is not proud. It does not dishonor others, it is not self-seeking, it is not easily angered, it keeps no record of wrongs. Love does not delight in evil but rejoices with the truth" (vv. 4–6, NIV). The prodigal's brother certainly struggles with envy, with seeking his own rights over others', with anger, and with too readily keeping track of his younger brother's wrongs. But love invites him instead to rejoice in the truth, in the fact that a life has been saved and restored. In the fact that justice includes mercy, a mercy born of love and respect for all life. Such love has been freely offered to us, and we should freely return it to others. Love takes joy in this truth.

NOTES

1. C. S. Lewis, *The Four Loves* (1960; reprinted, New York: Harcourt Brace, 1988). These are by no means the only four categories one can use to distinguish types of love. For example, Erich Fromm (*The Art of Loving* [New York: Bantam, 1956]) includes a fifth category, "self-love."

2. Lewis describes that while "friends and lovers feel that they are 'made for each other,'" the glory of affection "is that it can unite those who most emphatically, even comically, are not; people who, if they had not found themselves put down by fate in the same household or community, would have had nothing to do with each other." But Lewis also acknowledges that affection doesn't always develop in these relationships (*The Four Loves*, 36).

3. For an analysis of Mulder and Scully's relationship based on Aristotle's description of friendship, see Dean A. Kowalski and S. Evan Kreider, "*I Want to Believe* . . . But Now What?" in *The Philosophy of "The X-Files,"* ed. Dean A. Kowalski, updated ed., The Philosophy of Popular Culture (Lexington: University Press of Kentucky, 2009), 251–57.

4. Lewis, *The Four Loves*, 61, 66.

5. Chris Carter, "Inside the X-Files," Disc 6, *"The X-Files": The Complete Fifth Season, Collector's Edition*, DVD (Twentieth Century Fox Home Entertainment, 2002).

6. Before *I Want to Believe* was released, the comedy duo Rhett and Link composed a song and video titled, "I Want to Believe: *X-Files* Love Song." The lyrics focused on Mulder and Scully's relationship and hailed its "complexity" and "purity," their meaningful looks and elbow touches, and their fifteen-year courtship, especially in contrast to couples on *Lost* and *Desperate Housewives* (referencing hit shows at the time). See http://rhettandlink.com/blog/another-alien-returns.

7. Mulder and Scully bring to life the wisdom sayings from Ecclesiastes: "Two are better than one, because they have a good reward for their toil. For if they fall, one will lift up the other; but woe to the one who is alone and falls and does not have another to help. Again, if two lie together, they keep warm; but how can one keep warm alone? And though one might prevail against another, two will withstand one" (Ecclesiastes 4:9–12).

8. On gender reversals in *The X-Files*, see Rhonda Wilcox and J. P. Williams, "'What Do You Think?': *The X-Files*, Liminality, and Gender Pleasure," in *"Deny All Knowledge": Reading "The X-Files,"* ed. David Lavery et al., The Television Series (Syracuse, NY: Syracuse University Press, 1996), 99–120.

9. Lewis, *The Four Loves*, 67.

10. Lewis, *The Four Loves*, 94 (italics original).

11. Augustine, *Confessions*, trans. R. S. Pine-Coffin (London: Penguin, 1961), 80 (4.9).

12. Lewis, *The Four Loves*, 136–37.

13. Fyodor Dostoyevsky, *The Brothers Karamazov*, trans. David McDuff, rev. ed. (London: Penguin, 2003), 309.

14. In the novelization of the movie, during her final scene with Mulder, Scully refers to Father Joe as "a man who violated God's most sacred trust" (Max Allan Collins, *The X-Files: I Want to Believe*, based on the screenplay by Frank Spotnitz and Chris Carter [New York: HarperEntertainment, 2008], 232).

5

The Truth Is Out There

SCULLY: You're working down here in the basement . . . because they're afraid of you, of your relentlessness, and because they know that they could drop you in the middle of the desert, and tell you the truth is out there, and you'd ask them for a shovel.

MULDER: Is that what you think of me?

SCULLY: Well, maybe not a shovel. Maybe a backhoe. ("Piper Maru," 3x15)

At the end of the opening credits for each episode of *The X-Files*, the standard tagline tells us, "The Truth Is Out There." This statement is Mulder's mantra and the goal for his quest. Truth is the object of Mulder's faith and the source of his hope. Truth is a quality that he values, even loves, just as love "rejoices in the truth" (1 Corinthians 13:6). Mulder's persistent quest for truth is therefore fueled by the belief that there is a truth to be found and that it is worth searching for. This assumes that truth is concrete and attainable, that it is not transient or inaccessible. The truth Mulder seeks is solid and real. It can be proved and verified. But what is the truth, and who determines what is true? Is truth relative, so that it can be invented by those in power or redefined by any group or worldview? Or is there a more objective standard that determines whether such "truths" are valid?

Although Mulder continually encounters subjective answers and the clash between modernism and postmodernism, he pursues a truth that is clear cut, black and white—true and not false. Behind this pursuit is a notion of justice, of right and wrong, which presumes there are universal standards by which to determine what is right and to hold others accountable. That sense of justice drives Mulder and Scully forward in their work and in their lives, as they aim to reveal the lies and expose the truth for the sake of the people. At times, this leads the agents into a greater struggle between good and evil, vying against powers that transcend a human justice system. Yet always, the pair strives to fight for the side of what is true, just, and right, as they protect and serve.

TRUTH, OR A WHITE WHALE?

When the X-Files are shut down for the first of many times, Mulder tells Scully that "as long as the truth is out there," he will continue to search for it ("The Erlenmeyer Flask," 1x23). He will not let such a setback deter him from his true goal. But what is the truth that he seeks? The truth about what happened to his sister, about alien life, about various paranormal phenomena, about something greater beyond this world? The exact definition may vary, but what matters most is Mulder's belief that the truth exists and his reliance on that belief to empower his search each and every day. Mulder's desire is to dispel the lies that obscure the truth and liberate it from the powers that hold it in restraints. This is what he deems of highest value, and little else matters to him or will stand in his way.

It is because of such determination that Scully likens Mulder's pursuit of the truth to Captain Ahab's pursuit of the whale in *Moby Dick* ("Quagmire," 3x22). She sees both quests as obsessions for something impossible to capture and coming at a high cost. She recognizes that Mulder is often single minded in his quest, so focused on the goal that he loses sight of other factors along the way. Like

Ahab, Mulder also apparently doesn't consider that the end result of his pursuit may not be positive. When Mulder muses to his partner, "Did you ever look up into the night sky and feel certain that, not only was something up there, but it was looking down on you at that exact same moment and was just as curious about you as you are about it?" she cautions him, "Don't look *too* hard. You might not like what you find" ("War of the Coprophages," 3x12). At the end of the series, this in fact happens. In the finale, titled "The Truth" (9x19–20), when Mulder learns that the truth is the alien invasion is already scheduled and therefore inevitable, he feels defeated. At Scully's prompting, he considers whether this really is the truth he's been searching for all of these years. He must redefine what he believes to be true and refocus his goal: his focus is no longer on the truth about aliens but on the truth about "something greater than us, greater than any alien force."

But Mulder is not merely interested in finding out the truth to satisfy his own curiosity. He is also determined to reveal the facts to the general populace, especially those truths that are kept from them by the government and by men in power. Not only must the truth be known, it must be told. Mulder thus becomes a kind of Promethean figure, using his authority (and audacity) as an FBI agent to steal the truth from the powers that be in order to give it to the people. What Mulder struggles to understand on occasion is that the truth is like fire, both potent and dangerous, and there may be times when putting it in the wrong hands will do more harm than good. This is the case in "F. Emasculata" (2x22). Mulder and Scully are thrust into a situation where a convict infected with a deadly contagion is on the loose and can potentially spread the disease among the public. The government knows about the contagion, and Mulder wants to broadcast the truth that the government is hiding. As Scully tells him, though, releasing such information could cause a panic, which might endanger more people than the contagion itself. But as a representative of the government, Mulder is seen as complicit in the cover-up. This scenario only exemplifies that Mulder's ultimate goal is to release the truth to the general population, without regard for the reasons why the truth has been hidden and withheld. As he declares in "The Pine Bluff Variant" (5x18), "I want people to know the truth." But the CIA agent he is addressing, someone who is clearly concealing the facts, tells him, "Sometimes our job is to protect those people from knowing it."

The issue in such situations is who has a right to the truth, who decides what is the truth, and how true information is controlled. Mulder has this very conversation with his informant, Deep Throat, after Mulder finds out the man has just given him false data to put him on the wrong trail.

> DEEP THROAT: You and Scully are excellent investigators and your motives are just. However, there are still some secrets that should remain secret, some truths that people are just not ready to know.
>
> MULDER: Who are you to decide that for me?
>
> DEEP THROAT: The world's reaction to such knowledge would be far too dangerous.
>
> MULDER: Dangerous. You mean in a sense of outrage like the reaction to the Kennedy assassinations or MIAs or radiation experiments on terminal patients, Watergate, Iran-Contra, Roswell, the Tuskegee experiments—where will it end? Oh, I guess it won't end as long men like you decide what is truth. ("E.B.E.," 1x16)

As Deep Throat tells him at the end of the conversation, "A lie, Mr. Mulder, is most convincingly hidden between two truths." At times, Mulder is told so many "truths" that he has difficulty discerning the lies from the actual truth. Mulder believes that revealing the truth will bring down the powerful men who would twist it or hide it, the powers behind the types of experiments and conspiracies he named to Deep Throat. Later, however, Krycek tells him, "The truth, the truth. There's no truth! These men . . . make it up as they go along" ("Tunguska," 4x09). In a way, such men determine for other people what will be true by the information they choose to reveal or conceal, or by the narrative they weave and release for public consumption.

The X-Files is full of such varying narratives, often dangled before Mulder as answers. Season 5 and the faith crisis Mulder experiences is an excellent example. While Mulder has long held that the military is involved in covering up the truth about aliens, Michael Kritschgau weaves for Mulder an elaborate tale about how the government has invented aliens, and in a sense invented Mulder, in order to cover up the facts about their own unethical tests on the populace ("Redux," 5x02). After Kritschgau's account and the things that Mulder sees for himself inside the Department of Defense, Mulder is left doubting the existence of aliens, leading him to contend, "It's strongly held by believers in UFO phenomena that there is military complicity or involvement in abductions, but what if there is no complicity? What if there is simply just the military, seeking to develop an arsenal of weapons against which there is no defense: biological warfare?" ("Patient X," 5x13). But by the next episode, he has again seen evidence of alien involvement, once more swinging his opinion. Competing truths are told and controlled by those in power, often it seems merely for the purpose of toying with Mulder. Scully therefore warns him that his passion to believe could leave him vulnerable to deception: "Mulder, the truth is out there, but so are lies" ("E.B.E."). At the end of this episode, Mulder tells Deep Throat, "I'm wondering which lie to believe." In the midst of many purported truths that are presented to him, Mulder must discern which ones are actually true.

TRUTH IS AS SUBJECTIVE AS REALITY

The question, What is the truth? can also be reframed as, Whose truth? *The X-Files* often explores the various perspectives on what the truth is and how it can be explained, but one episode in particular stands out as the chief example of this: "Jose Chung's *From Outer Space*" (3x20).[1] When the novelist Jose Chung interviews Scully for his new manuscript based on the alleged alien abduction of two teenagers, she expresses her concern that even though his book is in part science fiction, he should represent the facts as accurately as possible.

> SCULLY: Well, just as long as you're attempting to record the truth.
>
> JOSE CHUNG: Oh, God, no. How can I possibly do that?
>
> SCULLY: What do you mean?
>
> JOSE CHUNG: I spent three months in Klass County and everybody there has a different version of what truly happened. Truth is as subjective as reality . . .
>
> SCULLY: So you're here to get my version of the truth?
>
> JOSE CHUNG: Exactly.

As the episode proceeds, Jose Chung recounts the various versions he has heard of "what truly happened" in Klass County. The descriptions in many ways are contradictory, but are true in the sense that each is reality as that individual perceives it. Truth is as subjective as the various experiences of reality.

One illustration of how truth is presented and perceived is the alleged alien-autopsy video (titled "Dead Alien! Truth or Humbug?") that Chung shows Scully, which turns out to be edited video of the autopsy she performed on a body found during their investigation into the abductions. The audience first sees the autopsy scene from an objective point of view, filmed as though merely documenting the event as it happens. Unlike many other parts of the episode, this scene does not appear to be filtered through a particular character's interpretation. This objective camera remains unseen, as merely the lens through which we observe, but there is another camera present. Blaine Faulkner, a UFO nut, bursts in with his own video camera, yelling, "You can't suppress the truth. The people have a right to know. Roswell! Roswell!" Mulder allows him to stay and videotape, so Blaine documents the event as someone who, like Mulder, wants to see and reveal the truth. However, when this footage is edited for the "Dead Alien!" video, it is spliced together, as Scully complains, "in such a way as to delete all the significant findings." This is her delicate way of saying that the truth was edited to create a complete fiction. Truth told in a selective way can create a new "truth," as often happens in propaganda. Of course, the most "significant finding" is that the alien she is seen autopsying isn't an alien at all, just a man in an alien costume. The video's subtitle asks if the alien autopsy is "Truth or Humbug?" but in fact the video itself is a humbug. The comparison of the edited video and the objective view of the autopsy symbolizes how the truth, or what is understood as truth, can vary based on one's perspective, which is often limited.

The recognition that "truth is as subjective as reality" is a main tenet of postmodernism. While modernism lauded science and rationality and reduced truth to what can be proved and quantified, postmodernism declares that such ideas are built on a false notion of objectivity. Instead, it claims, we all see reality with a specific worldview and therefore each have a different concept of what is true or real. The episode "El Mundo Gira" (4x11) exemplifies this. A fungal infection has been killing people, beyond what seems scientifically reasonable. Scully explains it in terms of a catalyzing enzyme; the Mexican community describes it as the work of El Chupacabra; Mulder thinks there might be an extraterrestrial connection. Agent Lozano, the immigration officer, says of the migrant workers, "These people love their stories." But when he overhears Mulder telling Scully his own theory involving a meteorite, Lozano remarks, "So, you got your own stories too, huh?" In the same way, postmodernism asserts that every person or group has their own story to explain what is true, how the world works, and how things came to be that way.

These varying accounts of reality are common on *The X-Files* and one reason why the show is seen as a reflection of its postmodern age. In most episodes, this is represented simply by the differing perspectives that Mulder and Scully bring to a case, and by the fact that many episodes are left open ended rather than providing one objective answer to what really happened. The show, then, is also postmodern in that it does not tell us what is true by offering a single, authoritative explanation but merely explores various possibilities of what *may* be true. At the end of "Jose Chung's *From Outer Space*," Mulder tells Chung, "You're a gifted writer, but no amount of talent could describe the events that occurred in any realistic vein because they deal with alternative realities that we're yet to comprehend. And when presented in the wrong way, in the wrong context, the incidents and the people involved in them can appear foolish, if not downright psychotic." (Of course, this is how Chung portrays Mulder in his book, as a "ticking time bomb of insanity.") Mulder's description could well apply to any number of X-Files investigations, which often explore "alternative realities that we're yet to comprehend." Rather than automatically dismissing such incomprehensible events as false or fictional, a postmodern approach allows that they may in some sense be real or true.

In "The Post-Modern Prometheus" (5x06)—a play on the subtitle of Mary Shelley's *Frankenstein: The Modern Prometheus*—Mulder and Scully discuss legends and unverified rumors, such as about monsters and ogres, and whether these tales reflect actual fact or are merely psychological constructions. Mulder argues that such stories are "unverifiable, and therefore true in the sense that they're believed to be true." To the people who believe in these kinds of stories, they are the truth. This highlights the connection between not only perception and truth but belief and truth. What is defined or accepted as truth depends on what a person believes is possible or likely. In this way, truth is subjective in the sense that what various groups or individuals claim to be true will vary, and sometimes these asserted truths are contradictory if not mutually exclusive. An illustration of this is the contrasting and sometimes conflicting theories on the afterlife portrayed in various *X-Files* episodes: ghosts ("Shadows," "How the Ghosts Stole Christmas"), reincarnation ("Born Again," "The List," "The Field Where I Died"), walk-ins ("Red Museum," "Closure"), and so forth. Rather than presenting one consistent worldview, the show offers multiple theories, representing the beliefs of whoever is the focus of that particular tale. The truth about the afterlife thus varies by episode, relative to the case at hand.

But is the truth itself subjective? Or only our *perception* of the truth? In "Firewalker" (2x09), a scientist named Trepkos recounts to Mulder a well-known story: "The truth is an elephant described by three blind men. The first man touches the tail and says it's a rope. The second man feels the rough leg, says it's a tree. The third man feels the trunk, says it's a snake." Because none of the three perceives the object to be an elephant, does that mean it is not an elephant? What is required to open the eyes of the blind men so they can see the whole picture for what it is? This kind of insight is what Mulder relentlessly chases after based on the conviction that, even if he only has a glimpse right now, he will eventually be able to see the whole truth. Mulder wants to see the elephant, and he wants to open the eyes of others so they can see the truth for what it really is.

In "Teliko" (4x04), Mulder offers a description of truth and perception that reflects the elephant metaphor in a way more familiar to *The X-Files*. When Scully asks him incredulously, "So you're basing [your] theory on a folktale?" Mulder replies, "It's just another way of describing the same truth, right? I mean, all new truths begin as heresies and end as superstitions. We fear the unknown, so we reduce it to the terms that are most familiar to us, whether that's a folktale, or a disease, or a conspiracy." While Scully seeks a medical explanation for how the suspect kills the victims, through a disease, Mulder turns instead to an African folktale. Although they each appeal to a different rendering of what is happening and how it is possible, that doesn't alter the facts of the case: young men are dying from something affecting their pituitary glands that is connected to a rare African seed. The agents' perceptions of the truth—how they explain the facts—are subjective and relative, but the truth itself does not change. We may all, therefore, have different understandings of the truth, so that what we individually accept to be true is relative, but that doesn't negate the existence of one absolute truth. The truth does not cease to be true simply because we are unaware of it or refuse to accept it. The elephant is still an elephant, even if the blind men can't see it.

As postmodern as the X-Files cases and theories may seem, one dichotomy that Scully and Mulder do not represent is the divide between modern and postmodern. While Scully's science is modernist, so is Mulder's pursuit of the truth. "They are both moderns: they both think the truth is out there, gather evidence, and reason from that evidence."[2] This is clear when Mulder explains to her why he wants to find the lake monster Big Blue: "Scully, so many of the things that we investigate are so intangible. But this creature, it exists within the specific earthly confines of this lake, and I want to find it . . . It would be a miraculous discovery. It could revolutionize evolutionary biological thinking" ("Quagmire"). The next season, he makes a similar statement about his eagerness to authenticate the alleged alien corpse found buried in old ice: "This is not some selfish pet project of mine, Scully . . . Definitive proof of sentient beings sharing time and existence with us, that would change everything. Every truth we live by would be shaken to the ground. There is no greater revelation imaginable, no greater scientific discovery" ("Gethsemane," 4x24). Mulder is searching for proof, scientific evidence to further human knowledge of evolution and the universe. He seeks truth that is verifiable and quantifiable. While Mulder represents postmodernism in the sense that he is willing to grant there is more to reality than merely what science can hypothesize, he still wants proof and validation; it isn't enough for him just to believe that it's true. For him, the truth that is "out there" to be found is an objective absolute, something that can be discovered and verified and then held by everyone to be universally true.

In spite of their different approaches, then, the partners' shared goal of the truth is their common ground and the solid foundation upon which they build their investigations. One example of this is "Born Again" (1x21). Mulder suspects that the girl who has committed the murders is channeling a past life, so he arranges for her to undergo regression hypnosis. When the session abruptly ends, he and Scully debate the value of attempting another regression. It is clear from the conversation that Scully seeks evidence they can use in court to give them an "actionable case" while Mulder's goal is "definitive proof of previous lifetimes." They may come at the case from different angles, but both agents want to find the truth about who committed the murders and why. Both of them are looking for evidence to determine what is true and to convince others as well—Mulder wants proof of the paranormal, and Scully wants proof of the crime. Both pursue a truth that is absolute and universal, even if it is described in contrasting ways by those who hold differing perspectives. They both believe the elephant is still an elephant, no matter what the blind men say, and they're looking for proof that they're right.

TRUTH, JUSTICE, AND THE AMERICAN WAY

"Proof" is the language of both science and law. Mulder may be interested in pushing the limits of science, but, as in "Born Again," Scully must remind him that their job is to find evidence that will stand up in court. The corollary to the assertion that there is such thing as a single, objective truth (and therefore such things as lies or untruths) is that there is right and wrong. As employees of the Department of Justice, the very justice system that Mulder and Scully participate in and uphold is built upon such assumptions. If "right" and "wrong" are entirely relative, based on the proposition that all truth is subjective, then there is no basis for a legal system that aims to administer justice equally for all, remaining fair and unbiased in its judgments. There must be some premise of commonly accepted absolutes in order for such a system to exist.

While court cases are presumably built on proof and evidence, they are not immune to the subjectivity of human experience and therefore the perceived relativity of truth. In American courts, witnesses are sworn in with an oath to tell "the truth, the whole truth, and nothing but the truth." That does not mean, however, that every witness—even the ones who intend to be honest—will give an identical account. Eyewitnesses may each attest to a slightly different version of events, based on their perspective or understanding. But the very fact that they are asked to give testimony is based on the notion that only one thing actually happened, and that by the telling of their various interpretations it is possible to arrive at the truth. The problem, of course, is when the testimonies are contradictory. At other times they are simply complementary, like puzzle pieces that fit together to compose the whole. As in the metaphor of the elephant, one witness may tell about the tail, another the trunk, another the legs, but the purpose of the court is to discern from the varying descriptions what the elephant may look like. Even if the end result is an incomplete picture, this does not change the goal of trying to reassemble it.

The episode "Bad Blood" (5x12) is an entertaining depiction of comparing varying eyewitness accounts and piecing together "what really happened." The first half of the story consists of Scully and Mulder each giving their own version of the events of the case up to that point. Each rendition is clearly biased (comically so), and because the characters seem caricatured in each retelling, the audience is left with the feeling that neither account gives an objective, and therefore true, description of events. In spite of this, we can discern "what really happened" based on what we know of the individuals and by comparing their accounts. For instance, was Mulder "characteristically exuberant" about the case, as Scully states? Or was Scully "characteristically less than exuberant," as Mulder says? Either way, what we do know from their separate accounts is that Mulder presented slides pertaining to the case, they discussed the dead cows and dead human, and suggestions about vampires and El Chupacabra were offered. The assumption is that what really happened—the truth—is somewhere in between the two accounts and can be gleaned by comparing the two subjective testimonies.

If Mulder represents the quest for truth, Scully represents the quest for justice. She turned to a career in the FBI because she believed that justice could be accomplished and that she could help further it. She tries to play by the rules of the legal system, focusing on things like warrants and evidence that is admissible in court. But the more Scully learns through their investigations, the more jaded she becomes about the ability for justice to be served. She proclaims before a Senate subcommittee, "I left behind a career in medicine to become an FBI agent four years ago because I believed in this country, because I wanted to uphold its laws, to punish the guilty and to protect the innocent. I still believe in this country, but I believe there are powerful men in this government who do not, men who have no respect for the law, and who flout it with impunity" ("Terma," 4x10). In the first half of this two-episode arc, just as Krycek has told Mulder there is no truth, he scoffs at Scully's naïve desire to bring such powerful figures to justice: "You can't bring these men to justice. They're protected. The laws of this country protect these men under the name of national security. They know no law" ("Tunguska").

This type of impunity, or at least an ineffectiveness of the legal system in prosecuting such crimes, is nowhere more apparent than in the murder of Scully's sister. Melissa Scully is murdered by Krycek with the help of another man, Luis Cardinal. Sitting by the empty hospital bed where her sister once lay, Scully tells Mulder, "There is no justice" ("Paper Clip," 3x02). She is echoing his words from earlier in the episode: she expressed concern that because they were on the run due to the sensitive information in Mulder's possession (truth about aliens that he wants to expose), they'd given up on any sense of justice. He answered her, "What makes you think there's any such thing as justice, Scully?" After the death of her sister, she's inclined to agree. A mere five months after the murder, in "Piper Maru" (3x15), the case is being shelved, and Assistant Director Skinner tells Scully he will appeal the decision. But when Skinner receives a warning to back off, and then is shot by Cardinal, it is clear that there are powers working against justice being served. By the end of the sequel episode, "Apocrypha" (3x16), Scully tracks down Cardinal and arrests him. She hopes this will bring closure, but she comes to realize that "the truth is, no court, no punishment is ever enough." Mulder tells her there is some justice, although not in a legal sense: Cardinal has been killed in his cell. What Mulder points to is that as much as the legal system tries to dispense justice, it can only do so much. For many people, true justice transcends a prison sentence or monetary award. Such justice can only be meted out by a higher force—like fate, or God.

ABSOLUTE TRUTH

Law, or justice, is just one of many disciplines that assume an objective truth exists and should be our goal. Most branches of science rely on objectivity as the basis of experiments and the scientific method. Thus, Scully the scientist can tell Mulder in the pilot episode, "The answers are there; you just have to know where to look." She too believes the truth is out there, science can find it, and the answers hold true for all people regardless of their subjective experience. Likewise, in many other aspects of life, such as basic arithmetic, tests and exams, disciplining children, and so forth, we depend on the fact that there is true and false, a right answer and a wrong answer. Absolute truth gives us common ground to work from, although it does not negate the variations in individual experience. Modernism, with its overemphasis on objectivity and on the notion that only what can be proved or reasoned can be true, erred by overlooking the subjectivity of the humans investigating such truth. Postmodernism, however, may at times react too strongly in the opposite direction. In Mulder we see a more moderate approach: while he remains open minded to the array of possibilities, he still seeks the truth as it can be argued and demonstrated to be valid for everyone. Like Mulder, in this postmodern sea many people long for some solid ground to stand on.

The need for a stable foundation is illustrated by the story of the man who built his house on sand, a parable that Jesus tells at the end of the Sermon on the Mount. After his discussion of the law, prayer, and the Golden Rule, Jesus summarizes: "Everyone then who hears these words of mine and acts on them will be like a wise man who built his house on rock. The rain fell, the floods came, and the winds blew and beat on that house, but it did not fall, because it had been founded on rock. And everyone who hears these words of mine and does not act on them will be like a foolish man who built his house on sand. The rain fell, and the floods came, and the winds blew and beat against that house, and it fell—and great was its fall!" (Matthew 7:24–27). People need something secure and unchanging to stand on, and Jesus offered his teachings as such a foundation. It's the same reason that any well-constructed house is built on a solid foundation, and on solid ground. Otherwise, if a house is built on earth that is unstable, it's as steady as a house of cards. Mulder makes a reference to this human desire for stability in "Signs & Wonders" (7x09): "Clear-cut right and wrong, black and white, no shades of gray. In a society where hard-and-fast rules are harder and harder to come by, I think some people would appreciate that." Even in this postmodern age, the world has not entirely rejected that there is such a thing as absolute truth.

The question, then, is: In the midst of relativity, what do humans hold in common, or commonly hold to be true? What makes cultures worldwide feel that killing another human is wrong and requires reaction, or that elders should be respected? This type of widespread morality is often termed "natural law." It is a universal sense of right and wrong built into humanity, by which all people share an innate understanding that certain behaviors should be praised or punished. This is the basis for the human conscience. Some laws and values vary by era or society, but others transcend culture. For example, we all understand "an eye for an eye," that a wrong done to a person deserves retribution against the offender—that's why it's our natural tendency when someone shoves us to shove them back. We all have a concept of justice or right and wrong when we are the ones who are wronged. Some of this is based on instinct, but it also includes a sense of ethics that goes beyond mere biology.[3] If natural law is built into nature, then to find the source we must look back to the origin of nature itself. For many people, natural law is evidence that humans were not an evolutionary accident but a creation intentionally formed with this inherent sense of morality. This points to an intentional Creator.

Saint Augustine found that with this internal morality, we all inherently "desire to rejoice in truth."[4] Although we all may bend the truth at times, no one likes to be deceived or lied to. We expect others to tell us the truth (e.g., truth in advertising, objective reporting on the news or in history books). We value honesty and therefore take pleasure in the truth. Mulder, of course, is a chief example of this, finding truth to be the supreme good. As the next logical step, Augustine also believed that the Truth is the ultimate source of happiness or pleasure: "True happiness is to rejoice in the truth, for to rejoice in the truth is to rejoice in you, O God, who are the Truth."[5] If God himself is the Truth, and we take pleasure in the truth, then it stands to reason that we would find joy in God. This is Augustine's own testimony. He tells the story of how he spent his youth seeking truth in many different places, in various philosophies and religions. But it was only once he turned to the source of all truth that he found happiness. What Augustine eventually came to believe at the end of this search is that all truth is God's truth.[6] This does not mean that every claim to truth has God's stamp of approval, but just the opposite. It is based on the notion that God, Truth himself, is the source of whatever is true. God is the creator of all good things; there is no other creator. Anything good or true that exists, therefore, by virtue of existing, has its origin in God. All genuine truth is traced back to him, and all other "truths" are measured by this absolute.

GOOD VERSUS EVIL

Related to the concepts of true and false, right and wrong, are good and evil. As with these other pairs, good and evil aren't simply two equal opposing forces. Good, like truth, is the absolute, the starting point, and evil is the lack of good or the mutation of good. It is similar to the relationship between light and darkness: darkness (//evil) exists only as the absence or diminishment of light (//good). God himself is the Good—he is the brightest light possible. What he created, he also declared good. Evil is not a creation but a removal or distortion of good things. The devil, therefore, as the prime representative of evil, is not another god equal in power with his own ability to create. The devil can only manipulate or attack the good for his own purposes; he can only "steal, kill, and destroy" (John 10:10). This is the same relationship that exists between truth and lies—God is Truth, the creator of all truth, whereas lies are the absence or distortion of truth. This is why the devil is known as "the father of lies" (John 8:44).

The initial encounter with the devil and with evil in the garden of Eden depicts this very thing. The serpent begins his temptation of Adam and Eve by citing God's own words, but he twists them to have a new, deceptive meaning. The serpent claims that by eating of the forbidden fruit, the pair will be "like God, knowing good and evil" (Genesis 3:5). The truth is that they are already like God, created in his image, and therefore themselves good. By disobeying, and trying to become godlike in one way, they actually become less like

God in another—they fall away from their good nature to give evil a foothold, and they abandon their access to the tree of life, which would have allowed them, like God, not to die. The serpent was right that they would attain knowledge through eating the forbidden fruit: their eyes have been opened to recognize their own evil. If they would have obeyed and kept away from the fruit, they wouldn't need to know both good and evil—they would only know the good.

Good and evil, like light and darkness, truth and lies, are seen as black and white: two poles on the same spectrum. Such extremes are vividly portrayed in "Signs & Wonders." This episode juxtaposes two churches: a charismatic, snake-handling congregation that is described as fundamentalist and intolerant, and a moderate community church depicted as free thinking and open minded. One scene in particular compares the two churches by going back and forth between them while both study the same passage from Revelation 3, God's words to the church of Laodicea: "I know your works; you are neither cold nor hot . . . So, because you are lukewarm, and neither cold nor hot, I am about to spit you out of my mouth" (vv. 15–16). The Church of God with Signs and Wonders represents black and white, hot and cold, while Blessing Community Church accepts the shades of gray—or, the lukewarm. First the fundamentalist Reverend O'Connor, and then later the moderate Reverend Mackey, each emphasize to Mulder that he may not realize which side he's on in this struggle, whether on the side of good or evil. Mackey says, as Mulder's eyes are being opened to the man's guilt, "Most people believe they're on the side of angels. But are they?"

As Mackey points out, most people tend to think we're on the side of good, yet many of us reside somewhere in the gray areas. But good and evil, white and black, are polar opposites. Where does the gray fit in? Just because gray isn't quite black doesn't make it white. White represents purity (pure as the driven snow, the white of a wedding dress), and gray is white dirtied or sullied. For instance, a bride doesn't look at her grayed wedding dress on the day of the ceremony and say, "Well, at least it's not black"; she wants the dress pure white. What many people think is that as long as they're not really evil, then they're good. But from the perspective of keeping the white pure, either you're pure or you're not—gray is just as unacceptable as black. This goes back to the relationship of good and evil. While the two are opposite, they are not equal. Good is the ideal, and evil is a falling away from or privation of good. White is pure, and gray is a diminishment of white's purity. Being lukewarm isn't acceptable; either you're on the side of good, or you're not. As the message to the church of Laodicea indicates, it is not God's desire for his people to be lukewarm, or to be living in the gray areas; he wants them to be pure white. This is how the bride of Christ, the universal church, is described in the Bible: wearing "fine linen, bright and pure" (Revelation 19:8), "without a spot or wrinkle . . . without blemish" (Ephesians 5:27). Just as no human bride wants her dress to be soiled, so God desires the same for his own bride.

Reverend Mackey stands as the chief example of the lukewarm and shades of gray in "Signs & Wonders"—and in the end, it turns out that not only is he guilty of the murders, but he appears to be the devil himself. As Mulder concludes, "People think the devil has horns and a tail. They're not used to looking for some kindly man who tells you what you want to hear." Mackey has used the gray, in the guise of tolerance and acceptance, to cloud the eyes of his congregation from seeing the truth, that his heart is utterly black. Tolerance is good when it is an expression of loving one's neighbor or valuing all people as formed in the image of God regardless of their actions or beliefs. The problem with Mackey's form of tolerance, however, is when it blurs the black and white so that there are no more absolutes; there is no standard for truth. If Adam and Eve can rewrite the rules for themselves, the fruit is no longer forbidden (at least, in their own minds it is not). But Mackey, the devil personified, does people a great disservice when he entices them into such logic and then they bite into the fruit and find out that actions still hold consequences. Black and white do not cease to exist simply because our vision to see them has been obscured by the devil's lies.

FALLEN ANGEL

If the devil isn't another god, then who is he? If God is the creator, everything he made was good, and nothing exists apart from what he created, then where did such an evil being come from? In "Fallen Angel" (1x09), the episode title is the code name given to a crashed

UFO. The name recalls the biblical reference to Lucifer, or Satan, as a star fallen from the sky along with his host of fallen angels. The story of Satan says that he too was created good, but that in his pride and selfishness he tried to elevate himself and so fell from grace. The name Lucifer refers to the morning star and was applied to the devil because of how brightly he shone, and then how far he fell: "How you are fallen from heaven, O Day Star [KJV: Lucifer], son of Dawn! . . . You said in your heart, 'I will ascend to heaven; I will raise my throne above the stars of God; . . . I will ascend to the tops of the clouds, I will make myself like the Most High.' But you are brought down to Sheol, to the depths of the Pit" (Isaiah 14:12–15). The familiar proverb "Pride goes before destruction, and a haughty spirit before a fall" (Proverbs 16:18) aptly applies to Satan, and to any who would follow in his footsteps. God allowed the angels, as well as humans, the freedom to choose whether to obey him. But the devil, in his arrogance, chose to disobey and tried to make himself like God. He rebels still and draws as many as possible down the same destructive path.

Not only did Satan fall, but also a number of the angels with him. This is depicted in apocryphal Jewish texts in a larger narrative about fallen angels, a story that serves as the basis for "All Souls" (5x17). As Father McCue rightly explains to Scully, the full story is not in the Bible. The biblical basis for the legend is a few verses in Genesis 6 that set up the reason for the great flood and therefore Noah's ark: "When people began to multiply on the face of the ground, and daughters were born to them, the sons of God [the angels] saw that they were fair; and they took wives for themselves of all that they chose . . . The Nephilim were on the earth in those days—and also afterward—when the sons of God went in to the daughters of humans, who bore children to them . . . The LORD saw that the wickedness of humankind was great in the earth, and that every inclination of the thoughts of their hearts was only evil continually" (Genesis 6:1–2, 4–5). This brief account led many to speculate on who exactly the nephilim were and how they related to the sinfulness of humanity. The result was an apocryphal elaboration, best described in The Book of the Watchers, part of 1 Enoch. (In the *X-Files* episode, Father Gregory's "Bible" contains a book of Enoch, likely referring to the same text.) Father McCue describes a version of the legend: "In the story, the angel descends from heaven and fathers four children with a mortal woman. Their offspring are the nephilim—the 'fallen ones.' They have the souls of angels, but they weren't meant to be. They're deformed, tormented. So the Lord sends the seraphim to earth to bring back the souls of the nephilim to keep the devil from claiming them as his own." In *1 Enoch*, the fallen angels are also responsible for providing humans with knowledge and technology that lead them into sin, which is why God sends the flood.

In this episode, the quadruplets that Scully encounters are identified with the nephilim, the offspring of angels and human women. They are called "fallen ones" because they are no longer angels, as the children of angels should be, but are fallen to earth, imitating their fathers, who have fallen from their high position in God's service. *The X-Files* also provides an analogy for this with the human-alien hybrids—such as Scully's daughter Emily, who parallels the girls in "All Souls." The hybrids are created from a mixture of DNA from aliens (beings from "the heavens") and ova from human women. It appears that at least some among the aliens consider such a mixture to be an abomination (see "Essence," 8x20). The alien DNA is referred to as "purity" (e.g., "The Erlenmeyer Flask"), so to mix human material with alien is a pollution, a watering down of the original or ideal. The fact that hybrids like Emily are sickly and cannot easily survive, and that the girls in "All Souls" are born deformed, symbolizes the sinfulness of their fathers, and the human sinfulness that these fallen angels helped to breed on the earth.[7]

In explaining the fate of the quadruplets to Mulder and Scully, Father Gregory says, "Unless you accept the truth of God's teachings that there is a struggle between good and evil for all souls and that we are losing that struggle, you're but fools rushing in." What he sees behind this tale of the nephilim, and happening right in front of them with the girls, is the larger battle between good and evil and the fact that the devil—the one who steals, kills, and destroys—wants to steal their souls. But this also represents what the devil would do with all of us: destroy and manipulate in order to claim our souls. He's trying to add to his number of the fallen. The name Satan itself means "adversary" (see Job 1:6–12). Whether the term refers to a specific being or just an adversarial spirit within us, it indicates the tension between right and wrong, the urge to do wrong when we know better—what in cartoons is often depicted as the devil on one shoulder, while an angel stands on the other. The devil sets himself up as an adversary to what is good and right, using lies to persuade us into following his bad example.

One of the most evil or demonic characters to appear on *The X-Files* is Donnie Pfaster. Perhaps what's most disturbing about him is his humanness, the fact that he's an ordinary boy next door—who just happens to like women's fingers with his peas and carrots. At times, though, Donnie is seen with a demonic face, which reveals the evil that has taken hold of him. In "Orison" (7x07), the Reverend Orison tells Scully, "Every moment of every day the devil waits for but an instant. As it is, it has always been. The devil's instant is our eternity." It is Orison who helps Donnie escape from prison, either in an attempt to show mercy and reform him, or, as the reverend eventually tries to do, to carry out the deserved death sentence that the justice system was too lenient to hand down. As Orison prepares to execute him, Donnie, taking on the persona of the devil, says, "My violence is always waiting, for an instant. For when His back is turned." Like a predator, the devil is crouching in the shadows, waiting for that moment when a person is off guard so he can step in and attack. That brief moment of vulnerability can have consequences that last a lifetime.

ORIGINAL SIN

The devil's instant in the garden of Eden has become an eternity for human history. The fallen angel himself deceived Adam and Eve into following his own path of pride and arrogance and trying to elevate themselves to God's level, and thereby caused them also to fall. They were created good, but they fell away from this ideal, marring their purity and innocence with the gray of sin. Their pride and disobedience became the original sin, and like a hereditary disease it has infected every human being since. Robert Modell makes passing reference to this in "Pusher" (3x17). After helplessly watching Modell "push" Agent Burst into suffering a heart attack, Mulder asks Modell, "You're dying, aren't you, Bob? What, do you want to take a few innocent people with you before you go?" Modell replies, "Biology tells us we're all dying, and original sin tells me ain't nobody innocent." The two halves of his statement are actually directly related: because of original sin and the fact that no one is completely innocent, the consequence for humans is our mortality. Adam and Eve were denied access to the tree of life, and ever since then humanity has experienced death.

"Signs & Wonders" makes mention of original sin and bookends the episode with references to the garden of Eden. In Mulder and Scully's opening discussion of the case, she says, "Serpents and religion have gone hand in hand. They've represented the temptation of Eve, original sin. They've been feared and hated throughout history as they've been thought to embody Satan, to serve evil itself." The closing scene of the episode shows Reverend Mackey (now Reverend Wells) in his office in a new church, as a congregant welcomes him and commends him for his "open and modern way of looking at God"—the scene begins by focusing on a painting hanging on the wall: Masaccio's *The Expulsion from the Garden of Eden*. The emphasis on snakes throughout the episode, then, illustrates what Scully has described: temptation and evil. In Genesis 3, before God delivers his punishment on Adam and Eve for their disobedience, he first sentences the serpent: "I will put enmity between you and the woman, and between your offspring and hers; he will strike your head, and you will strike his heel" (Genesis 3:15). This enmity is seen in "Signs & Wonders"—snakes are used as a tool of evil to murder, while the snake handlers represent mastery over evil and temptation. The serpent can still cause humans trouble, but they also have the ability to stomp him into the dust. Thus, when Reverend O'Connor is exorcising the snakes that have filled his daughter's womb, he quotes James 4:7: "Resist the devil and he shall flee." If only Adam and Eve had heeded such advice.

Even though the first man and woman did not resist the devil and his temptation, the offer remains open for each of us to choose better. Unfortunately, their son Cain did not. Before Cain murders his brother, Abel, God tells Cain, "Sin is lurking at the door; its desire is for you, but you must master it" (Genesis 3:7). Like an audible conscience, God warns Cain that he can make a better choice than his parents have, to ignore the hissing of the serpent in his ear and to stomp on its head. But in the moment of his anger, Cain is vulnerable. The devil takes advantage of that instant and sneaks in the door. That instant becomes an eternity for Cain as he forever pays the price for killing his brother. This warning from God is the same type of message that Mr. Burt tries to communicate to Wayne in "Improbable" (9x14). Mr. Burt continually gives Wayne signs and hints that although the deck is stacked against him, he can still play the game of life by the rules and come out a winner. At his most direct, Mr. Burt tells Wayne, "Choose better." But Wayne, like Cain, disregards God's words. He lets sin master him, making himself a slave to its desires.

In several *X-Files* episodes, sin or wrongdoing is depicted as a kind of appetite, an urge that people often feel controls them rather than vice versa (e.g., "Squeeze," "2Shy," "Leonard Betts"). This is particularly the case in "Hungry" (7x01). Rob Roberts is conflicted, feeling pulled in two directions: on the one hand, he has a biological hunger for human brains, which is apparently related to his unique physiology; on the other hand, he knows that killing is wrong and doesn't want to do it. His appetite is like sin lurking at his door, and he spends the entire episode struggling to master it. At the same time, Rob grapples with his own humanity and whether he is a person who is able to make moral choices that transcend his instincts or whether he is merely a monster, a creature that answers only to biology and is incapable of choosing between right and wrong. In their own ways, both Mulder and the counselor, Dr. Rinehart, try to convince Rob to let his humanity triumph over the monster inside. The counselor tells him, "I don't believe in monsters. But I do believe in people, and sometimes they do terrible things out of weakness or sickness or fear. But I do truly believe that deep down inside, even the worst of us wants to be good." Mulder takes a different approach, perhaps with a bit of reverse psychology, goading Rob by telling him their suspect is a "genetic freak, a carnivorous predator as yet unidentified. A monster, if you will . . . It has a biological imperative to eat . . . It knows that the more it feeds on humans, the closer it gets to getting caught. But the hunger is always there, and it satisfies it any way it can." But Mulder's parting words to Rob are, "Watch out for that monster." In the same way sin, or the tendency for evil, is an appetite residing inside each one of us. If we let it get the better of us, we can become monsters. But we have a choice to gain mastery over the appetite.

Another metaphor for sin or evil that plays a significant role in *The X-Files* is cancer. In fact, the Cigarette-Smoking Man, who is the personification of evil itself (he says to Assistant Director Skinner, "You think I'm the devil?" ["Memento Mori," 4x15]), is referred to as "Cancer Man." Cancer cells start out as normal cells, with several checks and balances to keep them healthy and on track. When the checks and balances, the protective genes, undergo mutations, the cell may become cancerous. The cancerous cell can then multiply rapidly, hence the common comparison that something "spreads like cancer."[8] Evil is like this. We have a natural system of checks and balances—our conscience and understanding of right and wrong—that prevents evil inclinations from getting the better of us. But when people stop listening to their conscience, or when their sense of right and wrong becomes twisted or erased somehow, evil can take over and spread like cancer. To continue with this metaphor, Leonard Betts then becomes the supreme example of someone who has let evil take over his life. His entire body is riddled with cancer cells, and he needs to feed on cancer in order to survive. Mulder calls him the next step in evolution, but Scully replies, "What you're describing is someone so radically evolved that you wouldn't even call him human" ("Leonard Betts," 4x14). Like Rob Roberts, Leonard has become more monster than human, as he has given in entirely to his biological imperative to kill in order to get what he needs. Like a monster, he is functioning strictly on instinct, placing his own survival above the rights of others.

More than becoming pervasive merely throughout an individual, however, evil that is allowed to spread like cancer can also run rampant through a community or society. One person who has given in to the evil can in turn influence the conscience or morals of someone else, weakening that individual's ethical immune system as well, so that evil can spread from person to person. One need look no further than the Nazi agenda that once infected Germany to see how morals can become compromised, right and wrong obscured, and wrong actions justified and transmitted from one person to the next. This kind of evil and its spread is visually depicted in *The X-Files* by the black oil, also called the "black cancer" (see "Terma").[9] The oil functions as a type of demon possession: it controls people, overriding their wills, giving them superhuman strength. But the oil can also body jump, moving from person to person. The only warning sign that someone is infected is the oily film swimming in their eyes.

The same transference of evil is portrayed in "Empedocles" (8x17) through the image of fire, which like cancer can spread out of control. Agents Doggett and Mulder discuss what it is that makes a person evil, or makes them do evil. Mulder explains,

> When I first came to work at the FBI, I worked at Violent Crimes, and I saw the worst of humanity. I saw monsters and I wondered how they became that way, how these men became so evil. I know there were psychological explanations—victims of their environment, victims of their parents—but the scientific explanations were never truly satisfying. And I began to think about evil like a disease. You know, that it goes from man to man or age to age. Most of us walk around thinking that we're incapable of any acts of evil, and we are. You know, we can stifle that momentary urge to kill or to hurt. We have some kind of immunity to it. But I think it's possible that there's an occurrence in somebody's life, a tragedy or a loss that leaves them vulnerable, hurts their immunity to evil, and all of a sudden at that point in their lives when they're weakened, they're open to evil, and they can become evil.

This is what happens to their suspect, Jeb Dukes. After he is fired, he gets fired up (literally), which we see as flames reflect in his eyes. His anger and sorrow make him vulnerable to the evil lurking outside; as his thoughts are focused only on his own rights and feelings rather than on the rights of others, he gives in to the evil and rampages into his workplace with gun blazing. But his rampage does not end there; once he has let the cancer take hold, it only spreads. Now that he has justified one murderous event, there is nothing to hold him back from justifying more. And then the cancerous evil spreads even further. From him, it goes on to infect his sister, in her own moment of vulnerability at the distress over her brother. Where will it end?

THE SPIRIT IS THE TRUTH

If sin is like a disease, and a weakening of the moral immune system is what makes a person vulnerable to evil thoughts and actions, then how can we bolster our immunity? We consume vitamins and antioxidants to defend our bodies from illness, so what is the moral equivalent? What daily supplements can we take to build up our immune system?

One way to protect our moral health is by strengthening our sense of right and wrong. Even apart from how our conscience advises us, there is something tangible already in place to help us determine right from wrong: the law. Most of the time it isn't necessary to wonder whether killing someone is bad, or to engage in deep philosophical contemplation on whether theft is okay. The law makes these things black and white for us: don't murder, don't steal. Don't harm another person or violate their rights. Of course, there will always be exceptions and extreme situations where it *is* necessary to have a deeper conversation, but in a just society, where the rights of individuals are valued equally, the law provides a solid foundation to avoid wrongdoing. That, in fact, is the purpose of the law—it was not created to challenge us to find loopholes or avoid being caught; it was instituted to protect us. As FBI agents, Mulder and Scully represent this purpose of the law, to protect and to serve. Scully states that she joined the FBI "to uphold its laws, to punish the guilty and to protect the innocent" ("Terma"). Even when there is corruption in the political and legal systems, which are meant to administer justice, these two agents continue to fight for the rights and protection of the people. They believe in the law and in its intended function to prevent harm. If we respect the law, it can protect us not only from others, but even from ourselves.

If this is true of human law, it is even more true of divine law. God instituted law not to restrict but to protect and to guide. The foundation and essence of the law is to love God and to love others, emphasized as *dos* rather than *don'ts*. It's meant to be quite simple: honor and respect your creator, and show the same honor and respect for all your fellow creatures. A daily dose of this basic formula can help make us all stronger during those moments of vulnerability. On the other hand, it is when we consider only our own good over the good of others, or turn the Golden Rule around to say, "do unto others what they've done unto me," that we do the most damage to our immunity and become the most open to evil. The story of Cain and Abel illustrates this well. Cain was thinking only of himself, his own rights and feelings, not of his brother's right to live and prosper. Natural law may have caused Cain to sense injustice when he was not rewarded as Abel was, but divine law enables us to see past ourselves, so that we can understand when our actions do injustice to others. Justice or punishment is the need for intervention and correction when people act contrary to love, when they put themselves first. If we obey the law by loving, it will help to protect us from the type of evil that took hold of Cain.

The law that God gave to Moses for Israel, encapsulated best in the Ten Commandments, was not in place during the time of Cain and Abel, or Adam and Eve. Rather, it was the sins of the first humans that made it necessary for God to put the basic principles of his law into writing. Even though Adam and Eve gained the ability to know good and evil by eating the forbidden fruit, they were but children in their understanding, not yet mature enough to have permission to eat of this tree (similar to when a child is not yet capable of processing certain information so the parents withhold it until they deem the child is ready). For Adam and Eve, just because they knew good and evil, right and wrong, did not yet translate into *choosing* good over evil. The law served this purpose, to help God's people not only recognize right and wrong but choose to do right. Human law, when it is just, serves the same purpose: to help us make right choices, for the good of everyone—to help those like Leonard Betts and Rob Roberts know that it is wrong to kill a human being, even when their instincts are telling them otherwise.

Unfortunately, the law that God gave to his people, including the Ten Commandments, did not fully accomplish the purpose for which he established it. The human tendency is to turn the law into legalism, so we can skate by with the bare minimum requirements and find loopholes to get around the consequences. Obeying the letter of the law then becomes a game to avoid punishment, or at least to avoid getting caught. Thus, the law itself, like the tree in Eden, becomes a source of temptation (see Romans 7:7–25). For example, we see a sign that says, "Don't touch"; before we saw the sign, it didn't even cross our minds to touch the object, but now that we've read the sign, we want to touch. In the Sermon on the Mount, Jesus points out that our attitude is more important than our legalism. It doesn't matter if we don't actually touch the object; the fact that we desire to touch it is already a transgression (Matthew 5). While this seems to make the law even more difficult to follow, the purpose is actually to redirect us from the letter of the law to the spirit of the law—from law to Spirit. "For the letter kills," by the penalty of death attached to the law, "but the Spirit gives life" (2 Corinthians 3:6b).

While the law and obedience to it, therefore, can provide one kind of immunity against evil, God offers another option, a kind of spiritual supervitamin. In contrast to evil spirits, which, like the black oil or fire, want to possess and consume, God offers his Holy Spirit. This Spirit took the place of Jesus after he left the earth, as an advocate and encourager who can help mediate between humans and God. The Spirit helps us pray when we're not sure how, or what to say. The Spirit can also reinforce our conscience, helping us to understand more clearly what is right in a given situation. More important, the Spirit can enable us to choose the right, to act out of love and so fulfill the law of God that might otherwise seem impossible. The Holy Spirit fills up that space in our lives where evil wants to come in and take hold—when evil lurks at the door, the Spirit answers by hanging up the "no vacancy" sign. Unlike evil, the Holy Spirit doesn't take control of us to act in a way that may be contrary to our will, but we can yield control to the Spirit at times when we feel like we have no control.

In "One Breath" (2x08), when Scully's mother prematurely orders Dana's tombstone, we see that it includes the verse, "The Spirit is the Truth."[10] Both the spirit world and truth are major themes on the show, as they are in Scully's life, in her roles as a Catholic, a scientist, and an FBI agent working on the X-Files. The phrase on her headstone echoes also the Gospel of John, where the Spirit and truth are often equated and the Spirit is referred to as "the Spirit of truth" (see John 4:24; 14:17; 15:26; 16:13). This is related to God's nature: God is spirit (John 4:24), and God is Truth, so the Spirit of God is the Spirit of truth. The character of the Spirit is to speak truth to our minds and hearts, and to communicate truth between God and us. This Spirit is a gift given by God to those who choose to trust in Jesus. The Spirit is a foretaste of our spiritual lives beyond this world, and a way in which God can remain with us always while we are still in this world. For those who want to accept this gift, their immunity to evil can be further bolstered. But notice, the Spirit, like the law, is a vitamin rather than a vaccine. As long as humans have free will, nothing can prevent us entirely from giving in to evil. Yet choosing the right is a lot easier when we can clearly hear the voices inside and outside of us telling us what the right thing is and empowering us to do it.

GOD'S ETERNAL RECOMPENSE

While the law is meant to protect and to guide, in order for it to be effective in that purpose it must be accompanied by judgment and punishment. There must be consequences for disobedience, for wrong actions—otherwise those who transgress will never learn their lesson and refrain from repeating the same mistakes. When the law is not enforced, it is useless, just as Scully asserts before the Senate subcommittee that there are men in the government (perhaps even some seated before her on the panel) who flout the law with impunity and therefore make it impossible to do her job pursuing justice ("Terma"). Judgment is necessary for justice to be served. The counterpart to justice is mercy: not repaying someone the full punishment they deserve. At times, mercy can be just as effective a deterrent as consequences, when the person realizes the price they should have paid and out of gratefulness vows never to repeat the offense. If the person is not truly repentant, however, mercy may not have this effect, and instead they may take the freedom as license to do the same thing again.

A story that exemplifies mercy and the wrong response to it is Jesus's parable of the man who was forgiven much (Matthew 18:23–35). A slave owes the king an exorbitant amount of money. When the king wants to collect the debt, the slave cannot repay, so the king orders the slave, his family, and his possessions sold to pay off the debt. The slave pleads for the king to be patient and allow him time to repay the money owed. The king has mercy on him: rather than simply granting the slave more time, the king completely cancels the debt. This is an incredible act of mercy by the king, to forgive a debt so great that it cannot be repaid. So when the same slave then comes across a fellow slave who owes him a small amount of money and who similarly pleads for patience, we expect that he will immediately forgive the debt, right? Unfortunately, no. The slave who has been forgiven much in turn throws the other slave into debtor's prison for owing such a small amount. Word gets back to the king, who is not happy about this turn of events. He revokes his earlier decision, reversing his act of mercy, and punishes his slave until the man can repay the original debt.

Some comparable examples to this parable may be seen in *X-Files* episodes where the criminal is caught and given a lenient sentence—a show of mercy—but does not learn a lesson. A similar pattern occurs with both Eugene Tooms ("Squeeze," "Tooms") and Donnie Pfaster ("Irresistible," "Orison"): the suspect in the case, who has committed a series of murders, attacks Scully, but he receives far less than the death penalty for his crimes (Tooms is briefly committed to a sanitarium for attacking Scully; Pfaster receives a life sentence because Scully has spoken to the judge on his behalf); however, when the criminal is released, he picks up his crime spree where he left off. And in both cases, the final result is that the criminal who could not be reformed by the justice system is killed by Mulder or Scully, thus receiving his just due.

We all understand the need for punishment when it is inflicted on someone who has wronged us (such as a criminal like Tooms or Pfaster). And we all understand and appreciate mercy when we are the ones who deserve the consequences but receive mercy instead (for example, when a judge dismisses your traffic ticket). What we often have difficulty with is accepting mercy shown to those who have wronged us or who have committed what may seem like an unforgiveable offense. Scully's reaction to Father Joe in the second *X-Files* movie, *I Want to Believe*, is a vivid example of this. She cannot accept that God would even hear Father Joe's prayers, let alone that God would forgive a man who committed such crimes. While Mulder asks in "All Souls" why bad things happen to good people, the reverse of this question points to the struggle Scully and others have with mercy: Why do good things happen to bad people? Along with this, to the question, Why do the innocent suffer? may be added, Why do the wicked prosper? One answer to such questions is that God permits us free will, which allows us to do bad things to each other; the justice we do not find in this world, then, we look for in the next (see chapter 3, above). But people still grapple with the question of how God can be called just when so much injustice continues to thrive in his creation. Or, to put it another way, How can a just God allow so much mercy for people who don't deserve it at the cost of not giving justice to those who have been wronged?

In Mulder's voiceover at the beginning of "Closure" (7x11), spoken against the backdrop of the shallow graves of murdered children being unearthed by the authorities, he addresses these issues: "They said the birds refused to sing and the thermometer fell suddenly as if God himself had his breath stolen away . . . These fates seemed too cruel, even for God to allow . . . I want to believe so badly, in a truth beyond our own, hidden and obscured from all but the most sensitive eyes, in the endless procession of souls, in what cannot and will not be destroyed. I want to believe we are unaware of God's eternal recompense and sadness. That we cannot see his truth." Part of the answer Mulder finds, or wishes to find, is that we simply cannot fully understand God's greater plan, that God cares for the innocent victims beyond this earth in ways that transcend what we can see and explain—"a truth beyond our own." Another part to Mulder's answer, as well, is the recognition that God himself shares in the grief over such loss. The pain God feels may be more than merely for the loss itself; it may be compounded by the agony of knowing that he has tied his own hands from preventing such loss by allowing us free will. Thus, in "Improbable," Mr. Burt (God) can only watch brokenhearted as Wayne continues to ignore his pleas and persists in killing, while Mr. Burt hopes that the FBI agents will finally read his signs and stop Wayne before the man kills again. As we see the murderers and child molesters go uncaught, and the innocent continue to suffer, we rail against God's injustice, while he may rail against ours.

When heinous crimes occur, we often expect a just God to intervene as judge, jury, and executioner—but only when the crimes are committed by *other* people. We frequently fail to recognize exactly what it would mean for God to step in and give summary judgment, for him to strike someone down with lightning (as people facetiously refer to), judging that person on the spot. We desire such judgment for what we consider to be greater crimes, but God's standard is much higher than ours. *Any* wrongdoing is wrong. To ask God to bring judgment on one person would be to ask him to judge all of us. Jesus makes this point when the Jewish leaders bring before him a woman who has been caught committing adultery and so according to their law deserves to be stoned to death. Their purpose is to test Jesus, to see if he will agree with the law. What Jesus says instead is, "Let anyone among you who is without sin be the first to throw a stone at her" (John 8:7). But none of them dares. In the same way, it is easy for us to bring before God those who have committed a crime deserving a harsh penalty (such as a pedophile like Father Joe, or a coldhearted killer like Donnie Pfaster), but we must be prepared to answer for ourselves whether we are completely without wrong. In the story of Jesus and the woman caught in adultery, once the crowd has left, rather than judge the woman Jesus says mercifully, "Neither do I condemn you. Go your way, and from now on do not sin again" (John 8:11). We hope that she will respond better than the man forgiven much, that she has learned her lesson and will gratefully accept Jesus's mercy and change her ways.

This expectation of God's judgment returns to the question by Reverend Mackey in "Signs & Wonders": Most people believe they're on the side of angels, or good, but are they? In other words, most people believe they're in the right because they're not mass murderers or despotic dictators or child molesters. But does not being extremely bad make you good? Does not being completely black make a piece of fabric white? From God's point of view, the standard by which we are measured is not the Donnie Pfasters of the world; the standard is God himself. God tells the Israelites, "Be holy, for I am holy" (e.g., Leviticus 11:44, 45); Jesus tells his followers, "Be perfect, therefore, as your heavenly Father is perfect" (Matthew 5:48). We have been created in the image of God, and God should be the mirror we look into to examine ourselves. Compared to this ideal, we all fall short.

In Genesis 6, when the nephilim are on the earth and just before God sends the flood, God recognizes that creation hasn't turned out quite the way he has hoped. When he sees the wickedness of humans and their continual evil thoughts, he is sorry that he has created humanity and it has "grieved him to his heart" (Genesis 6:6). He decides to undo creation, destroying with water what he once created out of the waters (see Genesis 1:2, 6). Yet Noah finds favor in God's sight, so God spares Noah, his family, and enough creatures to repopulate the earth after the flood. Through this family, God shows mercy to humanity. When the judgment is over and the waters have receded, God sends a rainbow and makes a covenant with Noah, and with all creation, that "the waters shall never again become a flood to destroy all flesh" (Genesis 9:15). This doesn't mean humanity has never again deserved such destruction. Surely there are many times when God looks around at the wickedness on the earth and it grieves him, when his breath is stolen away and we cannot see his sadness. But he has promised to withhold his ultimate judgment, which will not come until the last day. Then we will go before the Judge, and each will be rewarded or punished as we deserve. In the meantime, however, we all benefit from God's great mercy that he has spared creation and humanity in spite of our sins.

As for the wicked who continue to prosper, those who extort and maim and kill and never face consequences, our hope is that in God's final judgment they will receive what is coming to them. But we should also keep in mind that on that day, every one of us will be accountable for our thoughts and actions. Which one of us can claim to be holy as God is holy, or perfect as the heavenly Father is perfect? The bar is high, and none of us can reach it by ourselves. On our own merits, all of us deserve some kind of punishment. As Robert Modell says in "Pusher," "Original sin tells me ain't nobody innocent." Thanks to Adam and Eve, our access to the tree of life has been barred, so that the sentence awaiting everyone is death. But if God spared creation for the sake of one man, Noah, would he spare us again if one person were found worthy? This, in fact, is what has happened. The new Adam, Jesus Christ, has stepped forward to reopen the way into paradise, to once more allow us access to the tree and therefore to eternal life. His wooden cross has become an ark, and all who would cling to it will be spared, like Noah's family, when the final judgment comes.

THE TRUTH SHALL SET YOU FREE

In Dostoyevsky's *Brothers Karamazov*, the story of the Grand Inquisitor is set up in the preceding chapter by Ivan's diatribe concerning why he finds it too difficult to love his neighbor and why he considers the suffering of innocent children to be an insurmountable obstacle. After listening to his brother Ivan at length, Alyosha finally responds: "Brother, . . . just now you said: 'Is there in all the world a Being that could forgive and have the right to forgive?' Well, that Being does exist, and It can forgive everything, everyone, man and woman alike, *and for everything*, because It gave Its innocent blood for all things and all men. You have forgotten about It, but on It the edifice [of human fortune] is founded, and this it is that people will exclaim to It: 'Just and true art Thou, O Lord, for Thy ways are made plain.'" Ivan replies, "Ah, you mean 'the only sinless one' and His blood! No, I haven't forgotten about Him," and then proceeds into the narrative about the Grand Inquisitor.[11] Ivan has gone on about the blood of the innocent, and Alyosha answers that there is in fact an Innocent One, who shed his blood for everyone. That One alone has a right to judge (the right to cast the first stone), and a right to forgive and show mercy.

The role that Jesus played in saving the world is exemplified by Scully in "Redux II" (5x03). Lying on her hospital bed, knowing that Mulder is in danger of being arrested and charged with murder, she asks to take the fall for him, to take the punishment for his crime. She says, "If I can save you, let me." This is salvation; it is exactly what Jesus has done for us. We are the ones who are guilty, yet he has offered to take the guilt and punishment on himself to save us. He is innocent, while we deserve the death penalty, yet he stepped in to die on our behalf so we could go free: "In Christ God was reconciling the world to himself, not counting their trespasses against them . . . For our sake he made him to be sin who knew no sin, so that in him we might become the righteousness of God" (2 Corinthians 5:19, 21). While Jesus takes on our guilt, we take on his innocence and righteousness, so that in God's eyes we are made holy as Jesus is holy, and our dirty gray garments are washed pure white.

More than simply being innocent, Jesus is also himself the Judge. He is the one who has the right and authority to convict and sentence us. Instead, he has set down the gavel, walked over to the bailiff, and held out his hands to be shackled in our place. We are like the man who was forgiven much. The debt that we owe, the price we should have to pay, has been erased. How will we respond? The reaction of the ungrateful slave was to take his freedom as license to continue doing wrong. He suffered no consequences, so he didn't learn a lesson. Same with Eugene Tooms and Donnie Pfaster when their sentences were too lenient and they used their freedom as opportunity to continue killing. But we can follow a different path and respond with graciousness to the great mercy given to us. We can forgive others, as we have been forgiven. We can love God and other people because of the love that was first shown to us. Jesus, as God, loved us by paying the price for our wrongdoing, which was the supreme act of mercy.

When Scully offers to take the fall for Mulder, to save him and allow him to go free, he refuses to let her pay so great a price. He explains, "We all have our faith, and mine is in the truth." But so great a price has already been paid by Jesus; if we will accept his offer of taking the punishment for us, through his execution in our place, we may have life, abundant and eternal. Just as Mulder holds fast to the truth and it leads to his freedom, Jesus says that those who would heed his words and follow him "will know the truth, and the truth will make you free" (John 8:32). We will know the truth, what is right and good, through the Spirit of truth that God will give us. We will know what is solid and true in the midst of so much relativity. Out of God's great mercy, our acceptance of the truth in Jesus will set us free. This is the gospel, the good news—the truth of the cross.

NOTES

1. See, for example, Eileen Meehan, "Not Your Parents' FBI: *The X-Files* and 'Jose Chung's *From Outer Space*,'" in *The Postmodern Presence: Readings on Postmodernism in American Culture and Society*, ed. Alan A. Berger (Walnut Creek, CA: AltaMira, 1998), 125–56.

2. Richard Flannery and David Louzecky, "Postdemocratic Society and the Truth Out There," in *The Philosophy of "The X-Files,"* ed. Dean A. Kowalski, updated ed., The Philosophy of Popular Culture (Lexington: University Press of Kentucky, 2009), 67. In the same volume, see also V. Alan White, "Freedom and Worldviews in *The X-Files*," 44: "Clearly Mulder and Scully share far more axiologically than otherwise

in their worldviews, for they have agreeable senses of right and wrong, the nature of good and evil moral character, a high regard for the truth, and both seemed to root these values in some sort of sense of an ultimate ground of being." Cf. Robert Westerfelhaus and Teresa A. Combs, "Criminal Investigations and Spiritual Quests: *The X-Files* as an Example of Hegemonic Concordance in a Mass-Mediated Society," *Journal of Communication Inquiry* 22 (1998): 205–20 (esp. 216).

3. It should be acknowledged that the term "natural law" is variously defined in different contexts (such as law, theology, or philosophy); for an overview, see Howard P. Kainz, *Natural Law: An Introduction and Re-examination* (Chicago: Open Court, 2004).

4. Augustine, *Confessions*, trans. R. S. Pine-Coffin (London: Penguin, 1961), 229 (10.23).

5. Augustine, *Confessions*, 229 (10.23).

6. Cf. Arthur F. Holmes, *All Truth Is God's Truth* (Grand Rapids: Eerdmans, 1977).

7. There is another potential parallel in "Terms of Endearment" (6x06), in which apparently the devil himself sets up "a nine-to-five, *Make Room for Daddy* routine" to breed with human women, in an attempt to produce a normal human child, but the babies are all deformed (or demonic).

8. On cancer cells, especially as related to the episode "Leonard Betts," see Anne Simon, *The Real Science behind "The X-Files": Microbes, Meteorites, and Mutants* (New York: Simon & Schuster, 1999), 156–57.

9. The black oil, which can move on its own as an intact puddle, also brings to mind the *Star Trek: The Next Generation* episode "Skin of Evil" (1x22). In this story, a black, oily entity represents all the bad or evil aspects of individuals that a civilization left behind trapped on that planet. The entity delights in causing others suffering and pain, and seems to have no conscience or sense of mercy or justice that may be appealed to.

10. The verse reference then reads, "1 John 5:07." Since the extra zero isn't typical in citing Bible verses, "5:7" would be more accurate—and might've saved some money on the engraving. Note, however, that some Bible translations actually include this phrase in verse 6 rather than in verse 7.

11. Fyodor Dostoyevsky, *The Brothers Karamazov*, trans. David McDuff, rev. ed. (London: Penguin, 2003), 321 (italics original).

6

The Way of the Cross

Temptation, Death, and Resurrection

> SCULLY: You haven't heard the rumors? . . . That Luria is back from the dead? That he's risen from his grave?
>
> HERB BJUNES: What kind of Jew trick is this?
>
> MULDER: A Jew pulled it off two thousand years ago.
> ("Kaddish," 4x12)

Alongside Mulder's "I Want to Believe" poster, Scully's cross necklace is the other major motif of *The X-Files*. Scully wears it from day one, and Mulder even wears it for a time in her absence ("3," 2x07). The necklace therefore comes to represent Scully, but especially her own faith or desire to believe. It should be no surprise, then, that a show with such a ubiquitous symbol related to Christ would also frequently use imagery from the life and death of Jesus Christ, or Jesus the Messiah. *The X-Files* presents a number of themes from the Gospel story, from birth narrative to miracles to death and resurrection.

While no one character exclusively is portrayed as the Savior or Messiah, Mulder as a heroic figure most commonly represents the suffering, death, and resurrection of Christ. He undergoes a number of supposed deaths and resurrections, before his actual burial and resurrection in Season 8. Mulder is seen extended on a "cross" in "The Sixth Extinction II: Amor Fati" (7x04) as he reenacts the temptation scene from Nikos Kazantzakis's *Last Temptation of Christ*. But Mulder is a reluctant messiah. He does not set out to collect disciples, although he inevitably accumulates some along the way (most notably Scully and Assistant Director Skinner); he tells Max Fenig, a UFO aficionado who has been following Mulder's work, "I didn't think anybody was paying attention" ("Fallen Angel," 1x09). The only person Mulder sets out to save is Samantha, and at times Scully. When Mulder finds out, after he thinks Samantha has returned, that he has been duped by clones of his sister who want his help, he insists to them, "I'm not your savior" ("End Game," 2x17). If Mulder is a messiah, he's more like the title character in Monty Python's *Life of Brian*, who declares, "I'm not the Messiah!" to his unwanted followers. Like Brian, Mulder also does not intend to martyr himself for the cause, although he places little value on his own life in relation to the Truth. Mulder therefore takes many risks, some of which result in his death (assumed or real); but like a bad penny, or a good messiah, he keeps turning up.

UNTO US A CHILD IS BORN

To begin at the beginning, we must first turn to the account of Jesus's miraculous birth. Two of the Gospels, Matthew and Luke, begin with an infancy narrative, each containing some unique material. Matthew tells the tale of the magi who travel from the east and the animosity of King Herod toward the prophesied child. Luke recounts the journey to Bethlehem for the census and the angels' appearance to the shepherds. While there is no messianic imagery connected with Mulder's own infancy, there certainly is with the birth of his son, William. Themes from both Matthew's and Luke's infancy narratives make an appearance in William's story.

William's infancy narrative begins with his mother, Scully, who is in some ways compared to Mary, the mother of Jesus. The association is first made at the death of Scully's daughter, Emily. In the final scene before Emily dies, Scully climbs into the girl's hospital bed to lie down next to her. As the scene fades into the next, the image of Scully's face next to Emily's is superimposed on a stained-glass window of Mary and baby Jesus, Mother and Child. With William's conception, Scully again becomes a Mary figure, especially with the implication of a "virgin birth," or a miraculous conception. Scully, like Mary, is a woman who shouldn't be able to conceive. In Scully's case, she is left barren because of her abduction. Mary's conception is miraculous because, as she tells the angel Gabriel, she's never been intimate with a man (Luke 1:34). But the angel says to her, "The Holy Spirit will come upon you, and the power of the Most High will overshadow you; therefore the child to be born will be holy; he will be called Son of God" (v. 35). While it isn't directly suggested that Scully too is a virgin, she is never seen engaging in sexual activity, even to conceive William, so there is actually no evidence that she is not a virgin—at the very least, her character takes on a virginal quality by remaining essentially asexual onscreen.

It is also implied that Scully may have conceived through science's equivalent of the virgin birth, by in vitro fertilization (see "Per Manum," 8x08). Even Mulder, the presumed father (who also is the sperm donor for the IVF procedure), says in a voiceover, "How did this child come to be? What set its heart beating? Is it the product of a union? Or the work of a divine hand, an answered prayer, a true miracle? Or is it a wonder of technology, the intervention of other hands? What do I tell this child about to be born? What do I tell Scully? And what do I tell myself?" ("Essence," 8x20). While Mulder eventually refers to William as "my son," it is never clarified for the audience exactly how the baby came to be. Whatever the exact source, William is clearly a miracle baby, which is unfortunately what puts his life in danger. Alex Krycek tells Mulder and Scully later in "Essence," "Your baby was a miracle. Born of a barren mother's barren womb . . . [The aliens are] afraid of its implications. That it could somehow be greater than them. Something more human than human . . . I wanted to destroy the truth before they learn the truth." Connecting the dots, Mulder deduces what this truth is: "That there's a God, a higher power." Like the conception of Jesus, a miracle that shows the hand of God at work, William's conception is also seen to be something that defies both science and aliens, and thus evidence of God's intervention. Matthew 1:23 quotes from Isaiah 7:14, "Look, the virgin shall conceive and bear a son, and they shall name him Emmanuel," and explains that the name means, "God is with us." Like the birth of Jesus, the birth of William is taken as evidence that God is with us, with the humans, and may represent a power that the aliens cannot overcome.

Because William is seen as special and therefore is in danger from the aliens, his story also echoes the danger to Jesus at his birth. In Matthew 2, King Herod learns from the magi that a child was born who is being called "king of the Jews." Herod sends the magi on to find the baby, claiming that he too wants to pay homage; really, though, he wants to kill the potential usurper to his throne. So an angel appears to Joseph and warns him to flee to Egypt with his family. When the magi do not report back to Herod to tell him the child's location, he is infuriated and sends men to kill all of the boys in the Bethlehem area who were born around the time of the star the magi reported. Some of these same themes appear with William. In his situation, the flight from danger comes before he is born, as Scully is rushed off to a remote location by Agent Reyes ("Existence," 8x21). A bright light in the sky is seen over the place of his birth, like the star reported by the magi. The aliens are the ones who pose a threat to William's life. But the Gospel story of the slaughter of the innocents also recalls another biblical account that has implications for William: the story of Moses (Exodus 1–2). Like Herod, the pharaoh commands the death of Hebrew boys; like Jesus, Moses is spared and hidden away in Egypt for a time by his parents. It is in the months following William's birth that the parallels with Moses become most prominent (see below).

The remote location where William is born yields more allusions to Jesus's birth narrative. The rustic location where Scully goes to have the baby recalls the manger where baby Jesus was laid "because there was no place for them in the inn" (Luke 2:7). The abandoned building in which Scully gives birth has a painted window that reads, "Water from the Rock," above a picture of Jesus, referring in part to the dried-up hot springs there that used to provide healing. This is another allusion to Moses, since he brought forth water from a rock during the exodus to provide something for the Israelites to drink.[1] The bright light overhead may in fact be an alien ship rather than a star, like the one the magi followed; when Mulder is asked how he found Scully after the birth, since no one gave him exact coordinates, he replies simply, "There was a light. I followed it." But the magi who visit the baby, the three wise guys, are the Lone Gunmen; just as the three wise men came with their gifts of gold, frankincense, and myrrh (Matthew 2:9–11), Frohike, Langly, and Byers come to Scully's apartment, bearing gifts, after she and William have returned home. William's birth is also attended by a host of alien replicants, who could represent the shepherds who came to visit the baby in his rustic birthplace (Luke 2:15–18).

In the Gospel of Matthew, the reference to Jesus as "king of the Jews" and the association with the infancy narrative of Moses foreshadow the ministry and death of Jesus. He will come preaching a kingdom, the kingdom of heaven, and even though he will not attempt to claim Herod's throne for himself, he will mockingly be crucified as "king of the Jews." As a new Moses, he will lead his people, the Jews, out of their slavery to the law and to sin (although many would prefer that the Messiah lead them out of their servitude to the Roman Empire). This new exodus is illustrated first by Jesus's journey through the wilderness to undergo testing for a symbolic forty days, then by his emergence from the desert to guide his people to the territory that God has promised them (God's kingdom) and his retelling of the law from a mountain (i.e., the Sermon on the Mount, Matthew 5–7).

After narrating Jesus's return from the testing in the wilderness, Matthew sets up the beginning of Jesus's ministry with a quotation from Isaiah 9:1–2 (Matthew 4:16). This recalls the verses that follow in Isaiah 9, a text often quoted at Christmas: "For to us a child is born, to us a son is given, and the government will be on his shoulders. And he will be called Wonderful Counselor, Mighty God, Everlasting Father, Prince of Peace. Of the increase of his government and peace there will be no end. He will reign on David's throne and over his kingdom, establishing and upholding it with justice and righteousness from that time on and forever" (vv. 6–7). The Jews expected their messiah to come as a king like David. But while Moses was a slave who became royalty, Jesus was heavenly royalty who became lowly as a slave (see Philippians 2). He came not to rule but to serve. After his triumphal entry into Jerusalem like the king in Zechariah 9:9 (Matthew 21:1–11), Jesus's final victorious act was not to take up the sword against the Romans but to be beaten and crucified by them, labeled as king of the Jews. What he knew, though, and the people were yet to understand, was that the promised land into which he was leading them, rather than a physical territory, was the kingdom of heaven.

It is later into Season 9, during William's first year, that he more closely parallels the story of Moses. In particular, William, like Moses, is given over by his birth mother to be raised by strangers for his own protection (see chapter 4, above, and the section titled "Motherly Love"). After William's life is endangered a number of times, in "William" (9x17) Scully finally makes the difficult choice to give him up for adoption so that he may have a future apart from aliens and conspiracies. William's ultimate fate—what he will grow up to be, and whether he is still destined to become someone great, as his miraculous birth suggests—remains to be written. There are, however, characters who believe he will one day be a leader or savior, like Moses or Jesus. In "Providence" (9x11), the leader of a UFO cult has William kidnapped because of a prophecy about a miracle child, "a future savior coveted by forces of good and evil," who "will follow in his father's paths and try to stop the aliens' return, unless his father was to be killed." If the father, Mulder, is killed, then the boy can fulfill his "true destiny," which is to lead the aliens. It is because of people like these cultists that Scully decides she must give up her son to anonymity or he will never be left alone to live a normal childhood. But if he truly is like Moses, then William's adoption is part of the greater plan and will contribute to fulfilling his fate, rather than prevent it.

THE TEMPTATION OF CHRIST

The Moses imagery apparent in the Gospels first with Jesus's birth is reinforced at the beginning of his ministry with his testing in the wilderness. After his baptism, which could parallel the Israelites' crossing of the Red Sea, Jesus is led into his own exodus account, a period of wandering in the wilderness. He spends forty days there fasting, which symbolize the forty years that the Israelites spent wandering in the desert often with little more than manna to eat. At the end of this time, when Jesus is physically at his weakest, Satan appears and offers him a series of three temptations, starting by challenging the hungry Jesus to turn stones into bread. Jesus answers each of the three tests with quotations from Scripture, and finally Satan leaves him, proving that Jesus is victorious. Only then does Jesus return to civilization to begin his ministry, leading the Jews into a new exodus toward the promised kingdom of God.

In Dostoyevsky's *Brothers Karamazov*, the Grand Inquisitor narrative is primarily the Inquisitor's diatribe against Jesus for rejecting the three temptations in the wilderness by Satan. Following the order of the temptations in Matthew (4:1–11), the Inquisitor says that Jesus wrongly refused miracle (turning stones into bread), mystery (jumping from the pinnacle of the temple to see if the angels would save him), and authority (worshipping Satan in order to receive the kingdoms of the world), all to allow people free will and the choice whether or not to love him. While the parallel to the Grand Inquisitor dialogue in "Talitha Cumi" (3x24; see chapter 1, above) doesn't name the three temptations, it does mention the same trio: miracle, mystery, and authority. To these three temptations could also be added a fourth, a last temptation, when Jesus is on the cross. In language echoing the second temptation by Satan ("If you are the Son of God, throw yourself down" so that God could send angels to rescue him [Matthew 4:6]), the bystanders at the crucifixion mockingly tell Jesus, "If you are the Son of God, come down from the cross," and say, "He trusts in God; let God deliver him now, if he wants to" (Matthew 27:40b, 43a). Jesus gives no answer to the taunting, but just as he overcame the three temptations by Satan in the wilderness, he also resists the final test and remains on the cross to fulfill his calling.

Mulder likewise goes through periods of testing, most notably in "Redux II" (5x03).[2] As always, the Cigarette-Smoking Man (CSM) represents the devil, the one who encounters Mulder at his weakest (when Scully is in the hospital dying of cancer) and offers him wonderful things, if only he will sell his soul. The first temptation is the cure for Scully's cancer. Mulder has gained access to the Department of Defense in "Redux" (5x02) and retrieved a vial that may hold the key to Scully's remission. While at first Mulder thinks the vial contains only deionized water, CSM tells him that it actually contains a microchip (like the one once removed from Scully's neck) that is "essential to her survival." But is it really a cure? The second temptation is Mulder's sister. CSM arranges a meeting with a woman who looks exactly like the Samantha clones that Mulder met back during Season 2. The woman sounds like she is Samantha, all grown up with a life and family of her own, but she's not ready to build a relationship with her long-lost brother. Is this really Samantha, or another clone? The third temptation is the secrets of the pyramids—the Truth. The price is finally set: if Mulder will come work for CSM, Mulder will learn everything he ever wanted to know about aliens and government conspiracies; the irony, of course, is that by working for the bad guys, he won't be able to reveal the truth to the public, which has always been his desire. Eventually, Mulder overcomes the temptations. While he does seem to receive the miracle of Scully's cure (although it is possible it was an answer to her prayers, unrelated to the chip), he rejects the mystery and authority that CSM offers him. Emerging victorious, Mulder retains his soul and his freedom.

Another temptation that Mulder undergoes is a reenactment of the final temptation from *The Last Temptation of Christ*.[3] The temptation sequence is not a part of the Gospel narrative but is Nikos Kazantzakis's imaginative rendering of what Jesus could have experienced in his final minutes on the cross. In that moment, Jesus lived a lifetime: he was tempted by Satan to come down from the cross (just as the bystanders had encouraged) and leave behind his role as savior and Son of God to live a normal life. "Amor Fati" interweaves the *Last Temptation* retelling, which is an extended dream sequence by Mulder, with the real-world events dominated by Scully's efforts to find and save him. Mulder is seen lying in an operating bay, with his arms extended (as on a cross) and a metal halo around his head (his crown of thorns). While he's undergoing surgery—performed by CSM's surgeons in order to extract genetic material that supposedly allows Mulder to be "our savior" because of his immunity to the alien infection, material that CSM has implanted in himself—Mulder experiences an extended dream about CSM inviting him to rise from his hospital bed and come live in a kind of witness-protection program. There, Mulder meets first Deep Throat, who apparently is not dead but has been living in the neighborhood with his wife and daughters, then Samantha, who is also living a happy, peaceful life with her children. Diana Fowley plays the role of Mary Magdalene, seducing Mulder into his own blissful family life.

The scenes of this happy life flash quickly by in Mulder's mind's eye, until finally he finds himself to be a bedridden old man. As he lies in bed, we see what's going on beyond his window: the alien apocalypse has arrived and the sky is falling (in *The Last Temptation of Christ*, Jerusalem is burning). The one figure who has been notably absent from his dream, Scully, then makes her appearance. She is not aged, as he is, but is as young as when he last saw her. Scully plays Kazantzakis's red-haired, blue-eyed Judas, who is actually Jesus's dearest friend. She repeats the words of Judas in the novel, calling Mulder a traitor, deserter, and coward.

> SCULLY: You're not supposed to die, Mulder, not here . . . Not in a comfortable bed with the devil outside.
>
> MULDER: No, you don't understand. He's taken care of me.
>
> SCULLY: No, Mulder, he's lulled you to sleep. He's made you trade your true mission for creature comforts.
>
> MULDER: There was no mission. There were no aliens.
>
> SCULLY: No aliens. Have you looked outside, Mulder?
>
> MULDER: I can't. I'm too tired.
>
> SCULLY: No, Mulder, you must get up. You must get up and fight. Especially you. This isn't your place. Get up, Mulder. Get up and fight the fight.

The temptation in the dream is for Mulder, as Christ, to deny his role as the savior, to give up the fight, and to accept the common life of a husband and father. As CSM summarizes, "Extraordinary men are always most tempted by the most ordinary things." But Mulder, like the Jesus of the novel, finally rejects the temptation and returns to the reality of the cross to complete his mission. The calling of the messiah is not an easy one, and the road is often lonely, but the consequences for abandoning the role are too high. Mulder recognizes that he cannot simply bury his head in the sand.[4] Like Jesus, and with followers such as Scully who have already paid a high price for their loyalty, Mulder must stay in the game and fight the good fight, come what may.

SIGNS AND WONDERS

After his testing in the wilderness, Jesus set out on his ministry, which along with teaching consisted mainly of healings, exorcisms, and other miracles. While Mulder is not a healer or miracle worker, there are at least two other characters in *The X-Files* who are portrayed with messianic healing ministries. One is Jeremiah Smith. In "Talitha Cumi," Jeremiah is playing the part of Jesus from the Grand Inquisitor tale, alluded to in the episode title (which derives from one of Jesus's healing miracles—raising a girl from the dead, Jesus tells her, "Talitha cumi," or "Young girl, arise"; see Mark 5:41). In a restaurant, a crazed gunman begins to shoot, but Jeremiah heals all of the victims, including the shooter, who was himself wounded by police. Although this has the positive effect of changing the gunman's heart through his belief that God has spared him and given him a second chance, it negatively has attracted the attention of CSM, the "Inquisitor," leading to Jeremiah's incarceration. In the Gospels, while Jesus's healings are not necessarily the cause of his arrest, they certainly do attract attention, sometimes more than he wants.

Another character portrayed as a healer is Samuel Hartley in "Miracle Man" (1x17). In the teaser of the episode, Samuel begins his miraculous ways as a young boy by resurrecting a man who has died in a fire. As Samuel continues to perform miracles (as part of a tent ministry run by his father, Reverend Hartley), this man who was resurrected, Leonard Vance, becomes a regular part of the show, giving his testimony before others come forward to be healed by Samuel. Samuel's gift is to heal simply with a touch, and hospital records attest how he has healed people of ailments such as metastatic cancer. As it is said of Jesus, it could be said of Samuel, "So his fame spread . . . , and they brought to him all the sick; those who were afflicted with various diseases and pains, . . . epileptics, and paralytics, and he cured them" (Matthew 4:24). Samuel can also raise the dead, as Jesus raised Lazarus (John 11); Leonard Vance is even associated with Lazarus by the painting that hangs in his bedroom: *The Resurrection of Lazarus*, by Geertgen tot Sint Jans.

In Jesus's healings portrayed in the Gospels, the physical afflictions that people suffer are often associated with demons. By casting out, or exorcising, the demons, Jesus frees people from the effects on their bodies and thereby heals them. For example, the mute are freed to speak (Matthew 9:32–33), and the blind are freed to see (Matthew 12:22); an epileptic boy is restored to health (Matthew 17:14–18), and a crazy and violent man is restored to his right mind (Mark 5:2–22). It is no surprise, then, that in "Miracle Man," the movie *The Exorcist* is mentioned. Scully says that she doesn't believe Samuel is guilty of the murders they are investigating, because "I was raised a Catholic, and I have a certain familiarity with the Scripture. And God never lets the devil steal the show." Mulder says, "You must have really liked *The Exorcist*." Scully smiles and replies, "One of my favorite movies." While Samuel's healings are not described as exorcisms, in the Gospels the two actions go hand in hand.

If evil is like cancer in the way that it mutates and spreads within people (see chapter 5, above), then to fight cancer is comparable to exorcism. This is the association that Scully makes relative to her own cancer in a voiceover addressed to Mulder:

> In med school I learned that cancer arrives in the body unannounced, a dark stranger who takes up residence, turning its new home against itself. This is the evil of cancer, that it starts as an invader, but soon becomes one with the invaded, forcing you to destroy it but only at the risk of destroying yourself. It is science's demon possession; my treatments, science's attempt at exorcism. Mulder, I hope that in these terms you might know it and know me and accept this stranger so many recognize but cannot ever completely cast out. ("Memento Mori," 4x15)

The idea of exorcising cancer is also visually depicted through the black oil referred to as the black cancer (see "Terma," 4x10). This oil is a possessing force, like demon possession, and so to enable a person to recover, the oil must be cast out (which the Russians and the Consortium each attempt to do by developing a vaccine). In a more literal sense, exorcism is also depicted in "The Calusari" (2x21) when an exorcism is performed on a young boy to cast out the lingering ghost of his evil twin. Removing the evil is necessary to restore the boy to health and to his right mind.

Another exorcism of sorts occurs in "Signs & Wonders" (7x09) when snakes are cast out of the belly of a pregnant young woman. In this episode, snakes represent evil, Satan, and the temptation that caused original sin. To drive out the snakes shows that with God's help humans are able to have power over the devil and temptation. Similarly, the exorcisms that Jesus performs show his power and victory over evil. Not only does Jesus triumph over temptation in the wilderness, but he is able to triumph over the source of temptation. Jesus does battle with Satan, binding him in order to free those he would hold in bondage (see Matthew 12:29). The demons recognize Jesus's power; they know him by name and cower when he comes near (see Mark 1:23–26). As Scully says, Jesus doesn't let the devil steal the show.

TAKE UP YOUR CROSS AND FOLLOW ME

During his ministry, Jesus gathered twelve disciples, representing the twelve tribes of Israel, and a number of other followers and supporters. He taught them and prepared them to continue his ministry in his absence, but ultimately the road that Jesus must travel, to Jerusalem and to the cross, was an individual journey that he had to complete alone. The call to be a disciple often required sacrifice, of home, family, or livelihood. Mulder doesn't call disciples, as Jesus did, but as others around him come to understand and pursue the same truth, he naturally accumulates followers. While Scully is in many ways Mulder's equal and partner, she admits more than once that she has become a follower in his quest due to his passion and tenacity. But her devotion comes at a price, as often happens when one commits to single-minded pursuit of a high goal.

In the Gospels, when Jesus calls his first disciples he simply walks by and says, "Follow me" (e.g., Mark 1:17; 2:14). As far as we know, they don't have much knowledge of who Jesus is or what his purpose is. Even in his last days before the crucifixion, they clearly don't have a complete understanding of what he is about. But even if the disciples don't fully believe Jesus, they believe *in* him; they trust him enough to follow him. In the same way, Scully is willing to follow Mulder, not because she fully agrees with him or believes the same way he does, but because she believes *in* him. In "The Red and the Black" (5x14), she tells him, "Mulder, when I met you five years ago, you told me that your sister had been abducted, by aliens. That that event had marked you so deeply, that nothing else mattered. I didn't believe you, but I followed you, on nothing more than your faith that the truth was out there." At the end of the series, in "The Truth" (9x20), she reaffirms her commitment: "I know you—you can't give up. It's what I saw in you when we first met. It's what made me follow you, and why I'd do it all over again." Because of Mulder's strong belief in the truth and his persistence in pursuing it, Scully is drawn into his quest as well, determined to follow his lead in seeking the same goal.

To seek the same goal, however, may mean to pay the same price. Mulder is well aware of the cost to himself. In the opening voiceover in "Colony" (2x16), he says, "To believe as passionately as I did was not without sacrifice, but I always accepted the risks, to my career, my reputation, my relationships, to life itself." Mulder is willing to live a lonely life, without family, with few friends, and to risk his career or even his life. The *Last Temptation* theme in "Amor Fati" emphasizes the isolation and sacrifice of the messiah's role. Mulder, as Jesus, learns through the dream sequence that he must deny himself the opportunity to live a normal life as a family man in order to fulfill his calling, which eventually means suffering on the cross. Mulder can accept this destiny for himself, but those who would follow him may also have to make sacrifices. We see Scully begin to make such choices when she turns down a date to join him at the Smithsonian in "The Jersey Devil" (1x04); by Season 4 she bemoans that she has lost herself in the X-Files and no longer has a life of her own ("Never Again," 4x13).

The disciples of Jesus have to face the same choices. He tells fishermen to leave behind their nets (Mark 1:17–18), a tax collector to leave his tax booth (2:14), a rich man to sell his possessions and give the money to the poor (10:21), parents and children to set aside their families to become his brothers and sisters (Matthew 10:37; 12:49–50). The life of a disciple requires letting go of worldly goods and concerns to focus on a higher calling. Jesus summarizes this commitment: "If any want to become my followers, let them deny themselves and take up their cross and follow me. For those who want to save their life will lose it, and those who lose their life for my sake, and for the sake of the gospel, will save it. For what will it profit them to gain the whole world and forfeit their life?" (Mark 8:34–36). This final question is the same dilemma faced by Kazantzakis's Jesus, and by Mulder as well, in *The Last Temptation*: What good would it do him, or anyone else, if he gained all the creature comforts a man could ever want in this world, only to lose his life, or his soul, and the lives of so many others that he could have saved? A disciple must be willing to give up everything, as Jesus has, in order to follow him. The reward he has promised them is in the world to come. Thus, when Peter says to Jesus, "Look, we have left everything and followed you," Jesus replies, "Truly I tell you, there is no one who has left house or brothers or sisters or mother or father or children or fields, for my sake and for the sake of the good news, who will not receive a hundredfold now in this age—houses, brothers and sisters, mothers and children, and fields, with persecutions—and in the age to come eternal life" (Mark 10:28–30).

To follow Jesus may mean not only to give up one's livelihood, but also to be willing to literally give up one's life. That, after all, is the function of a cross. Scully too must face the possibility of losing her life for Mulder's quest. In "One Breath" (2x08), when Scully has been returned from her abduction and is lying in a coma, Mulder asks Assistant Director Skinner, "What if I knew the potential consequences, but I never told her?" She again faces the possible costs when she is fighting cancer and is told, as she explains to Mulder, that "the men behind this hoax, behind these lies, gave me this disease to make you believe" ("Gethsemane," 4x24). Other people may also have to lose their lives along the way, such as Agent Weiss in "Colony." The agent simply receives a phone call from Mulder and Scully to go check on a local house before they arrive, and he ends up dead. When his death is on their heads, Mulder seems less than sympathetic: "Those are the risks we take. You either accept them or you don't." It is true that working in law enforcement means being prepared to sacrifice one's life in the line of duty, but the body count around the X-Files seems a little higher than average. The same quest costs the life of

Mulder's father and Scully's sister, not to mention at least two of their informants (Deep Throat and Mr. X) and numerous minor characters along the way. Each of these in their own way has to take up their cross to follow Mulder in their pursuit of the truth.

In the end, though, the messiah must walk his own path alone. There is a limit to how far the disciples can follow. Scully points out more than once that she can only go so far with Mulder. In "Tunguska" (4x09), when Mulder is chasing a lead provided by Krycek—who, as Scully reminds her partner, is "a liar and a murderer"—she expresses her concern: "What I'm worried about is you, Mulder. How far you'll go. And how far I can follow you." Where he ends up going is Tunguska, Russia, without Scully. A similar situation occurs two seasons earlier, in "Colony." In their discussion about the death of Agent Weiss, she tells Mulder, "You'll pursue a case at the expense of everything, to the point of insanity, and expect me to follow you. There has to be somewhere to draw the line." In the sequel, "End Game," Mulder determines for her where the line is drawn. When he travels to northern Alaska to look for a downed UFO, he leaves Scully a note: "Scully, when you get this message I will be too far away for you to stop me, but where I'm going I cannot allow you to follow. I won't let you jeopardize your life and your career for reasons purely personal to me. You were right, Scully—you said a line has to be drawn somewhere. I'm drawing it for you here."

The words that Mulder writes echo the words of Jesus to his disciples in John 13:36, at the Last Supper: "Where I am going, you cannot follow me now" (see also 8:21–22). What Jesus refers to is his solitary journey to the cross. While he tells the disciples to be prepared to suffer the same fate (he continues, "but you will follow afterward"), it is his fate to go through his trial and crucifixion alone. Thus, while three of the disciples accompany him to the garden of Gethsemane, all three fall asleep, leaving him in solitude, and even his closest follower, Peter, will deny his association with Jesus three times before morning. A line is drawn between the garden and the cross, so that the final steps Jesus takes must be on his own. A similar sentiment is expressed by Scully in a journal entry to Mulder as she faces the reality of her cancer and her own mortality, and thus her lonely journey towards death: "Though we've traveled far together, this last distance must necessarily be traveled alone" ("Memento Mori"). Just as Jesus draws a line for his disciples at the Last Supper, during Mulder's own "Last Supper" in "Requiem" (7x22) he draws a line for Scully before he goes off to his "crucifixion" (abduction): "You're not going back out there. I'm not going to let you go back out there . . . It has to end sometime. That time is now . . . I'm not going to risk losing you." Mulder must face his fate on his own. That is the lot of the messiah.

PASSION AND PASCHA

The story surrounding Jesus's death is referred to as the Passion Narrative. "Passion" is derived from the Latin word for "suffer," and hence refers to the suffering of Christ in his beatings and crucifixion. Although the Jews of Jesus's day were looking for a triumphant, political messiah, Jesus's triumph came in his suffering on a cross and his resurrection into new life. His death was not an unfortunate tragedy, as some of his followers likely thought, but was always the end goal of his ministry. He told his disciples to take up their cross and follow him, and he set the example by taking up his cross first. What was once a symbol of a shameful, criminal death in the Roman Empire then became a symbol for victory over impossible odds. It is a symbol of faith that Scully would carry with her daily. But, like the cross itself, this faith and its implications may not always be easy to bear.

While Mulder repeatedly reflects aspects of Jesus's journey to the cross throughout *The X-Files*, much of Jesus's death and resurrection are also encapsulated in "Miracle Man" through the faith healer Samuel Hartley. Although Samuel is in some aspects more a wayward young man than a messiah, even in this there are some parallels with Jesus. Finding Samuel at a local bar, Sheriff Daniels comments, "Not a very likely place to be saving souls." Yet Jesus spent his time saving souls in just such company, earning himself a reputation among some as "a glutton and a drunkard, a friend of tax collectors and sinners" (Matthew 11:19). Like Jesus, Samuel is arrested for a crime of which he is innocent but does not try to defend himself at his trial. The authorities have him beaten and killed. But his tomb (Samuel's drawer at the morgue) is found empty. After his death, he appears to numerous witnesses, still bearing the marks from his death. Scully even echoes the charge of some of the Jewish priests, that the resurrection was actually a "body snatching" (see Matthew 28:11–15), although Mulder believes that "the boy did rise from the dead" and quips, "That kind of thing happens only once or twice every two thousand years or so." There is a parallel also in Samuel's Judas, Leonard Vance, who betrays him (here, by committing the murders himself, for which Samuel is blamed) and then later feels remorse and commits suicide. This episode, then, gives an overview of some of the themes that reappear throughout the series, usually with Mulder in the role of persecuted messiah.[5]

The Last Supper

Near the end of "Requiem," Mulder has a "Last Supper" that initiates a series of parallels with Jesus's death and resurrection, taking place from the end of Season 7 into Season 8. Mulder's last supper is more a visual allusion to Da Vinci's painting than an actual reenactment of the event. Over a conference table in Skinner's office a meal is spread out (a variety of fast food and take-out). Along three sides of the table, a group is assembled: Mulder is at the center, with three people to his right and four to his left. Probably not too much should be made of the exact positioning of each person, since that would identify Langly, at Mulder's right hand, with John, the beloved disciple—although the parallel may be intentional, given Langly's long hair (since John is portrayed effeminately by Da Vinci). The importance of the scene is that it foreshadows what will happen to Mulder later in the episode, and into the next season.

The Last Supper that Jesus had with his disciples took place during the Jewish Passover, or Pascha (a name that carried over to the Christian celebration otherwise known as Easter). The festival commemorates the exodus of the Israelites from Egypt and the last of the ten plagues: all the firstborn would be killed, unless the blood of a lamb was painted on the doorposts of a house, and then the angel of death would *pass over* and spare those within the home. The central part of the Passover meal, in Jesus's day, was the lamb sacrificed at the temple, hence the references to Jesus as the Lamb of God (John 1:29, 36; see also Revelation 7:17; 22:1) and to the blood of the Lamb (Revelation 7:14; 12:11). But during the meal, the elements that Jesus associated with himself and his upcoming death were the bread and the wine. The bread used during Passover is unleavened, or without yeast, so it is hard and brittle, like a cracker. So when Jesus broke the bread, it snapped like dry bones, and he told the disciples, "This is my body" (Mark 14:22). Wine is a symbol of celebration, such as at the wedding in Cana when Jesus turned water into wine (John 2), so after Jesus told them, "This is my blood," he promised never again to drink the fruit of the vine until they could celebrate together in his Father's kingdom (Mark 14:24–25)—at the wedding feast of the Lamb (Revelation 19:9).

The concept of eating flesh and drinking blood is certainly offensive to many people, such as ancient Jews, so the symbolic teaching of Jesus was not easy for everyone to understand (see John 6). In fact, some of the references to the Eucharist—the regular reenactment of the Lord's Supper—in *The X-Files* are to these offensive types of misinterpretation. For example, in "Our Town" (2x24), as Mulder and Scully discuss the possibility that the townsfolk are participating in cannibalism and that this may result in their prolonged life spans, Mulder argues, "From vampirism to Catholicism, whether literally or symbolically, the reward for eating flesh is eternal life." The association with vampirism is seen in the episode "3," in which a bloodsucking unholy trinity hunts for victims and manipulates Scripture. At the home of one murder victim, they write on the wall in blood, "He who eats of my flesh and drinks of my blood shall have eternal life and I will raise him up on the last day," from John 6:54, although they misidentify it as John 52:54. Mulder rightly says, "They have the same feeble literal grasp of the Bible as all those big-haired preachers do," indicating their misuse of the text and abuse of its meaning.

Despite such misinterpretations, what Jesus instituted was not vampirism or cannibalism. He recognized that people would find his words offensive (John 6:61), and he explained to them, "It is the spirit that gives life; the flesh is useless. The words that I have spoken to you are spirit and life" (v. 63). What Jesus teaches here is that he is the bread of life, provided from heaven just like the manna that God provided to sustain life in the wilderness during the exodus (vv. 48–51). Jesus then adds the second element, his blood, and says, "Those who eat my flesh and drink my blood abide in me, and I in them" (v. 56). To "abide" or "remain" is a favorite verb used by Jesus in the Gospel of John and often refers to a sense of unity or being of one mind (to remain in something or someone). In this way, Jesus is essentially encouraging his followers to become "one flesh" (cf. Genesis 2:24) with him by relying upon his sacrifice for their deliverance to eternal life, just as the sacrifice of the lamb delivered the lives of the Israelites, right before Moses delivered them from Egypt and they encountered the manna.

For all this symbolism, though, and Jesus's reference to "spirit," there is a teaching in the Christian tradition that claims the bread and wine in the Eucharist actually miraculously become the body and blood of Christ: transubstantiation. In "Underneath" (9x09), Agent Reyes appeals to this doctrine in her theory to explain a Jekyll-and-Hyde character. Their killer, Bob Fassl, is a devout Catholic, but in his desire for holiness he is unable to acknowledge his sinful side. His denial gives rise to a type of split personality, an evil, murderous persona—only, this second personality manages to have slightly different DNA. Reyes says, "There is a precedent in the Catholic canon itself: transubstantiation, the manipulation of matter and energy." Scully adds, "You mean, water into wine" (referring to the wedding at Cana; John 2:1–11). Reyes replies, "Or the communion wafer into the body of Christ." What Reyes argues is that in the same way the bread and wine miraculously transform into real flesh and blood, Fassl can also transform from one type of flesh into another. Although, Agent Doggett's rebuttal is valid: "I've slept through my share of Sunday schools, but I never heard the story about the guy becoming another guy."

Whether an actual physical transformation happens during the Eucharist or the elements are merely symbolic, what Jesus intended at his Last Supper was to depict for his disciples his death coming in a few short hours and the importance that act would have for their earthly lives and beyond. At the Last Supper, Jesus also foretold that one of the disciples would betray him, shortly before Judas left to do so, and that Peter would deny him three times before the cock crowed. This meal was the last time the entire group would be assembled together. It was the beginning of the end for Jesus, but also a new beginning for the church that would emerge after his resurrection and would regularly eat the bread and drink the fruit of the vine to "proclaim the Lord's death until he comes" (1 Corinthians 11:26).

The Garden of Gethsemane

In the Passion Narrative, after the Last Supper Jesus goes to the garden of Gethsemane with three of his closest disciples to pray. It is a time of great anguish for Jesus, and perhaps weeping (see Hebrews 5:7), as he pleads with God to intervene in his fate, if it is God's will. The scene ends with Judas arriving with an armed crowd to betray and arrest Jesus. Throughout *The X-Files*, there are various allusions to Gethsemane and Judas. In the context of the larger "passion narrative" beginning in "Requiem," if the meeting in Skinner's office is Mulder's last supper, then his nighttime trip into the outdoors with Skinner is the garden of Gethsemane, and the abduction from the outdoors is the arrest from the garden. The most direct reference to Jesus's night in the garden, however, is the episode titled "Gethsemane," back in Season 4. At the end of this episode, Mulder is alone in his apartment crying. But the title also foreshadows Mulder's alleged death (which is the cliffhanger into the next season). The apparent betrayal is by Scully, who is seen at the beginning and end of the episode testifying before an FBI panel to the "illegitimacy of Agent Mulder's work." In the sequel ("Redux"), of course, the audience learns that all is not as it seems, with Mulder's "death" or with Scully's testimony.

Another moment that may depict Gethsemane for Mulder comes later in the same story arc, in "Redux II." Late one evening, Mulder appears by Scully's hospital bed. Like the disciples who accompanied Jesus, she is asleep, while Mulder kneels beside her in a penitent position, distraught and weeping. (There is perhaps another parallel in "One Breath," when Mulder spends a nighttime vigil by Scully's hospital bed, and then returns to his apartment and crouches down, sobbing.) This scene in "Redux II" is also significant because it is connected to Mulder's temptation by "the devil" (CSM): Mulder has apparently turned down CSM's offer to sell his soul in order to gain the Truth, but as Mulder explains later to Scully, during that moment by her hospital bed he was feeling lost and was still contemplating taking the deal—he was still undergoing temptation. With his own arrest imminent, he was looking for a way to avoid it, but he struggled with the tension between what he wanted and what he knew was right.

The garden of Gethsemane, like the garden of Eden, is a place of testing and temptation. Just as later on the cross Jesus must endure taunts to throw himself down and see if God will rescue him, in the garden he genuinely struggles with his human desire to avoid the suffering and death awaiting him. Like the three temptations in the wilderness, there is a pattern of three in Gethsemane: three times Jesus prays to the Father and then goes to his three disciples to find that they are sleeping. He tells Peter, "Keep awake and pray that you may not come into the time of trial [or, "into temptation"]; the spirit indeed is willing, but the flesh is weak" (Mark 14:38). The weakness of Jesus's own flesh is highlighted by his prayers in the garden, as he asks God to take from him "this cup" (referring to his blood about to be poured out). Jesus admits that it is not impossible for God to change the circumstances, since, as he prays to his Father, "for you all things are possible" (v. 36). But while it may be possible, it may not be God's will, and that, in the end, is what Jesus asks for: "not my will but yours be done" (Luke 22:42).

As the letter to the Hebrews describes, "In the days of his flesh, Jesus offered up prayers and supplications, with loud cries and tears, to the one who was able to save him from death, and he was heard because of his reverent submission. Although he was a Son, he learned obedience through what he suffered; and having been made perfect, he became the source of eternal salvation for all who obey him" (Hebrews 5:7–9). While it was not Jesus's desire to suffer and die, this was necessary in the greater plan in order to pay the death sentence that reached back to Adam and to release the many into eternal life. But despite Jesus's hesitation, his human fear and weakness, he obediently submitted to God's will and followed the course set for him. Hebrews says that Jesus's prayers and cries were heard—but that doesn't mean they were answered in the way that his heart desired. The prayer God answered was to do his will, which Jesus knew was for the greater good. As Hebrews explains earlier, Jesus underwent this weakness of his flesh, and this time of testing in the garden, so that he could identify with us in our human frailty: "Because he himself was tested [or, "tempted"] by what he suffered, he is able to help those who are being tested" (Hebrews 2:18; see also vv. 10–17).

Another source of distress and sorrow for Jesus, of course, was that not only would he soon be handed over to the soldiers but it would happen at the hands (and lips) of one of his own disciples. While in "Amor Fati" Scully stands in for the Judas depicted in *The Last Temptation of Christ*, two other figures during the course of the series represent a more traditional Judas, with a Judas kiss. The first is Krycek, who initially appears as Mulder's partner and eager pupil in the paranormal, but soon shows his true colors as a turncoat. In "The Red and the Black," Krycek shows up at Mulder's apartment in the dark, holding a gun on him. Krycek comes to impart information, as a friend. Before he leaves, he kisses Mulder on the cheek—a Judas kiss from a character known for his duplicity. The other character who plays a possible Judas is Diana Fowley, whom Scully suspects of betrayal practically from day one. Diana is clearly playing both sides of the game, but it is unclear whether her true loyalties lie with Mulder and the X-Files or with the Consortium. In "One Son" (6x12), the tension between Mulder and Scully over Diana finally comes to a head, and Mulder goes to Diana's apartment looking for evidence of the deceit that Scully has accused her of. What he does find is CSM, who tells him an elaborate tale about the alien conspiracy. Mulder remains alone in Diana's apartment, contemplating what he's heard. When Diana arrives, they converse briefly; then the scene closes with her leaning in to give him a kiss. She has claimed that her loyalties are to him, but is this a Judas kiss, belying her own words and denoting her betrayal?

The Trial

The betrayal by Judas, while heartbreaking, brought about the arrest and then trial of Jesus that were necessary to result in his crucifixion. Mulder's own trial comes in the series finale, "The Truth." Although the trials of Mulder and Jesus serve different purposes within their own narratives, they have a number of features in common. The main similarity is that neither trial is meant to be fair; the verdict is determined before the trial begins, and the "evidence" is stacked against the defendant. In Mulder's story, this fact is revealed through a secret meeting between representatives of the military (General Mark Suveg of the Marines) and the FBI (Deputy Director Alvin Kersh) to set up the hearing:

> GENERAL SUVEG: We both got a problem with this man of yours, Agent Mulder.
>
> KERSH: Mulder's been a running problem for the FBI. But nothing this serious . . .
>
> GENERAL SUVEG: You wanted a chance to clear up this mess, Mr. Kersh, and I'm going to give it to you, give it to the FBI . . . A fair hearing for your agent by his own agency. Your prosecutor, your judges. Held in my court.
>
> KERSH: That can't be legal. Why do this?
>
> GENERAL SUVEG: I want a verdict. A guilty verdict. This man Mulder has made a lot of enemies. He's a crusader. And a lot of people do not like the crusade.

Such plotting begs the question, with both Mulder and Jesus, If the trial is just for show, why bother with it at all? Why are the authorities so determined to kill this man and to do it in this way?

The popularity of a figure like Mulder or Jesus serves as the reason why the authorities want him out of the picture, and why they have allowed him to live so many times before. In the Gospels, as animosity grows toward Jesus, it is repeatedly noted that his opponents want to kill him, but they are afraid that the crowds who follow him and hang on his every word might riot or attack them (e.g., Mark 11:18; 14:1–2; John 5:18; 7:1). Mulder too, although he is a nuisance to the shadow men in the government for so long, is often spared because they fear that by killing him they risk transforming him into a revered martyr, thereby "turning one man's quest into a crusade" (*Fight the Future*; see also "Ascension," "Anasazi," "Talitha Cumi"). Both Mulder and Jesus attempt to bring truth and justice to the people, often clashing with leadership in the process. Jesus is not an innocuous teacher of parables but a prophet and religious revolutionary. He voices truths that the religious leaders don't want to hear. His teachings are radical, and so is the forgiveness that he offers. He speaks as one with authority who, independent of the religious establishment, can restore health and community, forgive sins, and define for the people how to observe the Sabbath and fulfill the law. His act of overturning tables in the temple and his prophecy of its destruction are taken as a challenge to the priesthood and the Jewish leaders, and they respond by putting down the threat. Jesus, like Mulder after him, provokes the rulers one too many times, and they want him dead. In either case, the trial is not intended as a fair hearing to allow the accused to prove his innocence; it is merely a means to publicly justify his death by making the verdict and execution appear legal.

After Jesus's arrest, he is taken to a hearing before the high priest and the priestly council, and false witnesses are brought forward to give testimony against him. Jesus doesn't try to defend himself against the charges. But when the testimonies disagree, the high priest is determined to find something for which he can convict Jesus, so he asks Jesus a loaded question to find cause to charge him with blasphemy. The council agrees with the charge and condemns Jesus to death. The guards then mock him and beat him. In Mulder's situation, the beating precedes the trial, as he is repeatedly hit and kicked by a guard in the military prison until he will "confess" to murder, or simply become submissive enough not to resist the charges and defend himself. Mulder recognizes that the trial is just for show and the intention is to discredit and kill him regardless of the case he presents. As Mulder says, "My trial's a foregone conclusion. What they really want is for me to admit my guilt and help them out. What's really on trial here is the truth." But the truth won't save him. The evidence against him includes the body of the victim, who isn't actually the victim, and Scully isn't allowed to give testimony that the evidence is false. Scully asks Mulder to take the witness stand and testify on his own behalf, but he refuses. The panel's verdict against Mulder is guilty, with a sentence of death.

Another significant parallel between the trials of Jesus and of Mulder comes with the collaboration of two groups of authorities in order to make the execution "legal." For Jesus, he is brought first to the Jewish religious authorities, the priestly council (and in Luke, he is also later brought before Herod, the Jewish political ruler), then to the Roman authority, Pontius Pilate. While the Jewish leadership delivers Jesus's death sentence, the Roman collaboration is necessary to carry it out, especially by means of crucifixion. In the same way,

Mulder's trial and planned execution is a collaboration (or conspiracy) of the FBI and the military. Mulder is held in a military prison, and only the military has the power to convict and execute him through their courts, but the trial is actually put on by the FBI. The FBI panel serves as the council of priests before which Mulder must answer for himself; he is therefore tried and condemned by his own kind (the FBI), just as Jesus is convicted by his own people (the Jews). The military, then, as Pilate does, represents the political authority that makes the execution possible but tries to wash its hands of the condemned man by putting his death squarely on the shoulders of the other group (the Jews, or the FBI).

The Crucifixion

As the Passion Narrative continues, after Jesus is condemned by the priestly council and then by Pilate, he begins the final journey to the cross. It is an exercise in mockery and torture. First beaten by the Jewish guards, then flogged at Pilate's command, Jesus is already bloody and bruised when he is handed over to the soldiers who prepare him for crucifixion. The Romans have charged Jesus with declaring himself king of the Jews (and thus with being a political insurgent), so the soldiers mockingly clothe him in the purple robes of royalty and twist thorns into a crown to put on his head. They spit on him and scoff at him, derisively hailing him, "King of the Jews!" (The same title is later affixed to his cross.) Jesus is then led off to be executed, carrying his cross to Golgotha. His hands (or wrists) and feet are nailed to the cross, and he is left to hang there in pain until he dies. People continue to deride him and mock him, challenging him to prove that he is the messiah by saving himself. In his agony, Jesus calls out the words opening Psalm 22: "My God, my God, why have you forsaken me?" (Mark 15:34). Finally, with a loud cry, he gives up his last breath. When the Roman soldiers come by later, they pierce his side with a sword to ensure that he is dead, and out of his side flow blood and water. Before dark arrives, and with it the Sabbath, Jesus's followers take his body and lay him in a tomb, sealing it with a rock across the opening. The king of the Jews lies dead.

While Mulder never experiences such a gruesome and public death, he undergoes his own crucifixions, at least symbolically. After he is abducted at the end of Season 7 (following his last supper and Gethsemane in "Requiem"), Mulder appears at the beginning of Season 8 ("Within"/"Without") attached to what looks like a torture device, inside a spaceship. Although he is seated, his limbs are awkwardly extended, and rods pierce his ankles and forearms, binding him to the chair. Another device is attached to his face, piercing his skin at three points on each cheek and pulling the skin outward. When Mulder returns from the dead a few months later, he still has these marks on his face. Rather than his side being punctured, it is his chest, as a drill descends and starts to slice into him. Another symbolic crucifixion occurs during "Amor Fati," when Mulder lies on the operating table with his arms extended and a surgical halo around his head. In that instance, CSM appears in the reverse position, upside-down from Mulder, with their heads adjacent, and CSM has his own "crown"—he is trying to take the messiah's place, but as a hero, not a martyr.

One theme in "Amor Fati" that is not directly borrowed from *The Last Temptation of Christ* is the father-son relationship and its role in Mulder's "crucifixion." CSM appears in the first scene of Mulder's dream sequence and presents himself as Mulder's father. As CSM reaches out his hand to lead Mulder from his hospital bed into the fantasy world, he mimics the image in Mulder's dream-within-a-dream of a toddler learning to walk and his father reaching out to guide him. Later dialogue between CSM and Diana Fowley, while Mulder lies incapacitated before them, reinforces the man's role as Mulder's father. CSM muses, "A father has high hopes for his son, but he never dreams his boy's going to change the world. I'm so proud of this man, the depth of his capacity for suffering." Diana replies, "Like father, like son," which presages CSM's attempt to steal Mulder's position as hero. But Diana eventually seems to have a change of heart as she recognizes that the procedure they are doing on Mulder may be fatal. She tells CSM, "You're removing genetic material that may kill your son." But he remains unconcerned, focused rather on the fact that he himself can become the revered savior: "We're forcing the next step in evolution to save man. We're doing God's work, Diana. Without this immunity, everyone would die. This knowledge is God's blessing. I'll carry on for Mulder from here." As a father, CSM is willing to sacrifice his son for what he claims is the greater good, but it may really be only for his own pride and selfishness.

The motif of a parent sacrificing a child emerges early in *The X-Files* with the abduction of Samantha. Exactly what part her parents played in her disappearance remains ambiguous, but it is implied that giving up one of their children was a condition of throwing in with the aliens, and that they had a choice as to which of their children would be taken. Mulder receives various explanations for why Samantha was chosen, what happened to her after she was taken from their home, and the importance of the tests performed on her and on the other abductees for the good of humanity's or her own survival. But none of these answers is really sufficient. Mulder cannot accept that his own parents, especially his father, would willingly hand over one of their children. And Mulder must live with the fact that while Samantha was chosen to be taken, he was chosen to stay behind and survive. Mulder would gladly sacrifice himself in his sister's place, if only he were given the choice. We can certainly understand this desire, and we wonder along with him how any parent could hand over their child to such a fate.

Another story about a father sacrificing his child is told in the Bible, in Genesis 22. After God has miraculously blessed Abraham and his wife Sarah with a son, Isaac, God tests Abraham. God asks Abraham to "Take your son, your only son Isaac, whom you love, and go to the land of Moriah, and offer him there as a burnt offering on one of the mountains that I shall show you" (v. 2). So Abraham obediently gathers wood for the fire, takes his son and some servants, and begins the trek toward Moriah. When they arrive, Abraham gives Isaac the wood to carry, and the two of them make their way to the place of the sacrifice. Along the way, Isaac speaks up. "Father, . . . the fire and the wood are here, but where is the lamb for a burnt offering?" (v. 7). With Abraham's reply, we finally learn what he has been thinking along this journey. He tells Isaac, "God himself will provide the lamb for a burnt offering, my son." But as they arrive at the location, no sacrificial animal awaits them. Abraham begins to go through the motions. He builds an altar and places the wood on it. Then he binds Isaac and lays him on top of the wood. Abraham pulls out his knife and holds it over his son, ready to kill him—but then a voice speaks from heaven: "Abraham! . . . Do not lay your hand on the boy or do anything to him; for now I know that you fear God, since you have not withheld your son, your only son, from me" (vv. 11–12). Abraham looks over into the thicket and sees a ram caught by its horns; just as Abraham has told his son would happen, God has provided an animal for the sacrifice.

This story is seen as a testament to Abraham's loyalty to and faith in God, that Abraham is willing to give up the thing dearest to him—what God has promised to him and provided for him—if God asks it. The point of the account is not that God desires child sacrifice; it is clear elsewhere in the Bible that he finds the act reprehensible (e.g., Leviticus 18:21; Deuteronomy 12:31; Jeremiah 7:31; Ezekiel 16:20–21). Because such sacrifice is unthinkable, it is challenging for us to accept how Abraham can go so far in his actions. Yet for the same reason we can easily sympathize with the anguish of giving up his son—his only son—in this manner. In *The X-Files*, Bill Mulder has faced a similar dilemma. The aliens demanded that he and the other conspirators give up a family member as a form of collateral in the agreement between the Consortium and the aliens. CSM portrays the negative example: he has callously and readily given up his wife to the aliens; then later, in "Amor Fati," he coldheartedly sacrifices Mulder, a man he considers to be his son. Bill Mulder, on the other hand, apparently has not given in so easily to the aliens' demands. Mulder is told, however, that because his father did not follow through with the agreement, Samantha was taken anyway ("One Son").

The way Samantha was forcibly removed from her family is reminiscent of the fate of several teenagers in "Die Hand Die Verletzt" (2x14). Long ago, some of the locals made a deal with the devil and committed themselves to Satanic worship. But over time they became complacent and watered down their observance of the old rituals. One of these backslidden worshippers is Jim Ausbury, the father of a girl who is murdered. He explains to Mulder, "The blood of the young is considered very powerful. We'd include them in the ceremonies, against their will . . . But we never physically hurt them. We'd slip over the ancient rituals that we didn't want to do." Mulder replies, "Like drinking grape juice instead of wine at communion?" (Mulder thus points out the man's own hypocrisy, since Ausbury has just said that he was raised to believe "Christianity was synonymous with hypocrisy.") However, the devil is not content with their lukewarm observances and has come to claim payment, with interest. These people do not willingly offer up their children, so the devil, appearing as a kindly teacher and a slithering snake, seizes the children for himself, taking his own blood sacrifice.

There are notable differences between, on the one hand, what the devil does here and what the aliens have done to the Mulders, and on the other, what God has done in the story of Abraham and beyond. In the *X-Files* episode, the devil comes in and claims the children for himself. He wants blood, and when it is no longer offered willingly, he comes and takes it. God, however, does not want the blood of Abraham's son—he wants Abraham's faith and obedience (cf. 1 Samuel 15:22; Hosea 6:6; Matthew 9:13; 12:7). Rather than taking Isaac for himself, God provides a sacrifice so that Isaac will be spared. But as history has unfolded, the story of Abraham and Isaac also has taken on deeper meaning. Abraham tells his son, "God himself will provide the lamb," and when Jesus later came to the earth, that is exactly what God did. Jesus, the Lamb of God, came to be the sacrifice, to spare the lives of all of Abraham's children (as God promised and fulfilled, that Abraham would become the father of many nations—through the endangered Isaac). God, like Abraham, sacrificed his only son. Through Abraham's account, we can understand how that was no easy thing for a father to do. But if the story simply ended there, with a father offering his son on an altar, it would still be difficult for us to accept. Thankfully, there is more. God did not merely give up his son—he gave up himself. Jesus, as God, willingly came to earth to become the lamb. God himself suffered and died so that we, as the children of Abraham, could live.

In the garden of Gethsemane, Jesus called out to his Father, asking him to remove the calling to crucifixion if it was at all possible within God's will. Hebrews 5:7 says that Jesus's prayer was heard, and yet it was still necessary for him to die. In Jesus's pleas we can hear echoes of Isaac's questions to Abraham as they travel to Moriah, and we can imagine the distress of a father who knows that he must follow through with the sacrifice. But even in the crucifixion, God showed his Son mercy by not allowing Jesus to suffer on the cross any longer or any more than necessary. As painful as Jesus's death was, it was fairly swift for this type of execution. John 19 illustrates this point: because the Jews want to remove the bodies from the crosses before the Sabbath, the soldiers come by to break the legs of the criminals so they will die more quickly. But when they get to Jesus, they see that he is already dead and don't break his legs. Through his swift death and therefore the fact that his bones remain intact, Jesus is further identified with the Passover lamb, whose bones were not to be broken (v. 36; see Exodus 12:46; Numbers 9:12; cf. Psalm 34:20). Jesus willingly came to earth to become the sacrificial lamb for humanity, and so his death had to take place. But God heard Jesus's prayers from Gethsemane and had compassion on his Son, sparing him any excessive agony.[6] In this, God has shown his love both for his only Son and for all who would become his children through that one act of self-sacrifice. Most important, though, God gave his Son—and therefore all his children—victory over death by restoring him to life.

The Resurrection and the Ascension

Not only did God not allow Jesus to suffer on the cross any longer than necessary, God also did not keep Jesus in the grave any longer than he had to stay. Prophecy foretold that Jesus would rise on the third day. He died on a Friday, the first day; Saturday, the Sabbath, was the second; and by dawn on the third, Sunday morning, the stone had been rolled away from the tomb and Jesus was risen. The Gospels retell numerous resurrection appearances that follow as Jesus visits his disciples to show them that he has returned as promised. One disciple in particular earns his reputation as doubting Thomas because he can't accept, based merely on the testimony of others, that this is really Jesus and that he is physically raised. "Unless I see the marks of the nails in his hands, and put my fingers in the mark of the nails and my hand in his side," Thomas says, "I will not believe" (John 20:25). Jesus then appears to him and the other disciples, still bearing the marks of his crucifixion, so that Thomas can touch him and believe. After forty days, the time comes for Jesus to depart, so he ascends into heaven and leaves them the Spirit so they can carry on his work.

Mulder too has experienced resurrection. In fact, Mulder is presumed dead, or "crucified," and resurrected at least once every other season of *The X-Files* (not counting the number of times that he cheats death while on a case). At the end of Season 2, Mulder is caught in a train car that is bombed; while his body is not found inside, it is assumed that he has been killed. Soon after, however, he is found a short distance away, barely clinging to life. Before he returns home after he is restored to health, he makes a resurrection appearance, visiting Scully in a dream. When he comes home, to find Skinner and Scully having a standoff in his apartment, he tells them, "I was a dead man. Now, I'm back" ("Paper Clip," 3x02). Two years later, at the end of Season 4, the finale again closes with Mulder presumed dead, this time from an apparent suicide ("Gethsemane"). But as the next season opens, in "Redux" (i.e., "brought back"), we find out that Mulder is actually alive. When Mulder finally emerges from hiding in "Redux II," Skinner says, "You're moving pretty good for a dead man." Mulder replies, "I'm only half dead" (the "half" likely referring to Scully, who is dying of cancer), and he later quips to Scully, "I'm officially among the undead." At the end of Season 6, Mulder is hospitalized, and the story arc concludes at the beginning of Season 7 with Mulder on the cross in "Amor Fati," from which he is rescued as Scully literally raises him up.

The most overt parallels between Mulder and the death and resurrection of Jesus, however, come in Season 8. This is the story line that begins with Mulder's last supper and "arrest" by the aliens in "Requiem," and with the piercing of his flesh on the alien torture device ("Within," 8x01/"Without," 8x02). Midway through Season 8, Mulder returns to complete this narrative. At the end of "This Is Not Happening" (8x14), Mulder's body is found, and he is buried at the beginning of "DeadAlive" (8x15). Then, doing Jesus one better, Mulder is in the grave for three *months*. When another alien abductee turns up alive, it is realized that Mulder might not be dead, so he is exhumed and soon restored to life. For a time, he still bears the marks of his "crucifixion": scars on his face from the piercings by the aliens (just as Jesus still has scars that he can show to doubting Thomas). Although the intended parallels may end there, Mulder also imitates the end of Jesus's earthly story by remaining with his followers for only a few short weeks after his resurrection and then leaving them, at the beginning of Season 9. This final season becomes the next chapter in the narrative, with the followers attempting to pick up where the messiah left off, as the disciples of Jesus do in the book of Acts.

At Mulder's funeral in "DeadAlive," the minister reads a text from the Gospel of John: "I am the resurrection, and the life: he that believeth in me, though he were dead, yet shall he live. And whosoever liveth and believeth in me shall never die" (11:25–26, KJV). This quotation is also repeated by the necromancer in "Millennium" (7x05) while he is raising the dead, or trying to protect himself from the dead. In John, Jesus speaks these words to Martha before he resurrects her brother, Lazarus. Jesus is good friends with Lazarus and his sisters, Mary and Martha. When Lazarus is deathly ill, the family sends word to Jesus, knowing that Jesus will be able to heal him. But Jesus doesn't come right away; he deliberately waits two more days. By the time Jesus and his disciples arrive, Lazarus has been dead and buried for four days. Martha comes out to meet Jesus and tells him, "Lord, if you had been here, my brother would not have died" (11:21; later, Mary says exactly the same thing [v. 32]). Jesus responds by telling Martha, "I am the resurrection, and the life . . ." (vv. 25–26). Some of the mourners then have the same reaction as do Martha and Mary: "Could not he who opened the eyes of the blind man have kept this man from dying?" (v. 37). But Jesus has a different plan. He goes to the tomb and tells them to roll away the stone. Mary complains, "Lord, already there is a stench because he has been dead four days" (v. 39). Jesus says to her, "Did I not tell you that if you believed, you would see the glory of God?" (v. 40), and he calls Lazarus forth from the tomb. Lazarus emerges, still wrapped in his burial cloths, and Jesus tells them to unbind him and set him free.

The raising of Lazarus is a foreshadowing first and foremost of Jesus's resurrection. Only two chapters later in John, Jesus begins the final journey toward the cross. By resurrecting Lazarus, he gives his followers hope that the promise that he himself will rise from the dead can come true. But, as Jesus explains to Martha, Lazarus's resurrection is also an example for all who will come after him that faith in Jesus can lead to renewed life. While Martha already believes that all people will be resurrected for judgment on the last day (John

11:24), what Jesus promises is yet something more: resurrection to life—eternal life. The purpose of the resurrection Jesus offers isn't merely to raise the body or to keep people on earth in this mortal life only to die again; the purpose is to be raised into true life, life untainted by death. This is why Jesus, although grieved, is not concerned about the death of Lazarus: he knows it isn't permanent. For all who believe that Jesus is the resurrection and the life, then, as for Lazarus, death is only temporary; what awaits is resurrection into everlasting life.

This point, however—that Jesus's emphasis is on not earthly life but eternal life—seems to be missed at times by *X-Files* characters who attempt to resurrect the dead. "Millennium" is one illustration: the necromancer does succeed in bringing back to life the man that he dug up from the grave, but the man is little more than a zombie. His body has life, or at least animation, but doesn't appear to have much of a mind or a soul. The same problem emerges in "Kaddish" (4x12) when Ariel, with good intentions, constructs a golem of her slain fiancé. While Isaac is brought back to life, in a way, he is by no means the man she fell in love with. He is merely a monster, a creature without a soul, who can only react on impulse to avenge his own death. A more comical example occurs in "Je Souhaite" (7x21). After the genie grants Anson Stokes his wish to turn invisible, he runs out and gets hit by a truck because the driver can't see him. His brother Leslie then uses one of his own three wishes to, literally, "bring him back." Unfortunately, Leslie doesn't specify in what condition he wants Anson to come back. So Anson does return, but he still smells dead (like Lazarus), he can't talk until Leslie wishes that he can (and then, he can only scream, just as he was doing when he died), and his heart isn't beating. Anson may be "back," but what he has isn't life.

A different dilemma arises in the episode named after the story in John 11: "Lazarus" (1x14). When two men are dying in the emergency room, and both flatline, only one is brought back from the dead. The only problem is, he has the soul of the other guy. What results isn't truly "life" for either one of them, since one man exists only in body, and the other man no longer has the body that other people recognize, so what life he has is not his own. In "Miracle Man," another character who is identified with Lazarus, Leonard Vance, expresses what all of these resurrected characters may be feeling: "You call this life?" Leonard was killed in a fire before Samuel Hartley raised him from the dead, but even when Leonard was restored to life, his skin was permanently melted and scarred from the flames. In the biblical story of Lazarus, the account ends with Lazarus emerging from the tomb, but he doesn't get a chance to share his side of the story. Leonard provides an interesting take on "the rest of the story," showing us what life is like for a Lazarus figure after his resurrection. Rather than having faith in Samuel for this miracle, Leonard views Samuel as a wolf in sheep's clothing because he sees the gift of life instead as a curse ("Who else would bring me back," he says, "looking like this?"). Lazarus thus becomes Judas, but in his last moments, when he encounters the resurrected Samuel, he finally comes to truly believe. Before Leonard dies from an overdose, his last gasping words are, "He forgave me." It isn't until the very end that Leonard comes to understand Jesus's lesson in the Lazarus story—that the real focus of resurrection goes beyond life in this mortal, mutable flesh.

Unless you're Mulder, then, resurrection on *The X-Files* often turns out to be not such a good thing. While these characters may be raised in the flesh, they are not truly raised to life, and certainly not to life that will last (in fact, all of the resurrected characters just mentioned end up dead again by the close of the episodes in which they appear). The necromancer in "Millennium" may quote the words of Jesus, "I am the resurrection and the life," but he treats them merely as a magical formula. In the process, he misses their true meaning: Jesus is the resurrection to life everlasting, the life into which we will be raised beyond this world. In contrast to the undead in *The X-Files*, the story of Lazarus serves as a reminder for all of us that the death and decay of our bodies is only temporary—if we believe in Jesus. This too is part of the quotation from John's Gospel that the necromancer seems to have overlooked. As Jesus tells Martha, "those who believe in me" will have life. It is not enough simply to believe that eternal life is possible; we must trust in the source of that life, in Life himself. Although Jesus does raise Lazarus to life in the here and now, the point he is making by this action—about faith and eternal life—is much greater. The point of his own resurrection is greater still.

Besides John 11:25–26, another favorite verse of the necromancer in "Millennium" is Revelation 1:18: "I am he that liveth, and was dead; and, behold, I am alive for evermore, Amen; and have the keys of hell and of death" (KJV). The verse also makes an appearance in "The Field Where I Died" (4x05), spoken by the cult leader who believes he has lived past lives (see chapter 3, above). This statement is voiced by the resurrected Jesus in the book of Revelation. The keys he refers to show his authority or power over death, and by the end of the book, he uses that authority to reopen the way to the tree of life—the way to Eden. Through his resurrection Jesus has gained victory over death, not merely for himself, but for everyone who has been subject to death since Adam and Eve lost access to the tree of life. The Apostle Paul thus compares the life that comes through Jesus to the death that came through Adam: "For since death came through a human being, the resurrection of the dead has also come through a human being; for as all die in Adam, so all will be made alive in Christ" (1 Corinthians 15:21–22).[7] Jesus came as the new Adam to undo the damage done to creation when Adam and Eve fell away from God's ideal for them. Thus, the eternal life that Jesus offers to all who would believe in him is nothing less than eternity in Paradise.

THE GIFT

What Jesus demonstrated through his life, death, and resurrection, his followers carried on in his absence. The next generation was pioneered by Paul, and others like him, who explained the meaning of who Jesus was and what he had done. Paul often described Jesus's offer of eternal life as grace—a gift that is not earned or deserved but freely given; it can only be freely accepted, and never fully repaid. "But God, who is rich in mercy, out of the great love with which he loved us even when we were dead through our trespasses, made us alive together with Christ . . . For by grace you have been saved through faith, and this is not your own doing; it is the gift of God—not the result of works, so that no one may boast" (Ephesians 2:4–5, 8–9). The salvation that Jesus has provided, saving us from the sentence of death by taking it on himself, is offered gratis, a free gift. Faith is the means of accepting the gift, and obedience or good works (loving God and each other) is the thank-you note. The fact that the gift cannot be earned or repaid spares us from pride, the very thing that was the biggest stumbling block for Adam and Eve.

The generosity and expense of such grace is illustrated in "The Gift" (8x11). During Mulder's absence, Agent Doggett sets out to learn the truth about a case that Mulder once investigated involving a "soul eater" or "sin-catcher shaman." The soul eater is human to some degree but looks more like a monster as a result of his special gift: he is able to consume the sickness of others. But his special ability is really more of a gift to the others, as he takes their sickness within himself so that they can be made well. Their illnesses have left him looking sickly, giving him his monstrous appearance. The soul eater performs these miracles by literally consuming the sick; he then regurgitates them, as though rebirthing them, and they are restored to their original form whole, no longer diseased. As Doggett comes to understand that this is the nature of the creature that Mulder was researching, Doggett also realizes something else that Mulder knew: the soul eater lives in incredible suffering and pain because of the pain he takes into himself. Mulder tried to kill the soul eater, as a mercy killing, but the creature didn't die. Doggett likewise wants to take the soul eater away from the community that is abusing his gift, to treat the soul eater humanely, but Doggett is rewarded for his efforts by getting shot in the back by an angry mob. He falls to the ground, dead. We see the dirt thrown onto his face as he is buried. But then later, Doggett wakes, rebirthed. Near him, the soul eater lies motionless on the ground. The woman who cares for the creature tells Doggett, "All these years we didn't know what it could do. It took your death. You freed it." By taking on Doggett's death, the soul eater restores him to life and dies in Doggett's place. In that death is a release, as the soul eater's suffering has finally come to an end.

The soul eater in many ways parallels the role that Jesus played as a healer. The correspondence is especially clear in Isaiah 53, one of the Suffering Servant passages prophesied in the book of Isaiah that was fulfilled by Jesus (see Matthew 8:17):

> Surely he has borne our infirmities and carried our diseases; yet we accounted him stricken, struck down by God, and afflicted. But he was wounded for our transgressions, crushed for our iniquities; upon him was the punishment that made

us whole, and by his bruises we are healed. All we like sheep have gone astray; we have all turned to our own way, and the Lord has laid on him the iniquity of us all. He was oppressed, and he was afflicted, yet he did not open his mouth; like a lamb that is led to the slaughter, and like a sheep that before its shearers is silent, so he did not open his mouth. By a perversion of justice he was taken away. Who could have imagined his future? For he was cut off from the land of the living, stricken for the transgression of my people. (Isaiah 53:4–8)

In this passage, there are echoes of the trial, beatings, and death of Jesus. But the similarity with the soul eater is especially apparent in the references to infirmities and diseases that Jesus has taken on himself; and by his bruises or stripes we are healed. Our suffering has become his, and his suffering has made us whole. The soul eater is a visual depiction of this; his very appearance reveals what taking on such immense suffering would do to a person. This text from Isaiah also correlates infirmities and iniquities, diseases and transgressions. In other words, sickness is a representation of sin or evil (see chapter 5, above), and persistent wrongdoing can make a person physically or spiritually ill. Hence, the soul eater is also referred to as a "sin-catcher shaman" (recalling the British tradition of a sin eater who would consume food and drink over a dead person to consume their sins), so that to devour sickness is associated with devouring sin.

In a way, the soul eater is the antithesis of Leonard Betts ("Leonard Betts," 4x14). Leonard is completely riddled with cancer; it is his normal state of being. What he reflects is the person who has let sin or evil become the regular course of life. Leonard's gift is to see the sickness within people, to diagnose cancer. Like the soul eater, he too consumes their illness. But his motives, and the results, are quite the opposite of the soul eater's. Leonard devours people's cancer out of his own selfish appetite, to their harm and his gain, strengthening himself through their weakness and death. The soul eater instead consumes sickness out of selflessness; it is entirely for the benefit of the "victims," while the soul eater is harmed and becomes weak. Leonard, though he appears human, is monstrous in his callous preying on human life. The soul eater looks on the outside as Leonard (and others like him who are riddled with cancerous sin) appears on the inside; but for those who look closely at the soul eater, they can see his lingering humanity in his willingness to give of himself entirely for the good of others.

While there is similarity between the soul eater and the story of Jesus, there are also some contrasts, especially in how the sickness affects the healer. In the Gospels, the illnesses that Jesus heals are often described as uncleanness (leprosy, for example), and the demons he casts out are referred to as unclean spirits. This stems from Jewish notions of holiness and purity, especially as they relate to the temple, God's holy place. As the law of Moses describes repeatedly, particularly in the book of Leviticus, if someone touches a thing or person that is unclean, that individual will also become unclean and must undergo certain rituals in order to be clean again and restored to community or worship. With a disease like leprosy, it is easy to see how this is considered "unclean" (just as today we are urged to wash and sterilize when we're sick or exposed to others who are sick), and how anyone who comes into contact with such a person would become unclean. There is a simple logic here: if something clean touches something dirty, the clean becomes dirty. Jesus, however, reverses this logic. When he touches people who are physically or spiritually unclean, he doesn't become unclean himself; rather, his holiness, or purity, makes them whole. His touch heals them. An example is the woman with a long-standing flow of blood. The bleeding makes her ritually unclean; but by her merely touching the fringe of Jesus's garment, his wholeness becomes hers, and she is healed (Mark 5:24–34). In the case of the soul eater, the sickness of others makes him unhealthy, so that he takes on a sickly appearance. With Jesus, the opposite is true: when he takes on our infirmities, we acquire his holiness, so that both of us are whole.

The ultimate similarity between Jesus and the soul eater—the point at which healing is taken to its extreme—also reveals their greatest difference. The soul eater's supreme and final act of healing is to take on death in order to give life. The death he consumes then becomes his own. Like the soul eater, Jesus has taken not only our sickness but our death upon himself, which resulted in his own death. While the soul eater's story ends here, however, Jesus's story continues and in a sense is just beginning. Jesus died, but he was raised again in victory over death to claim the prize of everlasting life. Therefore, when we reach out like the woman with the flow of blood and take on Jesus's wholeness, we take on his life as well. There is another parallel in "The Gift" that illustrates how the consumption also goes both ways. The symbol used to summon the soul eater to the house of the sick is a circle containing a cross, which is painted on the door. In the episode, this symbol is described as a medicine wheel, but it also resembles a communion wafer: a round wafer with a square cross at the center. The wafer, the bread, is the flesh of Christ consumed in the Eucharist. It represents Christ's body broken for us, when he consumed our death. In commemorating that act, then, we consume his flesh as well, receiving within ourselves his holiness and wholeness and the life that death cannot overcome.

While Jesus's death was by no means a mercy killing, as is the soul eater's, and while Jesus was not permanently deformed by taking on our diseased thoughts and actions, it is still important to recognize the significance of his suffering. As for the soul eater, for Jesus to bear our infirmities meant that he must suffer, and eventually die. In "Paper Clip," when Albert Hosteen gets word that the mother of a rare white buffalo calf has died just days after giving birth, he recounts, "My father taught me when I was a boy that this is how life is. That for something to live, another thing must often be sacrificed." This is what happens with the soul eater. Through the suffering of the soul eater, even to the point of death, we can see the cost of healing and realize how precious a gift the rebirthing is for it to be purchased at such a high price. Likewise, through hearing the story of the suffering and death that Jesus went through for our sakes, we can appreciate that much more the value of his gift.

The fact that a guileless soul eater would suffer for the good of others, or that the Innocent One would be beaten and executed for others' crimes, recalls the problem of suffering that has surfaced in many ways throughout *The X-Files*. In "All Souls" (5x17), Mulder asks, "Why do bad things happen to good people?" In *I Want to Believe*, Scully says, "Why bring a kid into the world just to make him suffer?" The same issue arises as Mulder struggles over the deaths of the children in "Closure" (7x11), and it is alluded to in "Talitha Cumi" through the use of *The Brothers Karamazov* since it is the brothers' discussion about the suffering of children and of the Innocent One that prompts the telling of the Grand Inquisitor narrative. The question posed in these many and other ways can be encapsulated as, Why must the innocent suffer? Various answers have been offered or addressed in previous chapters, but there is one more to be presented here. It is not an answer, however, so much as a response. To the question, Why do the innocent suffer? the Bible replies, They don't suffer alone. The response God has given is to come down to earth and suffer alongside us.

The fact is, when we ask God the difficult questions or make our requests of him, sometimes the response he gives isn't the answer we want but the answer we need. That was true even for Jesus himself when he prayed in Gethsemane for God to spare him from impending death. Although Jesus reasoned with God, "for you all things are possible," he also accepted that what is possible isn't always what God desires. Martha and Mary too experienced this with the death of their brother. The women knew that Jesus was capable of healing Lazarus. But that wasn't Jesus's will in this situation. God may be able to change our circumstances, but his plan isn't always the same as ours. Sometimes, he has a greater purpose that we cannot see. This is essentially what Scully tells Mulder when she is struggling to understand the death of Dara Kernof, as well as the death of her daughter, Emily: "I was raised to believe that God has his reasons, however mysterious" ("All Souls"). Through the course of this episode, Scully's eyes are opened to God's greater purpose in this situation, which requires the physical death of the girls so that their souls may be released to a better life.

When we encounter human suffering, the response we often want from God is for him to remove it all immediately. Mulder illustrates this in "Je Souhaite" when he tries to "play God." What he attempts to do with his three wishes is what we expect God to do—to make it "a safer world, a happier world. There's going to be food for everyone, freedom for everyone, the end of the tyranny of the powerful over the weak." But Scully points out that maybe God's plan is different, maybe there's a reason for the struggles we go through—that the very purpose of our lives on this earth is for us to work together toward making the world safer and happier for everyone. Why must it happen this way? Why do the innocent suffer in the process? Because God allowed us the freedom to make our own choices; we chose to disobey, and that brought death and suffering into the world. But God didn't just sit up in heaven to watch, or to read the box scores, as Mulder puts it. God came down to earth to show us how to make our world a better place, and to offer beyond it a better place yet.

Jesus, who is God with us (see Matthew 1:23), came to suffer just as we do so that he can help us to walk through our own suffering (Hebrews 2:17-18). When Jesus taught to turn the other cheek, to go the extra mile, or to love those who persecute us (Matthew 5:38-48), he experienced it first himself and set the example by turning his cheek to be beaten, by dying even for those who would persecute him—dying for opponents like Saul, before he became the Apostle Paul (Acts 9:4-5). Paul too experienced sufferings (beatings, persecution, and imprisonment [see, for example, 2 Corinthians 11:23-29]), but he gladly accepted them as an opportunity to commiserate with others and to share with them the same comfort that he received through his own difficulties (2 Corinthians 1:3-5). The God we pray to in our time of need understands fully what we are going through because he came to earth as Jesus Christ to experience for himself human life and pain, and even human death. And as he helps us to walk through our own sufferings, we in turn can use the insight and comfort that we have received to help others go through similar challenges.

Although Jesus was God and had all the privileges that came with such power, he chose to come down and live as one of us, as someone who could hunger and thirst, who could weep, who could bleed, who could suffer and die (Philippians 2). This sense of solidarity, his utter humanity, may be what resonates so deeply about the account of Jesus, and why his story has continued to shape the lives of so many people. It is this human vulnerability in Jesus—especially through his temptations, suffering, and death—that has given rise to stories like "The Grand Inquisitor" and provides such prevalent motifs in the life of Mulder.[8] It is also this common thread of humanity that Mulder and Doggett recognize in the soul eater, enabling them to see him not as a senseless beast but as one of us, with rights and feelings. They see in the eyes of the soul eater the human pain that has become his own, and they understand the depth and cost of his gift.

Looking into the eyes of Jesus, we can also see the pain he experienced by taking on human flesh so that he could take on our sin and death. By giving up his throne in heaven to become the king of the Jews who would suffer and die, Jesus used his gifts—his power and his purity—to present us a gift of wiping clean the slate that was first messed up by Adam and Eve's disobedience. Since it is a gift, we are free to accept or reject it. By accepting it, that doesn't mean our suffering on this earth will automatically end, but we will walk through it with someone who has gone through suffering himself, and our suffering will have meaning. For, the Jesus who became a human being to live among us did not stay on earth; he ascended again to the throne he had once relinquished, where he sits next to God and remains the conduit between humanity and heaven, as our advocate in prayer, who knows firsthand what we're going through. He has also gone ahead to Paradise to prepare a place for us one day; the suffering we endure in this life will be no more than a blink of an eye compared with the peace and joy of abundant life that await us in the next.

This is the source of our hope, and the reason to have faith. The gift of life is freely offered to us, through the love of Jesus Christ—if we want to believe.

NOTES

1. See also 1 Corinthians 10:4, where the Apostle Paul identifies Jesus with the rock from which the Israelites drank in the wilderness. Note that in "Existence," the reference on the window reads, "Exodus 7:16"; however, the correct reference for the story of Moses drawing water from the rock is Exodus 17:6.

2. John J. Pierce ("The Spiritual Journey of Fox Mulder," *Spectrum* 8 [1997]: 2–9) also describes "The Three Temptations of Mulder" in "One Breath" (2x08), again when Mulder is emotionally weak because Scully is lying comatose in the hospital; the three temptations he rejects are (1) to walk away from it all, as Mr. X suggests, (2) to kill the Cigarette-Smoking Man, and (3) to stay in his apartment and kill the men who are coming to ransack it. Mulder chooses instead not to walk away or take revenge, but to go sit by Scully in the hospital, which may be the key to her waking from the coma.

3. For a fuller treatment of the parallels between this book and the episode "Amor Fati," see my article, "The Last Temptation of Mulder: Reading *The X-Files*

through the Christological Lens of Nikos Kazantzakis," in *"The X-Files" and Literature: Unweaving the Story, Unraveling the Lie to Find the Truth*, ed. Sharon R. Yang (Newcastle, UK: Cambridge Scholars, 2007), 2–29.

4. *I Want to Believe* provides an interesting parallel to the dream sequence in "Amor Fati," since it represents a Mulder who *has* given up the quest in exchange for a domestic life. Instead of facing his execution in the series finale, Mulder escapes (comes down from the cross) and runs off to live in hiding with the woman he loves. He becomes a hermit, secreted away in his new office, living as though with the blinds shut to the outside world and ignoring the coming alien apocalypse that he learned about before his arrest. Even the role of Deputy Director Kersh in the finale may have a parallel: in "Amor Fati," it is CSM who leads Mulder away from his road to martyrdom, just as in *The Last Temptation* it is Satan appearing in a friendly guise who leads Jesus away from the cross; so too Kersh, who until this point has always been a bad guy, suddenly appears to have a change of heart and helps Mulder escape from his upcoming execution to run off into a quiet life. In *I Want to Believe*, Mulder appears to be pulling his head back out of the sand to realize that he can't completely abandon the quest, that it is his fate and calling, but at the same time it stands in tension with a normal, domestic life (since Scully asks him to choose between the two). In this scenario, then, Scully is not Judas but Mary Magdalene.

5. Karen Wolf ("'Whosoever Believeth': Rereading the Bible through *The X-Files*," in Yang, *"The X-Files" and Literature*, 30–42) also describes Scully as a crucified and resurrected messiah during her abduction in Season 2: Scully is bound and gagged and taken up the mountain in "Ascension," like Christ's journey up to Golgotha. This happens in the first episode of her abduction arc; in the third episode (like on the third day), "One Breath," she returns to life. Her abduction is also a substitutionary sacrifice for Duane Barry, in whose place she is taken.

6. God no more wanted his son to suffer than he wants any of us to suffer: "Although [God] causes grief, he will have compassion according to the abundance of his steadfast love; for he does not willingly afflict or grieve anyone" (Lamentations 3:32–33).

7. Later in the same chapter, Paul continues,

> Thus it is written, "The first man, Adam, became a living being" [Genesis 2:7]; the last Adam became a life-giving spirit ... The first man was from the earth, a man of dust; the second man is from heaven ... Just as we have borne the image of the man of dust, we will also bear the image of the man of heaven ... When this perishable body puts on imperishability, and this mortal body puts on immortality, then the saying that is written will be fulfilled: "Death has been swallowed up in victory" [Isaiah 25:8]. "Where, O death, is your victory? Where, O death, is your sting?" [Hosea 13:14]. The sting of death is sin, and the power of sin is the law. But thanks be to God, who gives us the victory through our Lord Jesus Christ.
> (1 Corinthians 15:45, 47, 49, 54–57)

As Paul explains, through the first Adam, we have all been affected by death; through the second Adam, we can all have access to life. In this world, we bear the likeness of Adam in his earthly and perishable flesh. But Jesus has left us his Spirit, a foretaste of the spiritual life that awaits in the next world, where we can have heavenly bodies that no longer die or decay. Whoever chooses to believe in Jesus, though we will die, on this earth, yet shall we live in eternity.

8. In discussing the elements of *The Last Temptation of Christ* that he contributed to the script for "Amor Fati," David Duchovny refers to the humanity of Christ, especially through Kazantzakis's retelling, as what drew him to make the comparison with Mulder: "I wasn't saying Mulder is Christ; I'm not inflating Mulder. What I'm doing is using the very human model of Christ to make Mulder an everyman" (Paula Vitaris, "David Duchovny on 'The Unnatural' and 'Hollywood A.D.,'" *Morgan and Wong On-Line* [2004]; archived online at: http://etc1013.wordpress.com/2002/04/01/cinefantastique-7; a shorter version of this article was published as "David Duchovny's Grace Notes: Creating Episodes That Re-Think *The X-Files*," *Cinefantastique* 34, no. 2 [April 2002]: 54–55).

Epilogue

This book has only selectively addressed some of the many religious and spiritual themes in *The X-Files*. What these themes especially have in common is that the truth *out there* relates very much to the truth *right here*, namely the realities of the human condition. From the ethereal and sometimes elusive qualities of faith and belief, to the hope and love that give life meaning, to the humanity of a God who would become a man to suffer and die—the truths illuminated by the far-reaching tales of *The X-Files* are really the truths of what it means to live in this world.

The story of Mulder and Scully is in many ways the story of us all: people who grapple with the twists and turns that life hands them, when confronted with tragedy, suffering, and true evil, who try their best to make sense of it all through the human constants of faith, hope, and love. Mulder looks to the skies for his answers, Scully looks to the heavens, both out of the basic human desire to believe. While the series is built on the credos of wanting to believe and looking for truth out there, it is striking that so often the stories, and characters, return to the theme of the problem of evil and the suffering of the innocent. Whether intentionally or incidentally, the cross that Scully wears (or bears?) holds a key to both. The cross represents the One who took on human suffering, who suffered himself, in order to overcome evil, in the end.

For *The X-Files* itself, the end is still unwritten, and many questions remain unanswered. This too, however, is true to life. As long as we live on this earth, we are still in the middle of our stories—the end, and what follows, is yet to be told. We spend our lives searching for answers, but the ones we do find are not always to our satisfaction, and some answers are simply not to be found in the limitations of this lifetime. Like Mulder and Scully, though, we keep asking, we keep pursuing the elusive. Because, the truth is, we want to know—we want to believe. As long as this continues to be an essential part of humanity, there will be a place for religion, for faith and faith struggles, and for the message of the cross.

Appendix

Episodes Cited

(in order of airdate)

Pilot (1x79). Written by Chris Carter. Directed by Robert Mandel. Original airdate: September 10, 1993.

Deep Throat (1x01). Written by Chris Carter. Directed by Daniel Sackheim. Original airdate: September 17, 1993.

Squeeze (1x02). Written by Glen Morgan and James Wong. Directed by Harry Longstreet. Original airdate: September 24, 1993.

Conduit (1x03). Written by Alex Gansa and Howard Gordon. Directed by Daniel Sackheim. Original airdate: October 1, 1993.

The Jersey Devil (1x04). Written by Chris Carter. Directed by Joe Napolitano. Original airdate: October 8, 1993.

Shadows (1x05). Written by Glen Morgan and James Wong. Directed by Michael Katleman. Original airdate: October 22, 1993.

Fallen Angel (1x09). Written by Alex Gansa and Howard Gordon. Directed by Larry Shaw. Original airdate: November 19, 1993.

Eve (1x10). Written by Kenneth Biller and Chris Brancato. Directed by Fred Gerber. Original airdate: December 10, 1993.

Beyond the Sea (1x12). Written by Glen Morgan and James Wong. Directed by David Nutter. Original airdate: January 7, 1994.

Genderbender (1x13). Written by Larry Barber and Paul Barber. Directed by Rob Bowman. Original airdate: January 21, 1994.

Lazarus (1x14). Written by Alex Gansa and Howard Gordon. Directed by David Nutter. Original airdate: February 4, 1994.

E.B.E. (1x16). Written by Glen Morgan and James Wong. Directed by William Graham. Original airdate: February 18, 1994.

Miracle Man (1x17). Written by Howard Gordon and Chris Carter. Directed by Michael Lange. Original airdate: March 18, 1994.

Tooms (1x20). Written by Glen Morgan and James Wong. Directed by David Nutter. Original airdate: April 22, 1994.

APPENDIX

Born Again (1x21). Written by Alex Gansa and Howard Gordon. Directed by Jerrold Freedman. Original airdate: April 29, 1994.

The Erlenmeyer Flask (1x23). Written by Chris Carter. Directed by R. W. Goodwin. Original airdate: May 13, 1994.

Little Green Men (2x01). Written by Glen Morgan and James Wong. Directed by David Nutter. Original airdate: September 16, 1994.

Sleepless (2x04). Written by Howard Gordon. Directed by Rob Bowman. Original airdate: October 7, 1994.

Ascension (2x06). Written by Paul Brown. Directed by Michael Lange. Original airdate: October 21, 1994.

3 (2x07). Written by Chris Ruppenthal, and Glen Morgan and James Wong. Directed by David Nutter. Original airdate: November 4, 1994.

One Breath (2x08). Written by Glen Morgan and James Wong. Directed by R. W. Goodwin. Original airdate: November 11, 1994.

Firewalker (2x09). Written by Howard Gordon. Directed by David Nutter. Original airdate: November 18, 1994.

Red Museum (2x10). Written by Chris Carter. Directed by Win Phelps. Original airdate: December 9, 1994.

Excelsis Dei (2x11). Written by Paul Brown. Directed by Stephen Surjik. Original airdate: December 16, 1994.

Irresistible (2x13). Written by Chris Carter. Directed by David Nutter. Original airdate: January 13, 1995.

Die Hand Die Verletzt (2x14). Written by Glen Morgan and James Wong. Directed by Kim Manners. Original airdate: January 27, 1995.

Fresh Bones (2x15). Written by Howard Gordon. Directed by Rob Bowman. Original airdate: February 3, 1995.

Colony (2x16). Story by David Duchovny and Chris Carter. Teleplay by Chris Carter. Directed by Nick Marck. Original airdate: February 10, 1995.

End Game (2x17). Written by Frank Spotnitz. Directed by Rob Bowman. Original airdate: February 17, 1995.

Fearful Symmetry (2x18). Written by Steve De Jarnatt. Directed by James Whitmore Jr. Original airdate: February 24, 1995.

The Calusari (2x21). Written by Sara B. Charno. Directed by Michael Vejar. Original airdate: April 14, 1995.

F. Emasculata (2x22). Written by Chris Carter and Howard Gordon. Directed by Rob Bowman. Original airdate: April 28, 1995.

Our Town (2x24). Written by Frank Spotnitz. Directed by Rob Bowman. Original airdate: May 12, 1995.

Anasazi (2x25). Story by David Duchovny and Chris Carter. Teleplay by Chris Carter. Directed by R. W. Goodwin. Original airdate: May 19, 1995.

The Blessing Way (3x01). Written by Chris Carter. Directed by R. W. Goodwin. Original airdate: September 22, 1995.

Paper Clip (3x02). Written by Chris Carter. Directed by Rob Bowman. Original airdate: September 29, 1995.

D.P.O. (3x03). Written by Howard Gordon. Directed by Kim Manners. Original airdate: October 6, 1995.

Clyde Bruckman's Final Repose (3x04). Written by Darin Morgan. Directed by David Nutter. Original airdate: October 13, 1995.

The List (3x05). Written and directed by Chris Carter. Original airdate: October 20, 1995.

2Shy (3x06). Written by Jeffrey Vlaming. Directed by David Nutter. Original airdate: November 3, 1995.

Nisei (3x09). Written by Chris Carter, Howard Gordon, and Frank Spotnitz. Directed by David Nutter. Original airdate: November 24, 1995.

Revelations (3x11). Written by Kim Newton. Directed by David Nutter. Original airdate: December 15, 1995.

War of the Coprophages (3x12). Written by Darin Morgan. Directed by Kim Manners. Original airdate: January 5, 1996.

Grotesque (3x14). Written by Howard Gordon. Directed by Kim Manners. Original airdate: February 2, 1996.

Piper Maru (3x15). Written by Frank Spotnitz and Chris Carter. Directed by Rob Bowman. Original airdate: February 9, 1996.

Apocrypha (3x16). Written by Frank Spotnitz and Chris Carter. Directed by Kim Manners. Original airdate: February 16, 1996.

Pusher (3x17). Written by Vince Gilligan. Directed by Rob Bowman. Original airdate: February 23, 1996.

Teso Dos Bichos (3x18). Written by John Shiban. Directed by Kim Manners. Original airdate: March 8, 1996.

Hell Money (3x19). Written by Jeffrey Vlaming. Directed by Tucker Gates. Original airdate: March 29, 1996.

Jose Chung's *From Outer Space* (3x20). Written by Darin Morgan. Directed by Rob Bowman. Original airdate: April 12, 1996.

Quagmire (3x22). Written by Kim Newton. Directed by Kim Manners. Original airdate: May 3, 1996.

Wetwired (3x23). Written by Mat Beck. Directed by Rob Bowman. Original airdate: May 10, 1996.

Talitha Cumi (3x24). Story by David Duchovny and Chris Carter. Teleplay by Chris Carter. Directed by R. W. Goodwin. Original airdate: May 17, 1996.

Herrenvolk (4x01). Written by Chris Carter. Directed by R. W. Goodwin. Original airdate: October 4, 1996.

Home (4x03). Written by Glen Morgan and James Wong. Directed by Kim Manners. Original airdate: October 11, 1996.

Teliko (4x04). Written by Howard Gordon. Directed by James Charleston. Original airdate: October 18, 1996.

APPENDIX

The Field Where I Died (4x05). Written by Glen Morgan and James Wong. Directed by Rob Bowman. Original airdate: November 3, 1996.

Sanguinarium (4x06). Written by Valerie Mayhew and Vivian Mayhew. Directed by Kim Manners. Original airdate: November 10, 1996.

Tunguska (4x09). Written by Chris Carter and Frank Spotnitz. Directed by Kim Manners. Original airdate: November 24, 1996.

Terma (4x10). Written by Chris Carter and Frank Spotnitz. Directed by Rob Bowman. Original airdate: December 1, 1996.

Paper Hearts (4x08). Written by Vince Gilligan. Directed by Rob Bowman. Original airdate: December 15, 1996.

El Mundo Gira (4x11). Written by John Shiban. Directed by Tucker Gates. Original airdate: January 12, 1997.

Leonard Betts (4x14). Written by Vince Gilligan, John Shiban, and Frank Spotnitz. Directed by Kim Manners. Original airdate: January 26, 1997.

Never Again (4x13). Written by Glen Morgan and James Wong. Directed by Rob Bowman. Original airdate: February 2, 1997.

Memento Mori (4x15). Written by Chris Carter, Vince Gilligan, John Shiban, and Frank Spotnitz. Directed by Rob Bowman. Original airdate: February 9, 1997.

Kaddish (4x12). Written by Howard Gordon. Directed by Kim Manners. Original airdate: February 16, 1997.

Synchrony (4x19). Written by David Greenwalt and Howard Gordon. Directed by James Charleston. Original airdate: April 13, 1997.

Elegy (4x22). Written by John Shiban. Directed by James Charleston. Original airdate: May 4, 1997.

Gethsemane (4x24). Written by Chris Carter. Directed by R. W. Goodwin. Original airdate: May 18, 1997.

Redux (5x02). Written by Chris Carter. Directed by R. W. Goodwin. Original airdate: November 2, 1997.

Redux II (5x03). Written by Chris Carter. Directed by Kim Manners. Original airdate: November 9, 1997.

The Post-Modern Prometheus (5x06). Written and directed by Chris Carter. Original airdate: November 30, 1997.

Christmas Carol (5x05). Written by Vince Gilligan, John Shiban, and Frank Spotnitz. Directed by Peter Markle. Original airdate: December 7, 1997.

Emily (5x07). Written by Vince Gilligan, John Shiban, and Frank Spotnitz. Directed by Kim Manners. Original airdate: December 14, 1997.

Kitsunegari (5x08). Written by Vince Gilligan and Tim Minear. Directed by Daniel Sackheim. Original airdate: January 4, 1998.

Chinga (5x10). Written by Stephen King and Chris Carter. Directed by Kim Manners. Original airdate: February 8, 1998.

Bad Blood (5x12). Written by Vince Gilligan. Directed by Cliff Bole. Original airdate: February 22, 1998.

Patient X (5x13). Written by Frank Spotnitz and Chris Carter. Directed by Kim Manners. Original airdate: March 1, 1998.

The Red and the Black (5x14). Written by Frank Spotnitz and Chris Carter. Directed by Chris Carter. Original airdate: March 8, 1998.

All Souls (5x17). Story by Billy Brown and Dan Angel. Teleplay by Frank Spotnitz and John Shiban. Directed by Allen Coulter. Original airdate: April 26, 1998.

The Pine Bluff Variant (5x18). Written by John Shiban. Directed by Rob Bowman. Original airdate: May 3, 1998.

Folie à Deux (5x19). Written by Vince Gilligan. Directed by Kim Manners. Original airdate: May 10, 1998.

The End (5x20). Written by Chris Carter. Directed by R. W. Goodwin. Original airdate: May 17, 1998.

Fight the Future (1st movie). Story by Chris Carter and Frank Spotnitz. Screenplay by Chris Carter. Directed by Rob Bowman. Release date: June 19, 1998.

The Beginning (6x01). Written by Chris Carter. Directed by Kim Manners. Original airdate: November 8, 1998.

Triangle (6x03). Written and directed by Chris Carter. Original airdate: November 22, 1998.

How the Ghosts Stole Christmas (6x08). Written and directed by Chris Carter. Original airdate: December 13, 1998.

Terms of Endearment (6x06). Written by David Amann. Directed by Rob Bowman. Original airdate: January 3, 1999.

The Rain King (6x07). Written by Jeffrey Bell. Directed by Kim Manners. Original airdate: January 10, 1999.

Tithonus (6x09). Written by Vince Gilligan. Directed by Michael Watkins. Original airdate: January 24, 1999.

One Son (6x12). Written by Chris Carter and Frank Spotnitz. Directed by Rob Bowman. Original airdate: February 14, 1999.

Monday (6x15). Written by John Shiban and Vince Gilligan. Directed by Kim Manners. Original airdate: February 28, 1999.

Arcadia (6x13). Written by Daniel Arkin. Directed by Michael Watkins. Original airdate: March 7, 1999.

Biogenesis (6x22). Written by Chris Carter and Frank Spotnitz. Directed by Rob Bowman. Original airdate: May 16, 1999.

The Sixth Extinction (7x03). Written by Chris Carter. Directed by Kim Manners. Original airdate: November 7, 1999.

The Sixth Extinction II: Amor Fati (7x04). Written by David Duchovny and Chris Carter. Directed by Michael Watkins. Original airdate: November 14, 1999.

Hungry (7x01). Written by Vince Gilligan. Directed by Kim Manners. Original airdate: November 21, 1999.

Millennium (7x05). Written by Vince Gilligan and Frank Spotnitz. Directed by Thomas J. Wright. Original airdate: November 28, 1999.

The Goldberg Variation (7x02). Written by Jeffrey Bell. Directed by Thomas J. Wright. Original airdate: December 12, 1999.

Orison (7x07). Written by Chip Johannessen. Directed by Rob Bowman. Original airdate: January 9, 2000.

Signs & Wonders (7x09). Written by Jeffrey Bell. Directed by Kim Manners. Original airdate: January 23, 2000.

Sein und Zeit (7x10). Written by Chris Carter and Frank Spotnitz. Directed by Michael Watkins. Original airdate: February 6, 2000.

Closure (7x11). Written by Chris Carter and Frank Spotnitz. Directed by Kim Manners. Original airdate: February 13, 2000.

all things (7x17). Written and directed by Gillian Anderson. Original airdate: April 9, 2000.

Hollywood A.D. (7x18). Written and directed by David Duchovny. Original airdate: April 30, 2000.

Je Souhaite (7x21). Written and directed by Vince Gilligan. Original airdate: May 14, 2000.

Requiem (7x22). Written by Chris Carter. Directed by Kim Manners. Original airdate: May 21, 2000.

Within (8x01). Written by Chris Carter. Directed by Kim Manners. Original airdate: November 5, 2000.

Without (8x02). Written by Chris Carter. Directed by Kim Manners. Original airdate: November 12, 2000.

Patience (8x04). Written and directed by Chris Carter. Original airdate: November 19, 2000.

Roadrunners (8x05). Written by Vince Gilligan. Directed by Rod Hardy. Original airdate: November 26, 2000.

Via Negativa (8x07). Written by Frank Spotnitz. Directed by Tony Wharmby. Original airdate: December 17, 2000.

Badlaa (8x12). Written by John Shiban. Directed by Tony Wharmby. Original airdate: January 21, 2001.

The Gift (8x11). Written by Frank Spotnitz. Directed by Kim Manners. Original airdate: February 4, 2001.

Per Manum (8x08). Written by Chris Carter and Frank Spotnitz. Directed by Kim Manners. Original airdate: February 18, 2001.

This Is Not Happening (8x14). Written by Chris Carter and Frank Spotnitz. Directed by Kim Manners. Original airdate: February 25, 2001.

DeadAlive (8x15). Written by Chris Carter and Frank Spotnitz. Directed by Tony Wharmby. Original airdate: April 1, 2001.

Empedocles (8x17). Written by Greg Walker. Directed by Barry K. Thomas. Original airdate: April 22, 2001.

Essence (8x20). Written by Chris Carter. Directed by Kim Manners. Original airdate: May 13, 2001.
Existence (8x21). Written by Chris Carter. Directed by Kim Manners. Original airdate: May 20, 2001.

TrustNo1 (9x08). Written by Chris Carter and Frank Spotnitz. Directed by Tony Wharmby. Original airdate: January 6, 2002.
Provenance (9x10). Written by Chris Carter and Frank Spotnitz. Directed by Kim Manners. Original airdate: March 3, 2002.
Providence (9x11). Written by Chris Carter and Frank Spotnitz. Directed by Chris Carter. Original airdate: March 10, 2002.
Underneath (9x09). Written and directed by John Shiban. Original airdate: March 31, 2002.
Improbable (9x14). Written and directed by Chris Carter. Original airdate: April 7, 2002.
Scary Monsters (9x12). Written by Thomas Schnauz. Directed by Dwight Little. Original airdate: April 14, 2002.
William (9x17). Story by David Duchovny, Frank Spotnitz, and Chris Carter. Teleplay by Chris Carter. Directed by David Duchovny. Original airdate: April 28, 2002.
The Truth (9x19–20). Written by Chris Carter. Directed by Kim Manners. Original airdate: May 19, 2002.

I Want to Believe (2nd movie). Written by Chris Carter and Frank Spotnitz. Directed by Chris Carter. Release date: July 25, 2008.

Episode Index

2Shy (3x06), 164
3 (2x07), 12, 91, 119, 179, 196

All Souls (5x17), 6, 9–10, 16n7, 28, 42, 43–44, 47–49, 58, 62, 63n3, 75, 83, 84, 86, 160–61, 171, 217, 218
all things (7x17), 45, 82–83
Amor Fati. *See* The Sixth Extinction II: Amor Fati
Anasazi (2x25), 201
Apocrypha (3x16), 11, 154
Arcadia (6x13), 54
Ascension (2x06), 11, 46, 201, 221n5

Bad Blood (5x12), 153
Badlaa (8x12), 6, 56
The Beginning (6x01), 22, 27–28, 52, 114
Beyond the Sea (1x12), 53
Biogenesis (6x22), 8, 71–72, 117
The Blessing Way (3x01), 5
Born Again (1x21), 11, 150, 152

The Calusari (2x21), 5, 189–90
Chinga (5x10), 6
Christmas Carol (5x05), 125–26
Closure (7x11), 44–45, 60–61, 68–69, 72, 150, 172, 217
Clyde Bruckman's Final Repose (3x04), 68, 79–80

Colony (2x16), 18–19, 39, 113, 114, 191–93
Conduit (1x03), 38, 42

DeadAlive (8x15), 11, 209, 210
Deep Throat (1x01), 113, 114
Die Hand Die Verletzt (2x14), 6, 9, 206–7
D.P.O. (3x03), 112–13

E.B.E. (1x16), 35, 39, 114, 146, 147
Elegy (4x22), 53, 61
El Mundo Gira (4x11), 149
Emily (5x07), 47, 52, 75, 105
Empedocles (8x17), 53, 166
The End (5x20), 22
End Game (2x17), 40, 52, 53, 66, 116, 180, 193
The Erlenmeyer Flask (1x23), 35, 51–52, 65, 114, 144, 161
Essence (8x20), 161, 181
Eve (1x10), 11, 114
Excelsis Dei (2x11), 11
Existence (8x21), 11, 182, 220n1

Fallen Angel (1x09), 159–60, 180
Fearful Symmetry (2x18), 12
F. Emasculata (2x22), 145
The Field Where I Died (4x05), 7, 12, 90, 91, 150, 213
Fight the Future (1st movie), 110, 114, 118–19, 123, 201

Episode Index

Firewalker (2x09), 150
Folie à Deux (5x19), 55, 112, 116
Fresh Bones (2x15), 5

Genderbender (1x13), 8
Gethsemane (4x24), 11, 19, 36–37, 39, 40, 151, 192, 198, 209
The Gift (8x11), ix, 214–17
The Goldberg Variation (7x02), 83, 89
Grotesque (3x14), 116

Hell Money (3x19), 69–70
Herrenvolk (4x01), 27, 59, 65, 66–67
Hollywood A.D. (7x18), 10, 11, 35
Home (4x03), 107–8
How the Ghosts Stole Christmas (6x08), 150
Hungry (7x01), 164–65

Improbable (9x14), vii, 13, 30, 86–87, 127–28, 164, 172
Irresistible (2x13), 35, 171
I Want to Believe (2nd movie), 1, 4, 9, 11, 13, 29–30, 37, 45, 48–50, 53, 63n3, 70, 72, 73–75, 77, 101, 108, 119, 123, 128, 134, 137–40, 141n6, 171, 217, 221n4

The Jersey Devil (1x04), 191
Je Souhaite (7x21), 54–55, 84–85, 211, 218–19
Jose Chung's *From Outer Space* (3x20), 20–21, 23, 38, 53–54, 147–49

Kaddish (4x12), 5, 125, 132, 133, 179, 211
Kitsunegari (5x08), 56

Lazarus (1x14), 11, 211
Leonard Betts (4x14), 164, 165, 168, 215–16
The List (3x05), 150
Little Green Men (2x01), 18, 39, 40, 103, 109–10

Memento Mori (4x15), 165, 189, 193–94
Millennium (7x05), 11–12, 89–93, 210–13
Miracle Man (1x17), 6, 11, 42–44, 46, 57, 188–89, 194–95, 211–12
Monday (6x15), 81–83, 89

Never Again (4x13), 119, 191
Nisei (3x09), 37, 54

One Breath (2x08), 12, 169, 192, 198, 220n2, 221n5
One Son (6x12), 110–11, 115, 200, 206
Orison (7x07), 11, 30, 42, 44, 83, 84, 86, 162, 171
Our Town (2x24), 12, 196

Paper Clip (3x02), 71, 154, 209, 217
Paper Hearts (4x08), 43, 68
Patience (8x04), 112
Patient X (5x13), 19, 26, 147
Per Manum (8x08), 181
Pilot (1x79), 1, 17, 23, 38, 46, 51, 71, 101, 111, 113, 155
The Pine Bluff Variant (5x18), 145–46
Piper Maru (3x15), 143, 154
The Post-Modern Prometheus (5x06), 42, 57, 149–50
Provenance (9x10), 8
Providence (9x11), 8, 11, 184
Pusher (3x17), 56, 162–63, 174

Quagmire (3x22), 7, 12, 17, 67–68, 75–76, 144, 151

The Rain King (6x07), 121
The Red and the Black (5x14), 40–41, 191, 200
Red Museum (2x10), 7, 8, 150
Redux (5x02), 116, 146–47, 186, 198, 209
Redux II (5x03), 3–4, 29, 31, 38, 46, 47, 76–77, 115, 175–76, 185–86, 198, 209
Requiem (7x22), 11, 51, 53, 77, 133, 194, 195, 198, 204, 209

Revelations (3x11), 4, 6, 9–12, 28, 42, 46–47, 57, 58, 73, 83, 86–87
Roadrunners (8x05), 7–8

Sanguinarium (4x06), 6, 12
Scary Monsters (9x12), 56
Sein und Zeit (7x10), 43
Shadows (1x05), 54, 100–101, 150
Signs & Wonders (7x09), 6, 8–9, 11, 44, 156, 158–59, 163, 173, 190
The Sixth Extinction (7x03), 8, 117
The Sixth Extinction II: Amor Fati (7x04), 5, 8, 11, 117, 180, 186–87, 191, 200, 204–6, 209, 221n4, 222n8
Sleepless (2x04), 12–13, 56
Squeeze (1x02), 112, 164, 171
Synchrony (4x19), 68, 79–81

Talitha Cumi (3x24), 11, 14, 23–27, 30, 69, 88, 136, 185, 188, 201, 217
Teliko (4x04), 150–51
Terma (4x10), 116, 154, 166, 167, 170, 189

Terms of Endearment (6x06), 177n7
Teso Dos Bichos (3x18), 5
This Is Not Happening (8x14), 8, 209
Tithonus (6x09), 125
Tooms (1x20), 116, 171, 176
Triangle (6x03), 97, 113
TrustNo1 (9x08), 118
The Truth (9x19–20), 13–14, 36–37, 41, 45, 53, 66, 68, 69, 72–74, 93, 98, 123, 145, 191, 200–203
Tunguska (4x09), 146, 154, 193

Underneath (9x09), 12, 197

Via Negativa (8x07), 7

War of the Coprophages (3x12), 145
Wetwired (3x23), 35, 114
William (9x17), 106, 184
Within (8x01), 204, 209
Without (8x02), 204, 209

Scripture Index

Old Testament

Genesis
1:2	174
1:6	174
1:26–27	22
1:27	109
2:7	221n7
2:18	108
2:24	122, 133, 197
3	85
3:5	157
3:7	163
3:15	163
4:6–7	102
6:1–2	160
6:4–5	160
6:6	174
9:15	174
15:6	131
21	131
22	131, 205–6
22:2	205
22:7	205
22:11–12	206

Exodus
1–2	182
2:1–10	106–7
12:46	208
17:6	220n1

Leviticus
11:44	173
11:45	173
18:21	206
19:18	136, 139

Numbers
9:12	208
23:19	95n2

Deuteronomy
6:5	136
12:31	206

1 Samuel
1:1—2:11	105–6
15:22	207
15:29	95n2

1 Kings
3:16–28	107

Job
1:6–12	161
38–41	62

Psalms
22:1	203
34:20	208

Scripture Index

Proverbs
16:18	160
25:2	70, 86
27:6	117

Ecclesiastes
1:2	12
3:19	12
4:9–12	141n7
12:8	12

Song of Solomon
2:4	134
2:16	134
6:3	131
8:6–7	125

Isaiah
7:9	63n4
7:14	182
9:1–2	183
9:6–7	183
11:10	94
14:12–15	160
25:8	221n7
41:8	131
49:14–15	104
53:4–8	214–15
54:5–10	132
66:13	104

Jeremiah
7:31	206
29:11–14a	93

Lamentations
3:32–33	221n6

Ezekiel
1:4–5	8
16:20–21	206

Daniel
	93

Hosea
6:6	207
13:14	221n7

Jonah
3:9	78

Zechariah
9:9	184

New Testament

Matthew
1:23	182, 219
2	182
2:9–11	183
4:1–11	24, 185
4:6	185
4:16	183
4:24	188
5–7	183
5	169
5:38–48	219
5:45	137
5:48	173
7:7–11	78
7:12	99, 139
7:24–27	155
8:5–13	58
8:17	214
9:13	207
9:20–22	58
9:22	57
9:32–33	189
10:37	191
11:19	194
12:7	207
12:22	189
12:29	190
12:49–50	191
15:21–28	58
16:1–4	57

Matthew (continued)

17:14–18	189
17:20	62, 99
18:23–35	170–71
21:1–11	184
22:1–14	133
22:39	139
24:36	92
25:1–13	134
25:31–46	138–39
26:29	134
27:40	185
27:43	185
28:11–15	195

Mark

1:17–18	190, 191
1:23–26	190
2:14	190, 191
5:2–22	189
5:24–34	216
5:41	188
8:34–36	191–92
9:23–24	61
10:21	191
10:28–30	192
11:18	201
14:1–2	201
14:22	196
14:24–25	196
14:36	199
14:38	199
15:34	203

Luke

1:13, 30	20
1:34, 35	181
2:7	182
2:15–18	183
6:27–36	136
10:27–37	136
15:4	127
15:7	127
15:11–32	126–27
15:31–32	128
17:5–6	62
18:1–8	77–78
22:42	199

John

1:29	195
1:36	195
2:1–11	196, 197
4:17–18	138
4:24	169
5:18	201
6:30	57
6:48–58	196–97
6:54	12, 91, 196
6:61–63	196
6:66	57
7:1	201
8:7	138, 173
8:11	173
8:21–22	193
8:32	176
8:44	157
10:10	157
11	188, 210–11
11:5	131
11:11	131
11:24	94, 210–11
11:25–26	91, 94, 131, 210, 213
13:36	193
14:2–3	133
14:17	169
15:12–13	130
15:26	169
16:13	169
19:36	208
20:25	57–58, 208
20:29	58

Acts

1:6	93
1:7	92
9:4–5	219

Romans

5:3b–4	85
7:7–25	168
8	129
8:15–17	130
8:24	79
8:24–25	92
15:12–13	93–94

Scripture Index

1 Corinthians
8:1   99
10:4   220n1
10:23   99
10:24   99
11:26   198
13   98–99, 124
13:4–6 140
13:6   143
13:8   125
13:13   14, 98, 124
15   99, 221n7
15:21–22   213

2 Corinthians
1:3–5   219
3:6   169
5:19   175
5:21   175
11:23–29   219

Ephesians
2:4–5   213
2:8–9   213
5:25–32 132–33, 139
5:27   159

Philippians
2   184, 219
2:3   99
2:3–11 133
2:7–8   130

1 Thessalonians
5:17   78

Hebrews
2:10–18 130, 199
2:17–18 219
5:7   198, 207
5:7–9   199
11   58
11:1   3, 36–37, 66
11:6   62, 78
11:13–16   94

James
2:23   131
4:7   163

1 Peter
1:3–5   94

1 John
3:12   102, 130, 135
3:16   130
3:17–18 139
3:18   97
4:8   99
4:10   129
4:10–11 139
4:19   134
4:20   102
5:6   12

Revelation
1–3   90
1:16   90
1:17   20
1:18   91, 94, 213
2–3   7
3:15–16 9, 158
6   90
7:14   195
7:17   195
12:11   195
12:17   90
19:7–9 133
19:8   159
19:9   196
21:4   94
22:1   195
22:17   94

Subject Index

For episode-specific characters, see the Episode Index.

Abel. *See* Cain and Abel
Abraham, 131, 205–7
Adam and Eve, 85, 157–59, 162–63, 168, 174, 199, 213–14, 220, 221n7
affection, 100–109, 124. *See also* love: between family members
afterlife, 49, 68, 70, 75, 91, 93, 95, 150
Ahab. See *Moby Dick*
aliens: abduction by, 2, 18, 53, 113, 148; colonization by, 8, 74–75, 145, 187; and God, 3, 19, 22, 23, 36; as gods, 3, 19, 23; proof of, 39, 147, 151; and religious experience, 19–21, 38; search for, 2, 8, 18–20, 72; truth about, 146–47, 154
Anselm, Saint, 59–60
apocalypticism, 11, 14, 90–93
ascension: of Jesus, 93, 208–13, 220; of Mulder, 134
Augustine, Saint, 21–22, 26, 59, 126, 156–57

belief, 3, 6–7, 31, 35, 37; and sight, 43, 53–59, 62; and truth, 143–44, 150, 191. *See also* faith; trust
believe, wanting to, 2, 6, 13–14, 17–33, 39–40, 42–43, 58, 60, 67–68, 73, 95

black and white, 144, 156, 158–59, 167. *See also* good and evil; right and wrong
black oil, 165–66, 169, 177n9, 189
brother: love for, 101–103, 124, 135; of the prodigal, 128–29, 140. *See also* Cain and Abel; Jesus Christ: as brother; Mulder, Fox: as brother
Brothers Karamazov, The. *See* Grand Inquisitor, the

Cain and Abel, 102, 130, 163–64, 168
cancer, 188; as metaphor for evil, 165–66, 189, 215; Scully's, 3, 29–30, 40, 47–48, 53, 58, 76, 110, 185–86, 189, 192–93, 209
Carter, Chris, ix, 1, 3, 4, 11, 17, 36, 37, 51, 90, 111
Catholicism, 1, 4, 9–11, 196–97. *See also* Scully, Dana: as a Catholic
charity, 98, 124–34, 139. *See also* love: by God; love: for God
Christ. *See* Jesus Christ
Cigarette-Smoking Man, 24–26, 69–70, 88, 165, 185–88, 198, 200, 204–6, 221n4
Commandments, Ten. *See* Ten Commandments
commandments, two greatest, 98, 134–40, 167

240

communion. *See* Eucharist
conscience, 24–26, 88, 156, 163, 165, 167, 169
Consortium, 189, 200, 206
cross, 11, 14, 185–87, 190–94, 199, 203, 210; suffering on, 191, 207–8. *See also* crucifixion
cross necklace, 1, 13, 41, 45–47, 179, 194
crucifixion, 14, 133, 184–85, 190, 193–94, 200, 202, 203–8; of Mulder, 180, 186, 194, 203–4, 209. *See also* Jesus Christ: death of
CSM. *See* Cigarette-Smoking Man
cults, 4, 7–9, 19, 90–92, 184, 213

David, King, 93, 183–84
Deep Throat, 35, 114, 146–47, 187, 193
demon possession, 61, 166, 189–90, 216
determinism, 79, 82–83, 86, 90, 92–93
devil, the, 6, 9, 12, 24–25, 44, 46, 157, 159–65, 185–86, 189–90, 198, 206–7
disciples: of Jesus, 57, 61, 190–91, 193–98, 200, 208, 210; of Mulder, 180, 190, 209–10; sacrifice by, 190–91, 193
Doggett, John, 56, 86–87, 112, 122, 166, 197, 214, 219
"Don't give up." *See* giving up, not
Dostoyevsky, Fyodor. *See* Grand Inquisitor, the
doubting Thomas, 57–58, 208–9

Eden, garden of, 85, 94, 157, 162–63, 168, 199, 213
Emily, 47–50, 52, 104–6, 126, 161, 181, 218
eros. *See* love: romantic
eternal life. *See* life, eternal
Eucharist, 12, 196–97, 206, 217. *See also* Last Supper, the
Eve. *See* Adam and Eve
evidence: and faith, 2, 14, 17, 27–28, 36–37, 39, 57–60; and law, 152–53, 200, 202; and science, 2, 27–28, 51–52, 54, 120, 151
evil, 93, 94, 98, 138, 140, 159, 162–70, 173, 177n9, 190, 197; as cancer, 165–67, 189, 215; problem of, 84, 88–89, 223. *See also* good and evil
exorcism, 5, 61, 163, 188–90

faith, 4–13, 35–64; in God, 19, 26–29, 35, 36, 38, 42, 59, 206–7; in Jesus, 57, 131, 190, 210, 212–13, 221n7; and reason, 57, 59–63; in science, 14, 27–29, 47, 51, 53, 58–59, 67, 72; as a struggle, 3, 4, 37, 51. *See also* evidence: and faith
faith, hope, and love, 14–15, 36, 66, 95, 98–99, 124, 126
fate, 26, 31, 63, 74, 80, 90–91, 94–95, 154; and free will, 13, 14, 81–89
father. *See* Abraham; God: as father; parents; prodigal son
Father Joe, 4, 9, 11, 13, 29–30, 49–50, 70, 73–74, 77, 78, 128, 137–40, 171, 173
Father McCue. *See* McCue, Father
forgiveness, 170–71, 173, 176; by God, 11, 49–50, 74, 76–78, 128, 171, 175–76, 201
Fowley, Diana, 114–15, 117, 187, 200, 204
free will, 24–26, 81–89, 170, 185; and God, 30, 85–89, 172; and love, 24, 88, 95, 185. *See also* fate: and free will; Grand Inquisitor, the
friendship, 23, 100, 102, 108–21, 124, 130; between Mulder and Scully, 97, 101, 109–11, 115, 117–18, 120–22, 124, 130; and trust, 115, 130. *See also* love: between friends
future: hope and, 14, 66–68, 70, 72–75, 79, 93–95; knowledge of, 14, 41, 68, 72, 78–82, 92, 95

garden of Eden. *See* Eden, garden of

Subject Index

gender. *See* male and female
Gethsemane, garden of, 133, 193, 198–200, 204, 207–8, 218
giving up, not, 29–30, 50–51, 65–66, 71, 73–79, 86, 93, 95, 123, 191
God: changing the mind of, 78, 95n2; character of, 22–23, 78, 84–85, 92, 99, 120; as creator, 30, 83, 124, 156–57, 159, 167; existence of, 58–60, 63; as father, 78, 92, 102, 124, 126–29, 131, 134–35, 173–74, 199, 207–8; as friend, 124, 129–31, 135; grief of, 172, 174; intervention in the world, 14–15, 30–31, 42, 83–87, 89, 93, 182, 219; as judge, 138, 172, 174–76; as lover, 124, 131–32, 134–35, 159; as mother, 104, 134; search for, 1, 2, 8, 18–20; as Truth, 156–57, 169. *See also* aliens: and God; image of God
God-shaped hole, 21–22, 32n5
Golden Rule, 99, 136, 139, 155, 168
good and evil, 14, 25, 127, 157–59, 168, 184; battle between, 12, 90, 144, 161
Good Samaritan, 136
grace, 213–20
Grand Inquisitor, the, 14, 23–26, 30–31, 42, 69, 88, 95, 135–36, 175, 185, 188, 217–19

Hannah, 105–7
Hawking, Stephen, 28, 30, 32n11
healings, 5, 11, 24–25, 29, 43, 58, 61–62; by Jesus, 188–90, 201, 210, 214–18
heaven, 13, 48–49, 80, 90–92, 94, 127, 134, 160–61, 183–84, 196, 206, 208, 219–20. *See also* afterlife
Holy Spirit. *See* Spirit, Holy
hope, 2, 14, 7, 17, 26, 40, 50, 65–96, 126, 134; and despair, 41, 69, 72, 92; and faith, 3, 36, 66, 72–73, 95, 98–99, 143; nature of, 66–71

image of God, 22, 30, 60, 99, 109, 120, 139, 158–59, 173
infancy narrative. *See* Jesus Christ: birth narrative of
"I Want to Believe" poster, 1, 13, 17–18, 20, 39, 179

Jesus Christ: on belief, 57–58, 61–62; birth narrative of, 11, 179–84; as bridegroom, 132–35; as brother, 129–31, 135; death of, 92, 94, 129–30, 175, 179, 183–84, 193–95, 197, 199, 202–3, 209, 213, 215–16, 219–20; as friend, 130–31, 135, 139; as "king of the Jews," 182–84, 203, 220; as Lamb of God, 133–34, 195–96, 207–8, 215; ministry of, 183–84, 188, 190, 194; resurrection of, 92, 94, 129, 179–80, 194–95, 197, 208–13, 216–17; as Son of God, 129–30, 186, 199, 207–8; suffering of, 180, 194, 199, 207, 215, 217, 219–20; trial of, 193, 200–203, 215; trust in, 170, 190–91, 210, 212. *See also* ascension: of Jesus; crucifixion; messiah; miracles: of Jesus
Job, 50–51, 62–63
Jonah, 50–51, 62–63, 76–78
Judas, 32n7, 187, 195, 197–98, 200, 212
judgment, 13, 49–50, 76; day of, 89, 94, 138, 210; divine, 12, 26, 172–74; and punishment, 170, 174–76
justice, 14, 62, 87, 144, 168; of God, 50, 62, 84, 95, 154, 172; in the next world, 89, 92, 94, 172; pursuit of, 77, 110, 153, 170; Scully's trust in, 45, 153–54; truth and, 77, 101, 109, 152–54, 201

Kazantzakis, Nikos. See *Last Temptation of Christ, The*
Kersh, Alvin, 201, 221n4
Krycek, Alex, 113, 146, 154, 181, 193, 200

Last Supper, the, 11, 133–34, 193–98; of Mulder, 194, 195, 198, 204, 209
Last Temptation of Christ, The, 180, 186–87, 191–92, 200, 204, 222n8
law, 101, 152, 154–55; divine, 134, 167–69; of Moses, 25, 134, 136, 155, 173, 183, 201–2, 216; purpose of, 167–70. *See also* commandments, two greatest; justice; Ten Commandments
law, natural. *See* natural law
Lazarus, 94, 131, 188–89, 210–12, 218
Lewis, C. S., 98, 100, 109, 121, 126
life, eternal, 91–94, 126, 129, 131, 174, 176, 196–97, 199, 211–13, 217
Lone Gunmen, the, 11, 183, 195
love: in action, 97–100, 129, 139; for enemies, 32n7, 102, 124, 136–37, 139; between family members, 98, 100–108, 126, 135; between friends, 98, 108–21, 126, 135; by God, 14, 23, 30–31, 104, 124–34, 137–38; for God, 14, 24, 88, 98, 124, 134–35, 137, 167, 176, 213; between Mulder and Scully, 97–98, 111, 117, 121–24; for neighbors, 24, 102, 124, 135, 159, 175; for others, 14, 98, 102, 120–21, 124, 134–35, 167, 176, 213; romantic, 98, 102, 109, 120–25. *See also* faith, hope, and love; free will: and love
loyalty: between Mulder and Scully, 97, 111, 115–18, 122; and trust, 115, 118

male and female, 22–23, 109, 122; Mulder and Scully representing, 119–21
marriage, 123, 132–35, 138. *See also* wedding
Martha. *See* Mary and Martha
Mary, mother of Jesus, 20, 180–81

Mary and Martha, 94, 131, 210, 212, 218
Mary Magdalene, 187, 221n4
McCue, Father, 9, 47, 48, 160
mercy, 13, 50–51, 162; of God, 76–77, 93, 95, 137–38, 140, 173–76; and justice, 170–71
messiah, 11, 14, 25, 187, 191, 193–94, 203–4; expectations for, 92–93, 183–84, 194. *See also* Jesus Christ; Mulder, Fox: as Christ figure
Millennium Group, 11–12, 90–92
miracles, 3, 24–26, 29, 47, 69, 181–82, 185–86, 214; and faith, 42–43, 57–58, 60, 62, 212; of Jesus, 57–58, 179, 188, 196
Moby Dick, 75–77, 144
Modell, Robert, 162–63, 174
Moses, 106–7, 134, 168, 182–84, 197, 216, 220n1; mother of, 106–7, 184
mother: God as, 104, 134; love by, 103–8; sacrifice by, 105–7, 129. *See also* parents; Scully, Dana: as mother; Mulder, Fox: mother of
Mulder, Fox: as brother, 101–3, 116, 130, 186, 205; as Christ figure, 11, 133–34, 180, 186–88, 191–92, 194–95, 198, 200–204, 209–10, 219; faith journey of, 14, 38–45, 147; father of, 193, 204–6; and God, 4, 38, 42, 44–45, 58, 62–63, 84; mother of, 103–4, 116. *See also* relationship between Mulder and Scully
Mulder, Samantha: abduction of, 42, 44, 71, 73, 101, 103, 113, 205–6; clones of, 180, 186; fate of, 43, 45, 49, 60–61, 68–69, 72, 93, 187; Mulder's search for, 2, 18, 38, 42, 52, 65, 67, 71–72, 74, 101, 180. *See also* Mulder, Fox: as brother
Mulder, Teena. *See* Mulder, Fox: mother of

natural law, 156, 168, 177n3
nephilim, 160–61, 173

Noah, 132, 160, 173–74

occult, 4, 6
original sin, 162–66, 174, 190

parables, 77–78, 126–28, 136, 155, 170–71, 201
parents, 29, 47, 70, 98, 100, 108, 122, 168, 191; love by, 102, 104, 129, 135; participation in creation, 104, 122; sacrificing a child, 105, 108, 205. *See also* father; mother; Scully, Dana: as mother
Pascal, Blaise, 21–22, 26
Passion Narrative, 194–213. *See also* crucifixion; Jesus Christ: death of
Passover, 195–96, 208
Paul, Apostle, 10, 78, 79, 93–94, 99, 132, 213, 219
perception of reality. *See* reality, perception of
perseverance, 72–73, 75, 77–78, 85, 92, 95, 99, 190–91
Pfaster, Donnie, 162, 171, 173, 176
postmodernism, 14, 31, 144, 148–49, 151, 155–56
prayer, 77, 80, 89, 155, 169, 171, 219–20; answers to, 29, 30, 42, 78, 87, 186, 199, 218; of Jesus, 199, 207; persistence in, 77–79, 88, 95n1
predestination. *See* determinism
prodigal son, 126–30, 140
proof. *See* evidence

reality, perception of, 20, 55–57, 148–51
reincarnation, 91, 150
relationship between Mulder and Scully, 74, 101, 109–15, 119, 122–23, 133. *See also* friendship: between Mulder and Scully; love: between Mulder and Scully
respect, 99, 101–2, 135; and loyalty, 115, 122; between Mulder and Scully, 97, 111–13, 122
resurrection, 10, 11, 14, 31, 91, 94, 125, 188, 212–14; in the last day, 91, 94, 210–11; of Lazarus, 131, 188–89, 210; of Mulder, 11, 133–34, 180, 209–10. *See also* Jesus Christ: resurrection of
Reyes, Monica, 12, 86–87, 182, 197
right and wrong, 88, 144, 152, 155–57, 162, 164–65, 167–68

Sagan, Carl, 28, 32n10, 33n12
Samantha. *See* Mulder, Samantha
Sartre, Jean-Paul, 21, 26
Satan. *See* devil, the
Satanism, 6, 9, 206
science: faith in, 14, 27–29, 47, 51, 53, 58–59, 67, 72; and religion, 26, 27–31. *See also* evidence: and science; Scully, Dana: and science
Scully, Bill, 76, 135
Scully, Dana: abduction of, 101, 107, 110, 192; as a Catholic, 28–29, 46–49, 58, 137–38, 169, 189; as a doctor, 29, 47–49, 53, 108, 137–39; faith journey of, 14, 29, 45–53, 74, 179; and God, 46–50, 59, 74, 77, 86–87, 128, 218; as mother, 47, 103–8, 129, 180–81, 184, 218; and science, 28, 51–53, 58–59, 67, 72–73, 151, 155, 169; sister of, 101, 104, 154, 193. *See also* cancer: Scully's; relationship between Mulder and Scully
Scully, Melissa. *See* Scully, Dana: sister of
Sermon on the Mount, 155, 169, 183
serpent, 157–58, 163–64, 190, 207
signs: from God, 47, 57–58, 60, 83, 86–87, 164, 172; and wonders, 24, 188. *See also* miracles
sin, original. *See* original sin
sister: loss of, 72, 76–77, 101, 104. *See also* brother: love for; Mulder, Samantha; Scully, Dana: sister of
Skinner, Walter, 29, 53, 115–16, 154, 165, 180, 192, 195, 198, 209

Smith, Huston, 22, 28
Smith, Jeremiah, 24–26, 69, 88, 136, 188
snakes. *See* serpent
Spender, Cassandra, 19–20
Spirit, Holy, 23, 167–70, 176, 208
spirits, evil. *See* demon possession
Spotnitz, Frank, 36
Stargate SG-1, 2–3, 15n3
Star Trek: The Next Generation, 2–3, 15n3
suffering, 14, 85, 214–15, 220; of children, 24, 29, 49, 105, 175, 218; and free will, 88, 95, 219; of God, 207, 218; of the innocent, 42, 45, 49–50, 84, 93, 171, 217–19. *See also* Jesus Christ: suffering of

temptation, 168, 184–88, 199, 219; of Adam and Eve, 157, 163; of Christ, 24–25, 183–88, 199; of Mulder, 180, 185–88, 198. See also *Last Temptation of Christ, The*
Ten Commandments, 134, 168
testing: of Abraham, 205–6. *See also* temptation
theodicy. *See* evil: problem of
Thomas, doubting. *See* doubting Thomas
time travel, 68, 79–81
Tooms, Eugene, 171, 176
trust: and God, 62, 130–31; in Jesus Christ, 170, 190–91, 210, 212; between Mulder and Scully, 62, 97, 111, 113–15, 118, 130

truth, 2, 87, 143–54, 193; absolute, 14, 151–52, 155–57, 159; and lies, 146–47, 157–58; Mulder's faith in, 38, 72, 117–18, 143, 176; Mulder's pursuit of, 41, 143–44, 150–51, 153, 186, 191; and relativity, 144, 152, 156; subjectivity of, 31, 147–53. *See also* belief: and truth; reality, perception of
"The Truth Is Out There," 1, 2, 13, 39, 65, 143–44, 147, 191

vampires, 12, 91, 94, 153, 196
virtues. *See* faith, hope, and love

wedding, 131–33, 158; at Cana, 196, 197; of the Lamb, 133–34, 159, 196. *See also* marriage; Jesus Christ: as bridegroom
William, 11, 49–50, 105–8, 118, 122; adoption of, 106–7, 184; birth of, 106, 180–84; conception of, 106, 122, 181

X-Files, The: genre of, 3, 13; as postmodern, 149, 151; religion in, 3–13; and unanswered questions, 3–4, 6, 10, 13, 14–15, 29–30, 78–79, 149

zombies, 55, 91–92, 94, 211